Studies in European Culture and History

edited by

Eric D. Weitz and Jack Zipes
University of Minnesota

Since the fall of the Berlin Wall and the collapse of communism, the very meaning of Europe has been opened up and is in the process of being redefined. European states and societies are wrestling with the expansion of NATO and the European Union and with new streams of immigration, while a renewed and reinvigorated cultural engagement has emerged between East and West. But the fast-paced transformations of the last fifteen years also have deeper historical roots. The reconfiguring of contemporary Europe is entwined with the cataclysmic events of the twentieth century, two world wars and the Holocaust, and with the processes of modernity that, since the eighteenth century, have shaped Europe and its engagement with the rest of the world.

Studies in European Culture and History is dedicated to publishing books that explore major issues in Europe's past and present from a wide variety of disciplinary perspectives. The works in the series are interdisciplinary; they focus on culture and society and deal with significant developments in Western and Eastern Europe from the eighteenth century to the present within a social historical context. With its broad span of topics, geography, and chronology, the series aims to publish the most interesting and innovative work on modern Europe.

Published by Palgrave Macmillan:

Fascism and Neofascism: Critical Writings on the Radical Right in Europe
by Eric Weitz

Fictive Theories: Towards a Deconstructive and Utopian Political Imagination
by Susan McManus

German-Jewish Literature in the Wake of the Holocaust: Grete Weil, Ruth Klüger, and the Politics of Address
by Pascale Bos

Turkish Turn in Contemporary German Literature: Toward a New Critical Grammar of Migration
by Leslie Adelson

Terror and the Sublime in Art and Critical Theory: From Auschwitz to Hiroshima to September 11
by Gene Ray

WEIMAR CULTURE REVISITED

EDITED BY
JOHN ALEXANDER WILLIAMS

First published in 2011 by
PALGRAVE MACMILLAN®
in the United States—a division of St. Martin's Press LLC,
175 Fifth Avenue, New York, NY 10010.

Where this book is distributed in the UK, Europe and the rest of the world,
this is by Palgrave Macmillan, a division of Macmillan Publishers Limited,
registered in England, company number 785998, of Houndmills,
Basingstoke, Hampshire RG21 6XS.

Palgrave Macmillan is the global academic imprint of the above companies
and has companies and representatives throughout the world.

Palgrave® and Macmillan® are registered trademarks in the United States,
the United Kingdom, Europe and other countries.

ISBN: 978–0–230–10942–1

Library of Congress Cataloging-in-Publication Data is available from the
Library of Congress.

A catalogue record of the book is available from the British Library.

Design by Newgen Imaging Systems (P) Ltd., Chennai, India.

First edition: February 2011

10 9 8 7 6 5 4 3 2 1

Printed in the United States of America.

Contents

Illustrations

FOREWORD

John A. Williams

"The killing is over. The consequences of the war, need and misery, will burden us for many years...Be unified, loyal, and dutiful. The old and rotten, the monarchy, has collapsed. Long live the new. Long live the German republic."[1] These words, spoken by the Social Democrat Philip Scheidemann to a massive crowd at the Reichstag on November 9, 1918, inaugurated Germany's first true parliamentary democracy, soon to become known as the Weimar Republic. By the winter of 1933, the republic's enemies on the far right had prevailed, and Adolf Hitler was the new chancellor. Attempting to justify why he was dismantling the democratic system, Hitler announced in March that, "Over the past fourteen years, our nation has suffered a decline in all realms of life that has been worse than we could ever have imagined."[2] The revolutionary "November criminals" like Scheidemann and subsequent Weimar governments had brought near ruin to Germany, proclaimed Hitler. It was time to clean up the mess.

With this rhetoric, Hitler was furthering an antiliberal narrative of the recent past that presented the Weimar Republic as doomed from the beginning by its own weaknesses and political corruption. Indeed, democracy's enemies on both the Right and the Left had been honing this representation of Weimar as a miserable failure since 1918. One need only look to the "stab in the back legend" propagated by Hindenburg, Ludendorff, and others, or to the fetishistic images of mutilated war veterans, corrupt politicians, syphilitic prostitutes, and "lust murderers" in the paintings of Otto Dix and George Grosz.

Unfortunately, this pessimistic and openly antidemocratic disdain influenced most of the memories and historical representations of Weimar Germany up to the 1980s, in the two Germanies and everywhere else. The resulting doom-laden narrative of Weimar gained added historiographical credence, even among political moderates and liberals, because of the *Sonderweg* ("deviant path") thesis that dominated scholarship on modern Germany from the early 1960s onward. Pre-1933 Germany, these *Sonderweg* historians asserted, remained under the control of the conservative aristocracy, and its culture was shot through with chronically irrational, illiberal, and anti-modern tendencies. Together these politically and culturally reactionary continuities undermined the attempt at democracy in Weimar and enabled the rise of Nazism.[3]

Most scholars of the high arts and literature—of "Weimar culture" per se—took an equally teleological approach. Either implicitly or openly, they commenced their analyses with the Nazi takeover and worked backward in search of ideological flaws. Doom-laden titles, such as *Before the Deluge, The Weimar Chronicle: Prelude to Hitler*, and *Dancing on the Volcano*, abounded.[4] Moreover, scholars generally limited their analyses to the famous canon of artistically daring and politically ambiguous works. Starring roles were given to films like *The Cabinet of Dr. Caligari, The Last Laugh, Metropolis*, and *M*; novels like *The Magic Mountain* and *Berlin Alexanderplatz*; the works of Bertolt Brecht; the architectural novelties of the Bauhaus; and the paintings of Expressionism and New Objectivity (*Neue Sachlichkeit*).[5]

A strong emphasis on the supposed decadence of Weimar shaped popular postwar representations as well. The best-known film about Weimar Berlin, Bob Fosse's *Cabaret* (1972), is a good example of how historically flawed this view could be. *Cabaret* offers the Kit Kat Club as a metaphor for the country's slide into jadedness and fascism, with Liza Minnelli as a politically oblivious, hedonistic American singer, Joel Grey as the sinister and increasingly Hitleresque German emcee, and Michael York as a hapless British onlooker. But as beautifully as the movie succeeds on its own cinematic terms, it departs significantly from the original source material and, from the realities of Weimar culture itself.[6] *Cabaret* is very loosely based on Christopher Isherwood's semiautobiographical novel of 1935, *Good-Bye to Berlin*, in which we find a far less portentous meditation on everyday life in early 1930s Berlin. Sally Bowles and the first-person English narrator never fall in love, and Sally never sings in a cabaret. Instead she performs at a sleazy bar called The Lady Windermere. This is how Isherwood describes her show:

> I was curious to see how Sally would behave. I had imagined her, for some reason, rather nervous, but she wasn't, in the least. She had a surprisingly deep husky voice. She sang badly, without any expression, her hands hanging down at her sides—yet her performance was, in its own way, effective because of her startling appearance and her air of not caring a curse what

people thought of her...I decided, as so often before, never to visit a place of this sort again.[7]

That's all—no belted-out songs about hunger or the hedonistic life, no sexy decadence, no grotesque emcee to symbolize the slide into fascism. In fact, Isherwood's story is far closer to the truth of everyday Weimar culture, in which the mundane and not particularly innovative far outweighed the spectacular and aesthetically challenging. Most of the enduring canonical works would never have come into existence without heavy subsidies from the states and municipalities. *Metropolis*, *The Threepenny Opera*, et cetera did not reflect popular mentalities or behaviors in any obvious way. As historian Karl Christian Führer points out,

> Our understanding of Weimar culture is incomplete without a grasp of broader patterns of cultural production and consumption, and skewed if it does not take into account the conservative tastes and the forces of tradition which also characterized [culture]. Seen from this broader perspective, cultural life in the republic emerges as less spectacular and less experimental than it appears in many accounts.[8]

A scholarly re-evaluation of Weimar and its culture has been underway since the late 1980s, however. There are several reasons for this. First, the *Sonderweg* thesis of German deviance from "Western modernity" came under attack beginning in the early 1980s. This took the form of a vehement debate among historians, which they carried out in programmatic essays, scholarly monographs, and polemical exchanges. Many if not most scholars of Germany began to realize that the *Sonderweg* thesis was based on an idealized notion of "Western modernization" that had little to do with the real complexities of modernity. The demise of the *Sonderweg* has inspired scholars to rethink Germany's state, society, and culture since the nineteenth century. They have demonstrated convincingly that in this era of rapid industrialization, urbanization, and all of the accompanying social changes, Germany became an essentially *modern* nation.[9]

Second, a number of post-*Sonderweg* historians began in the late 1980s to interrogate the nature of Weimar Germany's "modernity"—most influentially the late Detlev Peukert. Peukert's 1987 book *The Weimar Republic* argues that Weimar faced the same political, social, and economic instabilities that every other Western industrial society has at one time or another faced. Yet the republic was burdened with all of these crises at once; it stood "at a crisis-ridden intersection of epochal social-cultural innovations." This was largely because the First World War and its legacies "narrowed the space available within which to reach any compromise which might have made the political and social innovations of the Weimar Republic acceptable to the various groups among the German population."[10] In contrast to the *Sonderweg* historians, who identified modernization with the rise of capitalism, liberalism, and rationalism, Peukert saw even those developments as deeply ambiguous. For him, modernity itself was "Janus-faced" and deeply ambiguous, both in an objective sense and as a subjective experience.

> The hectic sequence of events, the depths of the crisis shocks, and the innovative power of the social-cultural and political changes were not marginal; they were central characteristics of the epoch. From them grew an underlying sense of insecurity and absence of bearings—of changes in the framework of everyday life and of the calling into question of traditional generational and gender roles. Insecurity was the mark of the epoch.[11]

This insecurity weakened democracy and left it vulnerable to attack from both the far Left and the far Right. Authoritarian solutions to the nation's problems, always a danger in any troubled democracy, came to the fore in the early 1930s. With the Depression and the polarization of politics, the republic finally ran out of both the time and the *Handlungsspielraum* ("room to maneuver") that would have been necessary to create lasting democratic solutions.

Peukert interprets culture as a microcosm of the deeply modern uncertainty that characterized Weimar. Culture "elegantly and breathlessly played out all the positions and possibilities of modernity through to the end, put them to the test, and repudiated them almost simultaneously."[12] This "playing out" took place not only in intellectual life and the high arts, but also within the mass media, everyday consumerism, and organized associations and subcultures. The diverse concept of "culture" found in Peukert's work is only one way in which he offered a far more complex view of Weimar modernity than had previously been the case.

Many historians have engaged with Peukert's thesis by seeking to bring specificity to his notion of "classical modernity," as well as to his emphasis on the real and perceived crises of Weimar. One subject that has attracted renewed scholarly attention in the wake of Peukert's interventions is the First World War and its cultural repercussions.[13] Over two million men were killed on the battlefield, and the nearly 800,000 injured soldiers who returned to Germany became a constant reminder of the cost for young men and their families. On the home front, exhaustion, malnutrition, and epidemics led to an estimated 300,000 civilian fatalities, not including some 400,000 people who perished in the 1918–1919 flu pandemic.[14] In cultural terms, by causing a decline in traditional ideas and institutions of social order on the home front, the war deepened existing fears of social disorder. Civilians experienced the sudden collapse of established hierarchical relationships—men over women and children, adults over adolescents, the wealthy over the poor. The trauma of mass death and rapid social and political transformation greatly intensified preexisting fears that the moral, physical, and social health of the nation was in danger.[15]

Other scholars have interrogated or given added nuance to Peukert's pessimistic concept of the "pathologies of modernity," which he located in policies of state welfare and social discipline. Still others have begun to go even further, investigating not only the weaknesses, but also the very real and positive potentials in Weimar culture. This latter initiative shows the most promise for the field of Weimar studies, but it does involve some distancing from Peukert's pessimism. The best research on Weimar culture since 1990 has denied neither the damaging legacies of total war, nor that there were longer-term "pathological" tendencies that the war only intensified—most obviously racial nationalism with all its social darwinist, biopolitical, and anti-Semitic excretions. But these scholars have shown Peukert's pessimistic view of Weimar to be exaggerated and, in its own way, teleological. Combining this insight with a rejection of the simplistic *Sonderweg* view of modernization is the key to moving forward in researching the Weimar era. As Anthony McElligott puts it in a recent discussion of Peukert's legacy,

> There is an increasing acceptance that there was not a single path to modernity; nor indeed was modernity itself one-dimensional but polyvalent...On closer examination Weimar's "crisis" need not be interpreted as a "crisis of modernity" *per se*, but instead as one where there was an ongoing tension between these different paths to modernization.[16]

While those on the Left tended to see these crises as new opportunities for progress, traditional conservatives and the far Right clung to the selective notion of a unique and homogeneous "German culture." During Weimar The Nazi Fighting League for German Culture (*Kampfbund für deutsche Kultur*), for instance, trumpeted its "basic principle of rejecting all limited, partisan artistic creations in [favor of] an exclusive recognition, protection, and promotion of *German art and culture*."[17] Yet the Right's hysterical insistence on preserving homogeneously "Aryan" and canonical "German culture" only shows that they were fighting a losing battle. Real German culture was rapidly superseding this parched fantasy. Indeed, the far Right soon compromised with contemporary technological and political developments. It is no longer convincing to dismiss Nazi concepts of culture as simply anti-modern or "Romantic"; rather Nazism was just one of myriad projects of mastering modernity, all of which had a strong cultural component.[18] And if popular insecurities and reactionary ideas could now be more freely expressed than ever before, so could genuinely forward-looking, experimental, and sometimes startlingly progressive blueprints for change.[19]

Contemporary scholars of Weimar are looking beyond the handful of texts that comprise the canon of "Weimar culture" and overturning popular clichés of flappers dancing on the volcano. This challenge to stereotypical reductions of Weimar culture was prepared by the critique of the *Sonderweg* and by Peukert's complex view of modernity. A third inspiration has been the recent turn to everyday life in the historiography of Germany. *Alltagsgeschichte* ("the history of everyday life") first emerged in West Germany during the 1980s as a collaboration between social historians, anthropologists, and a network of local *Geschichtswerkstätte* (history workshops).[20] These scholars understood culture broadly as a diverse set of historically contingent "texts" that shape how people view the world and themselves, as well as how they act in their daily social relationships. As anthropologist Hans Medick put it, culture serves as "a central dynamic and formative movement in the everyday 'realization' and transformation of social, economic, and political relations."[21] Yet in this view, culture never wholly determines human agency; for there is also an ongoing process through which people's everyday language and actions either reproduce, contest, or transform cultural "texts."

Finally, alongside the practitioners of *Alltagsgeschichte*, scholars of women's history and gender relations have brought remarkable new insights to our understanding of Weimar culture. Women in interwar Germany faced some significantly different problems from men, and their opportunities differed as well. The most famous symbol of the complexities of gender in Weimar was the "New Woman." This icon of an economically and sexually independent young urban woman reflected a (limited) social reality for some single women in the middle classes. For many others, the New Woman became a daring kind of potentially alternative identity, especially for those who were disappointed by the republic's failed promises to help emancipate them in their everyday lives. Else Herrmann's 1929 essay "This

Is The New Woman" expressed this link between political disappointment and gender:

> Despite the fact that every war from time immemorial has entailed the liberation of an intellectually, spiritually, or physically fettered social group, the war and postwar period of our recent past has brought women nothing extraordinary in the slightest but only awakened them from their lethargy and laid upon them the responsibility for their own fate.[22]

The New Woman also became a lightning rod for antifeminist anger. The Right tended to perceive women's independence as a threat to social order and the biological vitality of the "race." Fears of female autonomy were reflected in various attempts to reassert male control, most prominently in the retrenchment of the ideology of motherhood and in new forms of misogyny.[23] But above and beyond the political struggle over the New Woman, gender was in a larger sense fundamental to debates about the moral order; about work, both domestic and public; about the audience for the new mass media; and even about Germany's relationship to the rest of the world.[24]

All of these recent developments in the field of Weimar history have enabled younger scholars to produce extraordinarily innovative work. *Weimar Culture Revisited* offers a cross-section. The book focuses on four thematic areas: visual and mass culture, transnational film and literature, political culture, and the body and nature.

The first three chapters look into Weimar visual and mass culture. Avant-garde art still commands the attention of innovative scholars, as exemplified by Debbie Lewer's essay, "Revolution and the Weimar Avant-Garde: Contesting the Politics of Art, 1919–1924."[25] In the heady days of the November Revolution, Expressionists and Dadaists sought to extend their political influence in order to benefit to the radical working class. The November Group, founded in late 1918, announced that, "Art and people must form a unity. Art shall no longer be the enjoyment of the few but the life and happiness of the masses."[26] Lewer interprets this kind of radical modernism not so much as a set of canonical works, but as a site of intertwined aesthetic and political experiments. She shows that avant-garde artists consciously propagated a new imagery of the spectacular, symbolizing their revolutionary aims with the image of a passionate, quasi-religious political agitator. Representations of this male "orator" also suggested a conflation of the figures of the artist, the agitator, and the religious prophet into the icon of the visionary outsider. Ironically, as Lewer shows, this very image of the agitator exposed the early Weimar avant-garde's political limitations, as well as its partial alienation from the far Left.

As the next two chapters remind us, Weimar was also an era of remarkable innovation in mass culture. Radio and film, in particular, excited the popular imagination and intensified public debates over free expression, the politics of mass-produced art, and the psychology of the audience itself.[27] Some scholars have suggested that the unprecedented circulation of sights and sounds via the mass media led not only to a gradual displacement of regional particularities, but also to a partial dismantling of class hierarchies. This thesis reflects in part the strong influence of one of Weimar Germany's most famous intellectuals, Siegfried Kracauer. Kracauer built his pessimistic critique of mass culture on the assertion that there existed a homogeneous, petty bourgeois, and easily deluded mass audience. This "mass" was distracted from the travails of real life by flashy entertainment, and it was thus becoming indoctrinated into a socially conservative, proto-fascist form of capitalism.

> Nearly all the [film] industry's productions work to legitimate the existing state of affairs by failing to examine either its excesses or its basic foundations. They numb the people with the pseudo-glamour of counterfeit social heights, just as hypnotists use shining objects to put their mediums to sleep. The same applies to the illustrated newspapers and the majority of magazines.[28]

In his essay "Cinema, Radio, and 'Mass Culture' in the Weimar Republic: Between Shared Experience and Social Division," Corey Ross questions whether the new mass culture actually leveled social distinctions enough to create such a homogeneous audience. Ross investigates how this supposedly homogenizing mass culture actually functioned in the fragmented society of Weimar, as well as the degree to which film and radio offered shared social experiences. The essay challenges notions of cultural standardization and audience uniformity, focusing instead on who was seeing or hearing what, and on the specific circumstances in which films and radio programs were created and received.[29] Ross finds that there was no homogeneous mass audience in Weimar, because of persistent divisions by class, region, age, gender, and other factors. In light of the diverse public revealed by research such as this, generalizations about a single "mass audience" should finally be laid to rest.

Whereas Corey Ross attends to mass cultural reception in the context of everyday Weimar society, David Imhoof provides in "Blue Angel, Brown

Culture: The Politics of Film Reception in Göttingen" a local case study of how a popular and famous movie became intertwined with everyday politics. Josef von Sternberg's *The Blue Angel*, with Marlene Dietrich as the sultry traveling nightclub singer Lola Lola, has been since its release in 1930 one of the most famous examples of Weimar cinema. As Imhoof writes, "The film's content—the legs, the songs, the decadent nightclub setting, and especially the iconic imagery of Dietrich—has become shorthand for 'Weimar culture.'" Yet while the film itself has been heavily analyzed, little is known about its critical and popular reception, or about the ways in which it influenced political culture. Imhoof offers a local case study, analyzing the reception of *The Blue Angel* in the mid-sized university town of Göttingen to illustrate the roles played by mass culture, gender representation, and local critics in a rapidly changing political landscape.

The next three chapters bring transnational analyses to Weimar representations of the Far East, Africa, and Germany's relationship with the "Other." The investigation of attitudes toward other cultures is an increasingly important theme in the historiography of modern Germany. As Young-Sun Hong writes, although the nation-state has certainly not disappeared from the concerns of German historians, its "conceptual and geographical borders are much more porous than was once believed to be the case."[30] We are just beginning to recognize that in the modern world, as more people have become exposed through culture or experience to the ways of other peoples, their sense of identity and of life itself has been based in part on notions of the foreign and the exotic.

The research presented here on transnational currents in Weimar culture is pioneering. In his "Middle-Class Heroes: Anti-Nationalism in the Popular Adventure Films of the Weimar Republic," Ofer Ashkenazi investigates one of the most popular genres in Weimar film, the exotic adventure. Although few of these films have made their way into the recognized canon, millions of Germans followed the heroes and heroines of these films to the palaces of Indian Maharajas, lost subterranean cities in Africa, opium dens in China, and soulless department stores in North America. Through a series of encounters with sometimes dangerous but often alluring foreigners, these films expressed some of the anxieties of Weimar's middle-class liberals about the threat of dysfunctional state authorities, the dangerous appeal of mysticism and irrational convictions, and the possibilities of social chaos and absolute rulers. As Ashkenazi shows, Weimar adventure films became one way for bourgeois filmmakers and audiences to envision an optimistic, postnationalist, and pluralistic future for Europe.

Luke Springman's essay "Exotic Attractions and Imperialist Fantasies in Weimar Youth Literature" analyzes mass-produced children's literature, a rich field of cultural production that has only begun to draw scholarly attention. Such literature echoed many of the popular ideas about Africa in the wake of Germany's loss of its colonies in 1919. Springman looks comparatively at three texts—Paul von Lettow-Vorbeck's World War I memoir *Heia Safari!* of 1920, Colin Ross' 1928 travelogue *With Camera, Kith, and Kin Through Africa*, and the popular children's magazine *Merry Fridolin*. These works contained complex and sometimes contradictory representations of race relations and the Other. Africa appeared as a distant exotic realm, but postcolonial nostalgia made the continent's potential riches and its wild and "primitive" state seem even more enticing than before. Children's books and magazines tended either to idealize life in the former colonies or to present Africa optimistically as a refuge, where the next generation might find a new homeland. Springman shows that racist views of Africans could be both perpetuated and undermined in these works.

In "How Can a War Be Holy? Weimar Attitudes Towards Eastern Spirituality," Tom Neuhaus examines the growing interest of educated elites in both Tibetan Buddhism and a wider Eastern spirituality. This trend reflected a desire to look for "alternatives to the mistakes of the past (such as those that had led to the outbreak of the First World War), to the rapidly increasing urbanization of Weimar society, and to the supposed over-reliance on science to explain the human condition." Because Tibet and its religion were little known but had nonetheless long intrigued Germans, they became a kind of blank screen onto which one could project fantasies, fears, and desires. This meant that alternative solutions to Germany's problems could be discussed relatively freely through references to the beneficial aspects of Eastern culture. In this sense, growing interest in the East became one way of contemplating how postwar German society might heal itself and advance toward peace and spiritual regeneration.

The next two chapters analyze political culture as a site of ideological struggle. Central to Weimar was the ideological struggle to control culture. Traditionalist conservatives, liberals, and moderate socialists debated the relationship between culture and politics.[31] The state was a particularly important actor in this regard, yet historians have long neglected its attempts to promote republican democracy. Instead, they have typically contrasted republican state representation negatively with the allegedly more determined and "successful" propaganda of the Nazi regime. In her "Visualizing the Republic: State Representation and Public Ritual in

Weimar Germany," Nadine Rossol overturns this stereotype of the central state as an ineffectual advocate for liberal democracy. Rossol demonstrates that key officials were well aware of the need to popularize the republican state and developed innovative means to do so. Their new methods of representation echoed modern cultural developments by stressing spectacle and democratic inclusiveness. As Rossol argues, "Innovative representative methods were combined with optimistic hopes that the young democracy could educate its citizens in better artistic taste, a deeper communal spirit, and more republican dedication."

Extremists of the Left and Right wanted to see Weimar democracy dead, and they fought it in large part by attacking it through language and imagery. At the same time, radical movements produced their own unique rhetoric and imagery, in which gender played a key role.[32] Sara Ann Sewell offers a case study in the gendering of radical political culture in "The Party Does Indeed Fight Like a Man: The Construction of a Masculine Ideal in the Weimar Communist Party." While the KPD consistently advocated women's rights, neither the rank and file nor the party's leaders ever fully committed themselves to everyday gender equality. As the KPD built a membership cadre that was committed to revolutionary struggle, its political culture increasingly prioritized not only men's issues, but also the male fighter. This fierce masculine ethos became even more pronounced during the final years of the republic, as Communists devoted increasing energy to fighting Nazis with a force that excluded women.

The last two chapters focus on the body and nature, respectively. In part because of the very real damage caused to the human body by total war, and in part stemming from a diverse array of naturist organizations that had originated in the late nineteenth century, health, the body, and rural nature became key sites of everyday cultural endeavor in Weimar Germany. Erik Jensen's chapter "Sweat Equity: Sports and the Self-Made German" shows that competitive sports were perfectly suited to the liberal context of the republic. By rewarding individual merit, they symbolized for many a new democratic openness and opportunity. Especially tennis and boxing, Jensen asserts, promoted individualism more than any social movement at the time. And the "self-made" quality of the champion athlete extended beyond the cultivation of biceps and stamina alone. Elite athletes had star power, which they converted into financial and social opportunities. Thus sports appealed particularly to those on the margins of society, such as single women, Jews, and working-class men. Successful male and female athletes provided the models for a new ideal of individual accomplishment in Weimar Germany.

My chapter "Friends of Nature: The Culture of Working-Class Hiking" concerns the *Touristenverein "Die Naturfreunde,"* a socialist cultural organization dedicated to bringing urban workers into closer contact with rural nature. Founded in 1898, the TVNF had by the mid-1920s won a substantial following of some 70,000 industrial workers throughout Germany. By means of organized hiking, the TVNF offered laborers opportunities for physical and mental recuperation, a new kind of everyday class solidarity in the rural countryside, and a sharp critique of capitalist exploitation. One of the organization's goals was to anchor republican, Social Democratic values in the minds of the working class; and a discourse and everyday method of "social hiking" became the preferred way to raise popular consciousness of capitalist injustice. At the same time, the *Naturfreunde* developed a reverent attitude toward rural nature, which manifested itself in conservationist activity. While the history of the TVNF's leadership reveals in microcosm the political divisions between moderate socialists and communists that weakened the Weimar Left, this organization also reminds us that there were in fact genuinely innovative ways in which the Left appealed to workers' everyday needs and desires.

The research presented in *Weimar Culture Revisited* replaces the teleological, doom-laden narrative with a view of Weimar culture as pluralistic, complex, and full of both authoritarian and democratic potentials. What made Weimar culture so diverse and energetic was the urge across the entire ideological spectrum to overcome the war's terrible legacies, to restore the nation's collective physical and psychological health, and to navigate the rough seas of rapid change. The November Revolution might have failed to democratize key institutions like the judiciary and the military, yet it brought a true change of course toward democratic pluralism. Weimar culture was shaped above all by a powerful sense of transition and by the inevitable accompaniment: an unstable mix of fear, expectation, and hope. Through culture, Germans created between 1918 and 1933 the sites and practices of a democratically functioning civil society. Indeed, this was one of the most vital ways in which the German people participated, consciously or not, in the ongoing transformation of their nation. Looked at in this way, Weimar culture was not a failure at all.

Notes

1. Quoted in Philip Scheidemann, "Bericht über den 9. November 1918," http://www.dhm.de/sammlungen/zendok/weimar. I wish to thank Michelle Eaton, Alan Gillett, Allison Jones, Justin Tabatabai, Karl Zdansky, and the anonymous reader for Palgrave-Macmillan for their helpful insights.

2. "Die Tagung des Reichstags in der Krolloper am 23. März 1933," http://www.royallibrary.sakura.ne.jp.

3. The sociopolitical *Sonderweg* thesis focuses largely on Imperial Germany, but it is explicitly extended to Weimar in Heinrich A. Winkler, *Weimar 1918–1933* (Munich, 1999) and *Der lange Weg nach Westen* (Munich, 2002, two vols.) The most important foundational histories of Germany's allegedly reactionary culture include Fritz Stern, *The Politics of Cultural Despair* (Berkeley, 1961), and George Mosse, *The Crisis of German Ideology* (New York, 1964).

4. Otto Friedrich, *Before the Deluge: A Portrait of Berlin in the 1920s* (New York, 1972); Alex De Jonge, *The Weimar Chronicle: Prelude to Hitler* (New York, 1978); Thomas Kniesche and Stephen Brockmann, eds., *Dancing on the Volcano: Essays on the Culture of the Weimar Republic* (Rochester, 1994); Landesmuseum für Technik und Arbeit in Mannheim, ed., *Tanz auf dem Vulkan: Die Goldenen 20er in Bildern, Szenen, und Objekten* (Mannheim, 1994). The last two titles indicate that that tendency persisted into the 1990s.

5. Peter Gay, *Weimar Culture* (New York, 1968); Walter Laqueur, *Weimar: A Cultural History, 1918–1933* (New York, 1974); Bärbel Schrader and Jürgen Schebera, *The "Golden" Twenties: Art and Literature in the Weimar Republic* (New Haven, 1978); Eberhard Kolb, *Die Weimarer Republik* (Munich, 1988); Hans Mommsen, *Die verspielte Freiheit: Der Weg der Republik von Weimar in den Untergang 1918 bis 1933* (Berlin, 1989). This tendency to focus on the canon persists in Andreas Wirsching, *Die Weimarer Republik* (Munich, 2008) and Eric Weitz, *Weimar Germany* (Princeton, 2007), even if they attend more to mass culture.

6. For a historically grounded analysis of cabaret, see Peter Jelavich, *Berlin Cabaret* (Cambridge, MA, 1996).

7. Christopher Isherwood, "Good-Bye to Berlin" in *The Berlin Stories* (New York, 1954, orig. 1935), 26.

8. Karl C. Führer, "High Brow and Low Brow Culture" in *Weimar Germany*, ed. Anthony McElligott (Oxford, 2009), 260.

9. The critique of the *Sonderweg* began with David Blackbourn and Geoff Eley, *The Peculiarities of German History* (Oxford, 1984). Subsequent research that vindicates this early critique is too voluminous to cite. The originators of the *Sonderweg* thesis in Germany still adhere to it, e.g. Heinrich A. Winkler, *Der lange Weg nach Westen* (Munich, 2002, two vols.); Hans-Ulrich Wehler, *Deutsche Gesellschaftsgeschichte* (Munich, 2008, five vols.). Two important works that challenged the *Sonderweg* focus on reactionary elements in Weimar culture were John Willett, *Art and Politics in the Weimar Period: The New Sobriety* (New York, 1980); Jost Hermand and Frank Trommler, *Die Kultur der Weimarer Republik* (Munich, 1984), both of which shifted their focus to the Left's struggle for cultural influence.

10. Detlev J. K. Peukert, *Die Weimarer Republik* (Frankfurt, 1987), 139.

11. Ibid., 266. Some of Peukert's critics fail to acknowledge this subjective angle in his analysis, e.g., Moritz Föllmer and Rudiger Graf, ed., *Die "Krise" der Weimarer Republik: Zur Kritik eines Deutungsmuster* (Frankfurt, 2005).

12. Peukert, *Weimarer Republik*, 140.

13. George Mosse, *Fallen Soldiers: Reshaping the Memory of the World Wars* (Oxford, 1990); Gerald Hirschfeld, et al, eds., *"Keiner fühlt sich hier mehr als Mensch...": Erlebnis und Wirkung des Ersten Weltkriegs* (Frankfurt, 1996); Anton Kaes, *Shell Shock Cinema: Weimar Cinema and the Wounds of War* (Princeton, 2009).

14. Reichsarbeitsminister Dr. Brauen, cited in *Frauenstimme* (May 15, 1924); Robert Whalen, *Bitter Wounds: German Victims of the Great War, 1914–1939* (Ithaca, 1984), 40; Kathleen Canning, "Weimar and the Politics of Gender" in McElligott, *Weimar Germany*, 147.

15. Richard Bessel, *Germany After the First World War* (Oxford, 1993); Roger Chickering, *Imperial Germany and the Great War, 1914–1918* (Cambridge, 1998); Belinda Davis, *Home Fires Burning: Food, Politics, and Everyday Life in World War I Berlin* (Chapel Hill, 2000).

16. Anthony McElligott, "Introduction" in idem, *Weimar Germany*, 7–8. Other works that address Peukert's work include Frank Bajohr, et al., eds., *Zivilization und Barbarei: Die widersprüchlichen Potenziale der Moderne* (Hamburg, 1991); Elizabeth Harvey, *Youth and the Welfare State in Weimar Germany* (Oxford, 1993); Geoff Eley, ed., *Society, Culture, and the State in Germany, 1870–1930* (Ann Arbor, 1996); Peter Fritzsche, "Did Weimar Fail?," *Journal of Modern History* (1996): 629–656; Young-Sun Hong, *Welfare, Modernity, and the Weimar State, 1919–1933* (Princeton, 1998); David Crew, *Germans on Welfare: From Weimar to Hitler* (Oxford, 1998); Föllmer and Graf, *Krise*.

17. Joseph Goebbels, "Kampfbund für Deutsche Kultur" (1932), reprinted in *The Weimar Republic Sourcebook*, ed. Anton Kaes, et al. (Berkeley, 1994), 143. On Nazi ideas of culture in late Weimar, see *Nazi Culture*, ed. George Mosse (New York, 1966); Peter Jelavich, *Berlin Alexanderplatz: Radio, Film, and the Death of Weimar Culture* (Berkeley, 2006).

18. Paul Weindling, *Health, Race, and German Politics Between National Unification and Nazism, 1870–1945* (Cambridge, 1989); John Alexander Williams, "Protecting Nature Between Democracy and Dictatorship: The Changing Ideology of the Bourgeois Conservationist Movement, 1925–1935" in *Germany's Nature: Cultural Landscapes and Environmental History*, ed. Thomas Lekan and Thomas Zeller (New Brunswick, 2005), 183–206.

19. See, for example, Mary Nolan, *Visions of Modernity: American Business and the Modernization of Germany* (Oxford, 1994); Thomas Rohrkrämer, *Eine andere Moderne? Zivilisationskritik, Natur, und Technik in Deutschland, 1880–1933* (Paderborn, 1999); John Alexander Williams, *Turning to Nature in Germany: Hiking, Nudism, and Conservation, 1900–1940* (Stanford, 2007); Rüdiger Graf, *Die Zukunft der Weimarer Republik: Krisen und Zukunftsaneignungen*

in Deutschland, 1918-1933 (Munich, 2008). For an illuminating discussion of modern Germans' repeated attempts to "remake the nation" in the face of upheaval, see Konrad Jarausch and Michael Geyer, *Shattered Past: Reconstructing German Histories* (Princeton, 2003).

20. Geoff Eley, "Labor History, Social History, *Alltagsgeschichte*: Experience, Culture, and the Politics of the Everyday—A New Direction for German Social History?," *Journal of Modern History* (1989): 297–343.

21. Hans Medick, "'Missionaries in the Row Boat'? Ethnological Ways of Knowing as a Challenge to Social History," *Comparative Studies in Society and History* (1987): 78. Key collections by *Alltagsgeschichte* scholars include Alf Lüdtke, ed., *Alltagsgeschichte: Zur Rekonstruktion historischer Erfahrungen und Lebensweisen* (Frankfurt, 1989); Belinda Davis, et al, eds., *Alltag, Erfahrung, Eigensinn* (Frankfurt, 2008). Bernd Widdig, *Culture and Inflation in Weimar Germany* (Berkeley, 2001), takes an *Alltagsgeschichte* approach to Weimar.

22. Elsa Herrmann, *So ist die neue Frau* (1929), reprinted in Kaes, et al, *Sourcebook*, 207. See Marsha Meskimmon and Shearer West, eds., *Visions of the "Neue Frau": Women and the Visual Arts in Weimar Germany* (Aldershot, UK, 1995); Katharina von Ankum, ed., *Women in the Metropolis: Gender and Modernity in Weimar Culture* (Berkeley, 1997); Richard McCormick, *Gender and Sexuality in Weimar Modernity* (New York, 2001); Canning, "Women."

23. Tim Mason, "Women in Germany, 1925–1940: Family, Welfare, and Work" in *History Workshop Journal* (1976); Renata Bridenthal, et al., eds., *When Biology Became Destiny: Women in Weimar and Nazi Germany* (New York, 1984); Klaus Theweleit, *Male Fantasies* (Minneapolis, 1987–1989, two vols., trans. Stephen Conwa); Maria Tatar, *Lustmord: Sexual Murder in Weimar Germany* (Princeton, 1997).

24. Eve Rosenhaft, "Women, Gender, and the Limits of Political History in the Age of 'Mass Politics'" in *Elections, Mass Politics, and Social Change in Modern Germany,* eds. James Retallack and Larry Eugene Jones (Cambridge, 1992), 149–74; Cornelie Usborne, *The Politics of the Body in Weimar Germany* (Hampshire, UK, 1992), and *Cultures of Abortion in Weimar Germany* (Providence, 2007); Atina Grossmann, *Reforming Sex: The German Movement for Birth Control and Abortion Reform, 1920–1950* (Oxford, 1995); Dorothy Rowe, *Representing Berlin: Sexuality and the City in Imperial and Weimar Germany* (London, 2003); Raffael Scheck, *Mothers of the Nation: Right-Wing Women in Weimar Germany* (Oxford, 2004); Kathleen Canning, *Gender History in Practice* (Ithaca, 2006).

25. See also Shearer West, *The Visual Arts in Germany, 1890–1937* (New Brunswick, 2001); Helmut Lethen, *Cool Conduct: The Culture of Distance in Weimar Germany* (Berkeley, 2003); Sabine Hake, *Topographies of Class: Modern Architecture and Mass Society in Weimar Berlin* (Ann Arbor, 2009).

26. "Work Council for Art Manifesto" (1919), reprinted in Kaes, et al., *Sourcebook*, 478.

27. Bruce Murray, *Film and the German Left in the Weimar Republic: From Caligari to Kuhle Wampe* (Austin, 1990); Kaspar Maase, *Grenzenloses Vergnügen: Der Aufstieg der Massenkultur, 1850–1970* (Frankfurt, 2007); Kaes et al., *Sourcebook.*

28. Siegfried Kracauer, *Die Angestellten* (1930), reprinted in Kaes, et al., *Sourcebook,* 190–91. See also Kracauer's *From Caligari to Hitler: A Psychological History of the German Film* (Princeton, 1947).

29. With this emphasis on reception and audience diversity, Ross builds on the insights of Patrice Petro's pioneering *Joyless Streets: Women and Melodramatic Representation in Weimar Germany* (Princeton, 1989).

30. Young-Sun Hong, "The Challenge of Transnational History" (2006), http://www.h-net.org/~german/discuss/Trans/forum_trans_index.htm. Examples of transnational analysis include Alf Lüdtke, et al., eds., *Amerikanisierung: Traum und Alptraum im Deutschland des 20. Jahrhunderts* (Stuttgart, 1996); Eric Ames, et al., eds., *Germany's Colonial Pasts* (Lincoln, 2009).

31. See Donna Harsch, *German Social Democracy and the Rise of Nazism* (Chapel Hill, 1993); Shelley Baranowski, *The Sanctity of Rural Life: Nobility, Protestantism, and Nazism in Weimar Prussia* (New York, 1995); David Barclay and Eric Weitz, eds., *Between Reform and Revolution: German Socialism and Communism from 1848 to 1990* (Providence, 1998); Julia Sneeringer, *Winning Women's Votes: Propaganda and Politics in Weimar Germany* (Chapel Hill, 2002); Wolfgang Hardtwig, ed., *Politische Kulturgeschichte der Zwischenkriegszeit, 1918–1939* (Göttingen, 2005); Kathleen Canning, et al, eds., *Weimar Publics/Weimar Subjects: Rethinking the Political Culture of Germany in the 1920s* (Providence, 2010).

32. See Eve Rosenhaft, *Beating the Fascists: The German Communists and Political Violence, 1929–1933* (Cambridge, 1983); Dietmar Petzina, ed., *Fahnen, Fäuste, Körper: Symbolik und Kultur der Arbeiterbewegung* (Cologne, 1986); Pamela Swett, *Neighbors and Enemies: The Culture of Radicalism in Berlin, 1929–1933* (Cambridge, 2007).

CONTRIBUTORS

Ofer Ashkenazi is a Fellow of the Koebner Institute for German History at the Hebrew University in Jerusalem. He is the author of *A Walk into the Night: Reason, Subjectivity and "Crisis" in the Films of the Weimar Republic* (Am-Oved, 2010).

David Imhoof is an Associate Professor of History at Susquehanna University in Pennsylvania. He is currently writing a book entitled *Becoming a Nazi Town: Cultural Life in Göttingen during the Weimar and Nazi Eras*.

Erik Jensen is an Associate Professor of History at Miami University in Ohio. He is the author of *Body by Weimar: Athletes, Gender, and German Modernity* (Oxford University Press, 2010).

Debbie Lewer is a Lecturer in Art History at the University of Glasgow and a Humboldt Research Fellow at the University of Bonn (2009–2010). She is editor of *Post-Impressionism to the Second World War: An Anthology* (Blackwell, 2005) and is currently writing a book on the Weimar avant-garde and its representations of German history.

Tom Neuhaus is a Lecturer in History at the University of Derby. He is currently writing a book entitled *Lost Horizons: British and German Representations of Tibet and the Himalayas, 1890–1959*.

Corey Ross is a Professor of Modern History at the University of Birmingham. He is the author of *Constructing Socialism at the Grass-Roots: The Transformation of East Germany, 1945–65* (Macmillan, 2000), *The East German Dictatorship: Problems and Perspectives in the Interpretation of the GDR* (Arnold, 2002), and *Media and the Making of Modern Germany: Mass Communications, Politics, and Society from the Empire to the Third Reich* (Oxford University Press, 2008).

Nadine Rossol is a Lecturer in European History at the University of Essex. She is the author of *Performing the Nation in Interwar Germany: Sport, Spectacle, and Political Symbolism, 1926–36* (Palgrave, 2010).

Sara Ann Sewell is an Associate Professor of History at Virginia Wesleyan College in Virginia. She is currently writing a book entitled *Everyday Communism: Political Culture, Gender, and Daily Life among Communists during the Weimar Republic.*

Luke Springman is an Associate Professor of German at Bloomsburg University in Pennsylvania. He is the author of *Comrades, Friends and Companions: Utopian Projections and Social Action in German Literature for Young People, 1926–1934* (Peter Lang, 1989) and *Carpe Mundum: German Youth Culture of the Weimar Republic* (Peter Lang, 2007).

John Alexander Williams is an Associate Professor of History at Bradley University in Illinois. He is the author of *Turning to Nature in Germany: Hiking, Nudism, and Conservation, 1900–1940* (Stanford University Press, 2007) and the editor of *Berlin Since the Wall's End: Shaping Society and Memory in the German Metropolis since 1989* (Cambridge Scholars Press, 2008).

I

REVOLUTION AND THE WEIMAR AVANT-GARDE: CONTESTING THE POLITICS OF ART, 1919–1924

Debbie Lewer

"The revolution has brought us the freedom to express and to realize desires held for years...The call 'Art for the People!' is no empty cry." [1] These were the words of the Expressionist painter Max Pechstein, writing in the November Group pamphlet *An alle Künstler* (To All Artists) in 1919. His declaration, based more on hope than actuality, caught the tenor of the age. In the wake of the collapse of the monarchy and the end of the First World War in November 1918, many avant-garde writers and artists engaged intensively with the prospect of revolution. In countless manifestos, poems, plays, articles, proclamations, and images infused with the "spirit of November," they articulated a sense of both subjective, individual liberation and objective, collective purpose. However, there were also conflicts within the already deeply factionalized German avant-garde. Focusing on late Expressionism and aspects of Berlin Dada's anti-Expressionist polemics, this chapter addresses some of the key debates surrounding art and politics in the period 1918–1924. It examines, in particular, these disparate groupings' visual iconography of political agitation. In so doing, it seeks to shed new light on some of these conflicts, as a well as to provide a more meaningful context for the common motif of the agitator than that of a nebulous "spirit of revolution." [2]

In the early years of the Weimar Republic, ideas, not only about modes of representation, but also about the relationship between art and politics itself, were bitterly contested. Critics then and now have seized on Expressionists' often naive political claims in order to attack the movement from a variety of perspectives.[3] Even before November 1918, the Dadaists in Berlin were denouncing what they called Expressionism's "bloodless abstraction."[4] In April 1920, the third issue of *Der Dada* published John Heartfield's small but trenchant parody of Expressionism. It is an abstract picture, inverted on the page, consisting of a monochrome scribble in negative. The heading is "Expressionistische Quintessenz," and the sardonic title below is "John Heartfield, *Dame in Blau* (Woman in Blue)." The image reinforced the Dadaist verdict on Expressionism as absurd and meaningless abstraction.

To the familiar art/politics tandem, we can add a third component: religion. Accordingly, this chapter also explores the significance of (chiefly Christian) religious motifs and models in relation to the imagery of agitation. The left-wing political agitator was a potent symbol for many "revolutionary" aspirations in German Expressionism and Dada.[5] Representations of agitators, speakers, orators, and revolutionaries were part of a developing iconography and typology of "class struggle" (*Klassenkampf*). Such imagery frequently cast the revolutionary proletariat as a dynamic, mass force. But it also often suggested an identification between the figures of the artist, the agitator, and the preacher or prophet as visionary outsiders.

Representations of revolutionary agitators, speakers, and so-called rabble-rousers (*Aufrührer*), either as single figures or together with their assembled audiences, appear in the visual work of several key Weimar artists, including Conrad Felixmüller, Käthe Kollwitz, and George Grosz. The political affiliations of these artists, and indeed the degree of their political engagement, varied. Still, for wide sections of the avant-garde, the symbolic figure of the agitator was able to embody both the spirit and act of revolution. Yet in the very image of the agitator, ironically, the German avant-garde's political limitations and partial separation from the radical Left were also exposed.

The so-called spirit of November fueled the political hopes and engagement of Expressionist artists. At the same time, it lent a new intensity and apparent relevance to the chiliastic visions of upheaval that were already part of Expressionism. It has even been argued that this worked both ways: that, for a time, there was a "unity between political Expressionism and expressionist politics," in the case of Karl Liebknecht and Rosa Luxemburg, for example.[6] It was not merely that economic and political conditions in 1918–1920 seemed ripe for a restructuring of the institutions of art in Germany along council lines, though this was important. Within the discourse of art, the political and the theological often came together too.[7] In keeping with the ethical zeal of the movement, many voices in Expressionist circles expressed this fusion. Not long before his appointment to the Weimar Bauhaus, Lothar Schreyer evoked the terms, potent since Wassily Kandinsky's *On the Spiritual in Art* (1911), of a coming, boundless, inner "realm of the spirit" (*Reich des Geistes*). For Schreyer, in this epoch, the false light (*Irrlicht*) of the Enlightenment is overcome, and the empire of seers, ecstatics, followers of Buddha, and people of the German Middle Ages "is today resurrected."[8] Other voices articulated hopes for a new political vitality and solidarity with the proletariat in the same breath as they expressed faith in a new messianic purpose for art and a liberation of the artist's individual subjectivity. In Dresden, during what the artist Conrad Felixmüller called in retrospect "the most exciting days of the Revolution,"[9] the editors of the Expressionist journal *Menschen*, who were adopting an increasingly political tone, declared Expressionism to be a "spiritual attitude that has not emerged since today or yesterday, but which has existed for millennia in the history of humanity." They defined its political equivalent as "anational Socialism" and called for "unequivocal believers" to join in the work of its "holy task."[10] In Berlin at the same time, a manifesto-like proclamation by one of Expressionism's leading artists, Ludwig Meidner, appeared in the journal *Der Anbruch* and elsewhere, demanding that "socialism must be our new creed!"[11] The text's conclusion exemplifies Expressionism's theocratic, humanitarian socialism: "With body and soul, with our hands, we must join in. For it is Socialism that is at stake—that is: justice, freedom, equality and the love of humanity—*at stake is God's order in the world.*"[12]

The Expressionist avant-garde's intense investment in a redemptive artistic and political practice also developed into the search for a universal language of response to the keenly felt *failure* of the revolution. This quest became most urgent following the state-sanctioned *Freikorps*' counterrevolutionary brutality of early 1919, the March uprising, and the Kapp Putsch. It could take the form of a resigned pragmatism or, in the case of radicalized artists and writers, a fascination with ideas of "Bolshevism."[13] Part of the perceived disintegration that they were responding to was the increasing division of the Left. Following the Majority Social Democrats' "betrayal" of the revolution, a wave of counterrevolutionary murders further weakened the labor movement, including the violent deaths in January and February 1919 of the Spartacists Rosa Luxemburg and Karl Liebknecht and the prime minister of the Bavarian Republic, Kurt Eisner. These were the three symbolic leaders most celebrated, mourned, and beatified in avant-garde circles. The response of avant-garde artists such as Kollwitz, Felixmüller, Grosz, and Franz Wilhelm Seiwert to these deaths often involved an unambiguous visual iconography of martyrdom, redemption, and resurrection. The portfolio of woodcuts published in Cologne in 1919 under the title *Lebendige* (The Living) is a case in point.[14] It consists of stark, icon-like portraits of Luxemburg, Liebknecht, Jean Jaurès, Eisner, Eugen Leviné, and Gustav Landauer. The portfolio commemorates the dead—their deaths marked by the sign of the cross beside their prominent names cut into the black-inked wood block—as the "living." The paradox is resolved in the symbolism of apotheosis and the suggestion of the continued life, after death, of the ideas for which these figures stood.

The *Lebendige* portfolio exemplifies just one of a range of ways in which avant-garde artists sought to articulate in visual terms their disillusionment and a shared stance of righteous admonishment in the face of the events of the immediate postwar years. In this embittered ideological climate, representations of revolutionary agitators in Expressionist art were significant. They offer a particularly interesting case for analysis because of what they reveal about the aesthetics and politics of both Expressionism and that movement's critics. The majority of such works keep specific narrative content to a minimum. They rarely indicate the agitator's affiliation to a particular party or organization, for example. Instead, he evangelizes for a general sense of unity, for a commonality of purpose and direction.[15]

A key example is the painting by Magnus Zeller, now known as "The Orator," of 1919.[16] At two meters wide, it is a large work, characterized by a composition full of agitated diagonals and a queasy palette of greens, blues, and reds. The lighting of the scene suggests a nighttime interior. On a shallow platform, a nattily dressed speaker in declamatory posture gesticulates wildly as he shouts his message. He is surrounded by a throng of upturned faces, their mouths also opened to cry out, hands stretching toward the speaker. The assembled audience includes young and older figures, workers and bowler-hatted *Bürger*. Most are men, though in their midst we glimpse the figure of a naked woman. Her incongruous presence suggests a loosely allegorical dimension at the same time that it references the contemporary figure of the urban prostitute, a staple in Expressionist iconography. For many broadly left-wing artists, the prostitute was also the female pendant to the wounded war veteran, the two united as common victims of society. The "revolutionary" dimension of Zeller's painting is very much in the realm of subjective experience here. There are no signs of the content of this orator's speech. We gain little sense of an objective exchange of ideas or information, only of emotion. The stock ciphers of revolution—a single clenched fist in the foreground, a hint of a wafting red flag in the background—are dimly realized, and literally marginalized.

Zeller actively experienced the November Revolution as a member of Berlin's revolutionary soldiers' council and attended speeches by Liebknecht and others, so he had firsthand experience of the kind of assembly his painting evokes. But how should we read an image like this in political terms? Significantly, this painting was reproduced as an illustration to accompany an article on "Modern Revolutionary Art" in the USPD (Independent Social Democratic Party) paper *Freie Welt* by Felix Stössinger, the paper's editor.[17] Stössinger's discussion is in keeping with the USPD's relative openness to avant-garde and modern art, in contrast to the more resistant, even hostile attitude of the KPD. Zeller's painting appeared under the revealing title "Redeeming Cry [*Erlösungsschrei*] in the People's Assembly," which underlined its messianic symbolism.[18] Stössinger's pedagogic tone in the plural first person and the content of the text make clear that his article aimed firmly at the paper's working-class readership and intended to win them over to "modern art." Stössinger lamented (and exploited) the fact that both the worker *and* the "bourgeois" were baffled and put off by "modern art." Understandably, he selected for discussion figurative, fairly unambiguous, "readable" works by Grosz, Meidner, and others that, he claimed, "already through their content testify to a revolutionary sensibility." We can only wonder how successful his attempt was to convince his readership that these were the works of "revolutionaries of the studio." Of Zeller's painting, he wrote:

> The picture by Magnus Zeller represents a political atmosphere, spiritual [*vergeistigt*], ecstatically heightened. Certainly workers in assemblies do not raise their arms like that, they do not cry out like a theatre choir, they do not plunge with outstretched hands toward the speaker's platform. If the artist had painted a people's assembly with all its everyday details, then he would only have presented the incidental, outward appearance. The stylized picture by Zeller expresses more, however, namely the mass yearning for a leader, the excitement of the masses, who receive the leader's redeeming word.[19]

Stössinger implies a parallel between the agitator and a preacher or messiah as carrier of the "redeeming word" (*Erlösungswort*). In this way, his appraisal of the painting is complicit with its own iconography and theatricalization of the subject. Stössinger concludes his description of Zeller's painting with a remark that further underlines the political and the messianic, prophetic, and indeed transforming function of Zeller's agitator: "The picture was surely inspired by the assembly scene in Ernst Toller's play, *Die Wandlung* [The Transformation]."[20]

The comparison is apt, though some ambiguity remains. Toller's famous play ends with two scenes that bear close comparison with the painting: the eleventh, in a people's assembly and the final, thirteenth scene, before the church. Stössinger himself seems to refer only to the eleventh. In this "assembly scene," there is an aggressive agitator—a "*Kommis*"—who takes the speaker's platform and gives a blood-thirsty speech to whip up his audience. In response, the play's hero, Friedrich, a benevolent artist-agitator-prophet, takes over to preach a (superior) message of redemption through unity and fraternal love. If Stössinger's comparative reference was to Friedrich's oration, then viewers would indeed understand the agitator in Zeller's painting as a redemptive figure. However, there is room for another possibility. In singling out the "assembly scene" for comparison rather than the more unequivocally redemptive final scene, Stössinger may have been conveying some ambivalence. The rabble-rousing *Kommis*, after all, embodies the ultimately destructive force of an inauthentic (here, Bolshevist) revolution.[21] Toller probably drew for the scene on his own experience of addressing a mass meeting for the first time during the strike of January 1918 in Munich.[22] Indeed, a common perception of Toller himself is as "a utopian idealist, and an orator intoxicated by his own words."[23] Within the works of literary and artistic Expressionism, the motif of the self-intoxicated orator is a recurring one. In this light, it is striking that there are similarities—for example, in physical posture—between Zeller's representations of agitators and his works depicting men in the grip of drunkenness or cocaine-fueled intoxication.

For all the tropes and commonalities that can be found in artistic and literary responses to the political conflicts of the period, it is nonetheless clear that Expressionist notions of revolution were remarkably elastic. They could encompass a quasimystical, inward "revolution of the spirit," an idea that was often implicitly elitist, even aristocratic in character. Yet they could also embrace a concept of active revolution as class struggle. However, precisely because ideas about revolution were central to late Expressionism, commentators often equated the *failure* of the German revolution to bring about radical change with the waning of the movement. This view was already being voiced in 1919.[24] In 1924, in a text laden with disillusionment and ironic resignation, Alfred Kuhn assessed the situation in Germany thus:

> A few years ago we gorged ourselves on revolutionary energy and now reaction is here...The intoxication of the great words has been dampened, the

various Messiahs have not come and if one had come, he would surely have been put in jail. As far as visual art is concerned, one has become rather tired of the violet cows; for there emerged, understandably, a whole horde of nice young painters, who copied the aforementioned violet cows just as keenly as they had done before with the products of the Impressionists.[25]

The passage links the failure of the revolution with the political and aesthetic enervation of painterly Expressionism. It also suggests, in the context of the counterrevolution, an equation between the elusive "various Messiahs" and the reality of the imprisonment (or worse) of political revolutionaries. Such statements served to cement the perception that Expressionism ceded to a cooler, more objective pragmatism, classicism, or what Toller disparagingly called "a modern form of Biedermeierism" around 1923.[26] That was the year in which that problematic term, the one that stuck—*"Neue Sachlichkeit"* (approximately translatable as "new objectivity")—was coined. It was also the year identified in radical Left circles as that of "the complete triumph of capital over the proletariat."[27] We can draw an analogy in visual terms by comparing two images by Max Pechstein (a supporter of the SPD). One shows the flailing limbs and burning/bleeding heart of the revolutionary artist on the lithograph cover image of the 1919 pamphlet *An alle Künstler!* quoted at the start of this chapter. In the other, a poster of 1927, these vitalist features have given way to the clean lines and strident posture of the agitator, accompanied by the symbolic "tools" of Socialism and class solidarity (hammer and sickle within a red star).[28]

The radical Left's appraisal of cultural politics in Germany at this time revolved around two key issues, both of which had implications for the avant-garde. The first was the legacy of bourgeois culture. In the putative new revolutionary order, how should the politicized proletariat approach the historical tradition of high art and the contents of the museums? Stössinger's perception, for example, in the aforementioned essay on "Modern Revolutionary Art" was that "The working class is indeed revolutionary in its economic thought, but in art, religion, attitudes to nature and literature, it is completely bourgeois."[29] His USPD viewpoint and understanding of "revolution" was different from that of the KPD or the more radical KAPD (Communist Workers Party). Nonetheless, the complaint was common. At around the same time, in May 1920, the KAPD's program also made the claim that "The ideology of the proletariat is still partially in thrall to bourgeois or petit-bourgeois elements of the imagination." Its conclusion was that, "the problem of the German

Revolution is the problem of the *development of the self-awareness of the German proletariat.*"[30]

Emerging from a radical Marxist view of history, such discussions inevitably raised another question concerning the autonomy of art. In 1919 this issue hung over the notorious *Kunstlumpdebatte* (Art Scab debate).[31] This dispute erupted when George Grosz and John Heartfield published a scathing attack in the journal *Der Gegner* (The Opponent) on Oskar Kokoschka, professor of art in Dresden, for what they saw as his betrayal of the revolution. Following the scarring of a Rubens painting by a stray bullet, Kokoschka had publicly called on fighting revolutionary factions in Dresden to avoid further damage to the city's finest artworks. In turn, Grosz and Heartfield suggested that they would welcome the destruction of paintings rather than the prospect of bullets whizzing through workers' housing.[32]

As the discussion gathered momentum, a gulf opened up between the Communist sympathizers in Berlin Dada—such as Grosz and Heartfield—and the German Communist Party's paper *Die Rote Fahne*. The paper's cultural editor, Gertrud Alexander, stridently took issue with Grosz and Heartfield for what she saw as their call to nothing more than vandalism.[33] Alexander, a vocal critic of Dada, regarded the movement as a symptom of bourgeois decadence. She argued that the German working class had the right to appropriate and enjoy the legacy of Rembrandt, Rubens, and the highest artistic achievements of the past. Others joined in the debate. August Thalheimer, a founding member of the KPD, dismissed the "bourgeois slogan" of the destruction of art as "a reflection of the praxis of the declining and decaying bourgeoisie."[34] The quarrel highlighted the divisions between the party and even those artists most in tune with its political program. One of these, Franz Seiwert of the Cologne Progressives group, added his voice in support of Grosz and Heartfield. This was in a text in *Die Aktion* that was even more explicitly iconoclastic: "Comrades! Away with respect for this whole bourgeois culture! Smash the old idols! In the name of the coming proletarian culture!"[35]

A third issue was the possibility of a truly proletarian art.[36] Catalyzed by awareness of the *Proletkult* (proletarian culture) movement in Soviet Russia, debates on the far Left in papers like *Die Rote Fahne* questioned the extent to which art should be *by* or *for* the proletariat. They asked whether *non*-bourgeois art was even a theoretical possibility under the ongoing conditions of advanced capitalism. A key text in this connection was the German translation of Alexander Bogdanov's text *Die Kunst und das Proletariat* (Art and the Proletariat). It addressed both historical art (chiefly literature) and the potential for an independent "workers' poetry." In German avant-garde circles, the text must have affirmed for many readers the gulf between *Proletkult* and Expressionism. Bogdanov argued forcefully that what is crucial about workers' poetry is precisely that it relinquishes any focus on the self—the "Ich" —and is characterized instead by the "spirit of comradeship." [37]

The Dadaist Raoul Hausmann, however, parodied the aspirations of *Proletkult* and took on the wider problem of art and class-consciousness in an essay, published in *Die Aktion* in 1921, that featured "Puffke," Hausmann's literary personification of the German philistine or *Spiessbürger*. It is Christmastime, and "Puffke" is feeling sentimental. He reflects on the comforting effects of art: "Art, the only means of getting away from all this mess we call 'reality' and escaping to a better beyond!... How cheering to be able to believe, somewhere in the corner of one's heart, that man is good! Oh, it's as comforting as whipped cream or fruit ice!" [38] Puffke dreams on, pondering a world in which coal miners can barely wait to get home in the evening to read art history books, compare the drawings of Grünewald, Dürer, and Altdorfer, and listen to Wagner and Busoni until dawn before going back to work in the mines refreshed and elevated: "We'll allow them their bit of Communism then... Even the bourgeoisie will be Communists. With a decent profit rate it's all the same anyway, and the worker will have been so purified and elevated by the fine arts that there will barely be any class differences any more." [39]

Hausmann's parodistic inversion of the Marxist model of class struggle ends with Puffke's apocalyptic vision of culture rising like a deluge, engulfing class difference. A new kind of absurd and culturally induced chaos ensues, with the proletariat running as if possessed to attend Greek dramas and the capitalists barely their own class any longer, having sunk all of their dividends for the benefit of the workers into Puffke's "great non-plus-ultra *Proletkult*." At the end, Puffke congratulates himself for single-handedly saving culture from its downfall. In a phrase that calls to mind the ironic Dada inducement to "Invest in Dada: It's worth it!" Puffke concludes that "capital is a fine thing, it always pays!" [40]

Several references in the text make it clear that the serious target of Hausmann's cynicism was the cultural line taken by the KPD's *Die Rote Fahne* and others within the Communist movement. Given these tensions and contradictions, how do we read the iconography of revolution and agitation in the work of the German avant-garde? How meaningful is the politicization it implies? Are these merely habitual, aesthetic gestures, in revolutionary guise? This is the implication of a caricature that appeared in the *Freie Welt* in October 1920. Titled *Unsere Salonbolschewisten* (Our Salon Bolsheviks), the drawing shows an elegant, artistic-looking couple, seated in a comfortable interior. An abstract work of modern art hangs on the wall and the woman has a volume of Nietzsche beside her. Her companion berates her "Read Lenin, Arabella; hurry! Who knows, maybe next year they'll be supporting our Kaiser Wilhelm again." [41]

While the caricature image provides a humorous take on the relationship between modern art, bourgeois taste, and revolution, many members of the German avant-garde were in fact seriously interested in and in some cases involved in revolutionary politics. As one polemical defense of Expressionist politics put it in 1986, "That Expressionism conceived of itself as moral idealism does not contradict the meaning and purpose of revolution." [42] However, beyond the superficial "fashion" for revolution that the *Freie Welt* cartoon satirizes, it is clear that the avant-garde's relationship with the politics and the aesthetics of revolution was often deeply ambivalent. When it came to the politics of class, the narcissism that sometimes characterized the avant-garde's revolutionary role-play and theatricalized agitational stances underscored *difference* more than it affirmed solidarity with the proletariat. Expressionists and Dadaists alike were part of a wider literary, artistic, and social *bohème*. Many Expressionists, as Douglas Kellner has put it, "glorified 'lumpen' elements, such as prostitutes, the destitute and unemployed, or the criminal." [43] Among the Dadaists, as Hubert van den Berg has written, "there was wide interest and sympathy for criminals, outlaws, barbarians, primitive peoples, but also for the radical Left." [44] From this perspective, the recurrent figure of the agitator may *generally* signify sympathy with the Left and class struggle. However, we can also understand it as a trope in an older discourse of a particular urban exoticism.

A deeply embittered article on "Proletarians and Intellectuals," published in the radical *Allgemeine Arbeiter-Union* (General Worker's Union) journal *Der Kampfruf* (The Cry of Struggle), describes some symptoms of this exoticizing and primitivizing tendency among "the intellectuals":

> The proletarian is the prole, the prole is to one man the uneducated, the mentally deficient, an object of pity, who could taste neither the caviar of the classics nor the differentiated sauces of the present; to the other man he is the muck-raker, rowdy and immoral, the cave-dweller and the uncivilized beast. [45]

We can unpack this a little more by considering Expressionist images of revolutionaries and agitators, even if such figures are not necessarily "proletarians." Clichés of one form of wildness or another are evident in such images, which frequently emphasize the unruliness of the body and the instability of the revolutionary temperament. Conrad Felixmüller's portrait of leading Communist Otto Rühle in mid-speech, bloodshot eyes bulging and body taut with visceral energy, is one prominent example.[46]

There are several Expressionist representations of enraged or traumatized revolutionaries showing signs of extreme emotion, disorder, violence, loss of control, and even madness.[47] In Felixmüller's other work, similarities are evident in his depictions of traumatized soldiers in an insane asylum and of revolutionaries. By contrast, physical and (implicitly) *political* stability mark the KPD's own typical propaganda icon of a symbolically monolithic agitator, straddling manfully an industrial cityscape, as Sándor Ék's KPD election poster *Vote for a Red Saxony* of 1920 shows.[48]

Precisely because of the commonplace of representing the agitator as gripped by violence or intoxicated by the power of his own ideas, and perhaps even because of the *failure* of revolutionary agitation in Germany, it is possible to see the avant-garde's agitating class-warrior as part of an exoticized cast of marginal, disenfranchised, and antiauthoritarian male figures. This cast of types also included the fighters, vagabonds, pimps, gold-diggers, sailors, bandits, pirates, sadists, drug addicts, spies, and sex attackers that people the works of artists like George Grosz, Otto Dix, and Rudolf Schlichter, all three of whom were connected with both Expressionism and Dada.

As we have seen, Expressionist conceptions of the agitator figure tend to abstract, stylize, and dramatize the subject. Contemporary left-wing sources, however, indicate that the actual practice of agitation on behalf of various groups and parties was conceived in very different terms. The work of the agitator involved much more than public speaking. It also meant visiting door-to-door to solicit new members and funds, organizing meetings, distributing pamphlets, pasting up posters, and so on. It is interesting to consider the Expressionist imagery of agitators in relation to examples of internal party literature. Three examples of this kind of material from different political contexts suggest that the practicalities of agitation work were often remote from the spectacular oration singled out and dramatized in Expressionist images. In 1917, for example, the Swiss Social Democratic Party published a booklet devoted to "Tips for Agitation," which describes party agitators as "mostly quiet, serious men and women...without the desire for praise and fame."[49] The personal qualities it lists as necessary for the successful agitator are "knowledge, tact, understanding of people, perseverance, punctuality, [and] zeal."[50] A 1919 German Communist booklet on agitation among farm workers is still drier, indeed numbingly bureau-cratic, in its listing of points, subpoints, and organizational instructions for the "agitation commission." There is no mention of any requisite personal, let alone emotional, qualities.[51] Several pamphlets from the period advise on techniques of political public speaking. One, which reprints a lecture given in a political training course for the right-wing German People's Party (DVP), contains numerous practical tips—for example, it is better to speak in a crowded small room than an empty large one, speakers should not respond to hecklers unless relevant, and so on. It also emphasizes that, "Above all, the *articulation* should be clear and *quiet*. *Quiet*, not to be con-fused with lack of temperament, is always the sign of inner certainty."[52]

Of course, the Swiss, rural Communist, and right-wing contexts, respectively, are all culturally and politically distinct from the examples of images of chiefly urban Communist agitation discussed here. The exis-tence of such guidelines does not necessarily mean that all agitators com-plied with them or conducted themselves in such a decorous manner in practice. Nonetheless, Expressionist representations of agitators clearly bear little relation to the characteristics—including the possible gender—of the working agitator and his or her everyday tasks.[53] Instead, they are sym-bolic representations that attribute to the act of agitation untamed zeal and unbridled physicality.

Within the imagery of the German avant-garde, the agitator as visual type draws not only on contemporary politics of dissent, but also on the religious iconography of transformation. There are many images that employ Christian iconography in the representation of revolution. In 1920, for instance, Felixmüller made a small, two-color woodcut to adorn the cover of the New Year's (1921) issue of *Die Aktion*. The journal issue was an important one, marking the tenth anniversary of *Die Aktion*'s existence. Unusually, Felixmüller gives the role of the agitator here to a female nude. She appears, perhaps as a nocturnal vision, to the tired and enervated artist-revolutionary and emits her message in the manner of a gender role–reversed Annunciation. Through comparing the woodcut not only with the Christian iconography of Annunciation, but also with the iconography of the conversion of St. Paul and others in German art, important con-nections emerge. In both kinds of images, the conversion—one political, one religious—is enacted by materialized speech, visible language. The word(s) appear both as text and material, and in Felixmüller's case, they are in meaningful red.

In this context, it is noteworthy that the idea of transformative "con-version" (*Bekehrung*) was highlighted by the pacifist Expressionist writer

Ludwig Rubiner, who championed the idea of the politically effective artist or poet. In a text titled "Renewal" (*Die Erneuerung*), he wrote about the imminent transformation of the spirit (*Geist*) to come from the proletariat, the "mass." He was writing in late 1918 or early 1919, that is, when revolution was still a possibility and before the "despondency" of Felixmüller's symbolically isolated figure had set in. In the context of my argument, this text is significant not only because of its employment of metaphysical imagery to describe political movement, but also because Rubiner explicitly identifies "conversion" as the means for the reconciliation of spiritual and material "renewal." Articulating his abstracted yet nonetheless political vision in the language of faith and prophecy, he writes:

> Those of us who believe in the path of the creative spirit, we see: before the renewal, a great conversion will have to come…The goal is eternal and absolute—we ourselves are finite and our means are finite. Conversion is the way of negotiation with all, with all our finite means to the eternal goal. The path of conversion: immersion in the mass. To be the mass. To be the mass does not mean to disappear behind the back of the foremost. It means: with responsibility, with the most burning tensing of your will to plunge into the will of your countless comrades.[54]

There are many such instances in Expressionism of the desire for the annihilation of the self in the mass. We can read them as a dialectical companion to the intense individualism, sometimes described in terms of the all-flooding "Ich" that also characterized the movement's art and literature.[55]

In light of such Expressionist representations of agitators and related imagery of annunciation and conversion, it is now possible consider some aspects of Berlin Dada's own radicalism from a new perspective. Polemic annunciations of a different kind, yet still comparable with the Felixmüller image, were produced for the First International Dada Fair in Berlin in the summer of 1920. One of the posters there showed a photograph of the head of John Heartfield, hands cupped around his wide open mouth and the words "Dada is great and John is its prophet" spilling out of it.

The poster ironically casts Heartfield as the prophet-agitator of Dada. It also articulates an absurdist version of the phrase, in Islam, "Allah is great and Mohammed is his prophet." Given Dada's antipathy to what Hausmann disparagingly called the "Expressionism of the German patriot," it is reasonable to read the image as a conscious parody of the tropes of both the agitator and the prophet in Expressionism.[56] The image of the active, dynamic hollerer of this absurd battle cry can also be considered in

Figure 1.1 Poster at the First International Dada Fair in Berlin (1920). Courtesy of Berlinische Galerie.

the light of Huelsenbeck's anti-Expressionist "Dadaist Manifesto," which declared:

> Expressionism, which was discovered abroad and which, typically, has become in Germany a fat idyll with the expectation of a good pension has nothing more to do with the efforts of active people. The signatories of this manifesto have assembled under the battle-cry "DADA!!!!" to propagandize for an art which they expect to realize new ideals.[57]

With one Dadaist annunciating the words of another, the poster image of Heartfield as Dada prophet exemplifies the self-reflexive play of Dada. It also highlights the proclamations of the Dadaist as slogans. And it inverts hierarchies blasphemously; for with "John" as its prophet, Dada takes the place of God.

Considering this kind of Dadaist imagery in the light of the Expressionist iconography of agitation, we can read Berlin Dada as parodying Expressionism in two ways. First, it debunks the inward self-intoxication of the Expressionist orator. Second, it divests the modernist prophets' annunciations of their meaning and power. Such radical skepticism toward esoteric self-seriousness and spiritual quackery was a feature of Berlin Dada's critique of contemporary culture. In 1919, the first issue of the Malik Verlag's gleefully bellicose Dada journal, *Die Pleite*, included a short proclamation "An die Geistigen!" ("To the intellectuals!") by Carl Einstein. It demanded, "Away with the non-committal other-worldly prophets, defrauders of the here-and-now, . . . sickly apothecaries of mystical redemption pills."[58]

Many of what the Berlin Dadaists called their "products" (*Erzeugnisse*) in rejection of the term "artwork," and many of their actions were related to a wider political and cultural discourse of agitation. Not only did the Dadaists issue manifestos and organize demonstrations to expose the failings of dominant German culture, but their own language is also full of the noise of street protest. We need only look at other photographs of the First International Dada Fair to see that the Dadaists' love of a good slogan knew no bounds: "Dada triumphs! Dada is political! Down with art! Dilettantes rise up! Invest in Dada!" and "Art is Dead! Long live the new machine art of Tatlin." For Wieland Herzfelde, 1920 and the Dada Fair represented the climax of a process of development "from improvised provocation to revolutionary *agitation*."[59] A widely used slogan of the counterrevolutionary movement in early Weimar Germany and thus the counter to the left-wing agitator's actions, intentions, and loud cry was "*Ruhe und Ordnung*"

("Quiet and Order.")[60] During the bloodiest months of the early Weimar Republic, the term *Ordnung*, which in right-wing circles often meant the "old order" lost in the chaos of the revolutionary republic, took on a paradoxical meaning. Particularly in the Communist press, *Ordnung* came to stand as a synonym for counterrevolutionary *violence*. The May 6, 1919 issue of *Die Rote Fahne*, for example, reported mass arrests and murders of Spartacists in a wave of "white terror" in the Munich. Its front-page headline was *"Ordnungsorgien in München"* ("Orgies of Order in Munich"). Both Expressionism and Dada envisaged and enunciated the experience of the war and revolution in terms of its noise, its clamor, and its *dis*order. In 1920, Dada's ironic appropriation of the rhetoric of *"Ordnung"* was made explicit in a Cologne Dada poster. Under the familiar slogan "Dada Triumphs" (*Dada Siegt!*), the phrase *"Dada ist für Ruhe und Orden"* appears. The statement is a sardonic pun on the ubiquitous postwar slogan commanding *"Ruhe und Ordnung"* (quiet and order). Slyly distorted, it reads in approximate translation: "Dada is for quiet and military honors (or medals)."[61]

The agitator—left-wing, right-wing, or Dadaist—has a prominent place in the iconography of Dada.[62] Text has multiple functions in images such as these. It is material, and it also relates to Dadaist sound poetry. Text often appears as an emission from the body. In this sense, it is related to the sacral imagery of annunciation discussed above, as well as to the basely secular, such as when Heartfield and other Dadaists appear spewing text like circus barkers across the pages of Dada publications. These representations are closely connected to a stylization of the agitator figure. In my view, much of this imagery was an acknowledgment and subsequent critique of revolution in the Expressionist mode, its *Schrei*. Dada's noisiness was the racket of the city street or the advertising cry of the market trader, not the existential cry of the soul. Dada appropriated the agitator's passion and disassembled it, mechanizing it. In so doing, Dada made visible the semiotic and political limits of the Expressionist cry. By 1926, Magnus Zeller himself was expressing disappointment at how, as he saw it, the revolution in Germany had quickly devolved into a "wage movement" (*Lohnbewegung*). Tellingly, he linked to this the similar tendency in painting, which had also become a "matter of the economy" (*eine Konjunkturangelegenheit*), leading painters to mass produce their saleable "cry" (*Schrei*).[63]

Finally, Dadaist practices broke down and critiqued the conventional relationship between the agitator-as-preacher and the masses-as-congregation as it was encouraged in revolutionary idealism. When the Dadaists spoke into the void or hermetically, into the ear of another

Dadaist, they were interchangeably both prophets *and* converts.[64] For all their loudness, the Dadaists inverted the function of the agitator. Their slogans and gestures were locked in private communication and trapped, willingly, in the exclusivity of Club Dada and its love of in-jokes, private codes, hoaxes, and pseudonyms.[65] As such, they represent facets not only of Dada's play and humor, but also of its rhetorical upending of the conventional performance of public politics. Representations of the agitator also visualized and critically re-enacted the crisis of representation in Expressionist art. That crisis was itself triggered by the failure of the German revolution to bring about material and spiritual change. Dada responded by appropriating and subverting the aesthetics of both Expressionism and class struggle. This was offered not as a remedy, but as a diagnosis of a world about which Hausmann remarked, in Berlin on May Day of 1920: "Of course God has melted away into butter, of course the black marketeer must traffic in his goods and there must be order [*Ordnung muss sind* (sic)], only this spirit, this art, this science: this bourgeois filth makes us puke." [66]

Notes

1. Max Pechstein, "Was wir wollen" in *An alle Künstler!* (Berlin, 1919), 18–22. Beginning in December, 1918, Pechstein put his art in the service of the new (largely SPD) government's Publicity Office (*Werbedienst*) and against Spartacist politics. Joan Weinstein, *The End of Expressionism: Art and the November Revolution in Germany 1918–1919* (Chicago, 1990), 32–33. The early stages of research for this essay were generously supported by a research travel grant from the Carnegie Trust for the Universities of Scotland.
2. On the ambivalent relationship between Expressionism and Dada, see Richard Sheppard, *Modernism-Dada-Postmodernism* (Evanston, 2000), 236–65.
3. See in particular the texts by Ernst Bloch (in defense), Georg Lukács (in attack), and others in *Die Expressionismusdebatte: Materialien zu einer marxistischen Realismuskonzeption*, ed. Hans-Jürgen Schmitt (Frankfurt, 1973); Frederic Jameson, ed., *Aesthetics and Politics* (London, 1977).
4. Richard Huelsenbeck, "Dadaistisches Manifest" (April, 1918) in *Dada Almanach*, ed. Richard Huelsenbeck (New York, 1966, orig. 1920), 35–41.
5. The agitator motif is discussed in Diether Schmidt, "Die Gestalt des Agitators in der proletarisch-revolutionären Kunst," *Bildende Kunst*, vol. 11 (November, 1964). The term "Expressionism" has varied over time in meaning. See Charles Haxthausen, "A Critical Illusion: 'Expressionism' in the Writings of Wilhelm Hausenstein" in *The Ideological Crisis of Expressionism: The Literary and Artistic German War Colony in Belgium, 1914–1918*, ed. Rainer Rumold and O.K. Werckmeister (Columbia, S.C., 1990), 169–91.

6. Erhard Frommheld, "Politischer Expressionismus—expressionistische Politik" in Staatliche Museen zu Berlin, Nationalgalerie und Kupferstichkabinett, *Expressionisten: Die Avantgarde in Deutschland, 1905–1920* (East Berlin, 1986), 67.

7. On the relationship of the avant-garde to the politics of the Left, see Weinstein, *Expressionism*; John Zammito, *The Great Debate: "Bolshevism" and the Literary Left in Germany, 1917–1930* (New York, 1984); Barbara McCloskey, *George Grosz and the Communist Party: Art and Radicalism in Crisis, 1918 to 1936* (Princeton, 1997).

8. Lothar Schreyer, "Expressionistische Dichtung" in *Theorie des Expressionismus*, ed. Otto Best (Stuttgart, 1976), 170–72. Schreyer worked at the Bauhaus in Weimar, mainly in the Theatre Workshop, between 1920 and 1923.

9. Conrad Felixmüller, *Legenden* (1977), quoted in *Conrad Felixmüller: Das druckgraphische Werk 1912 bis 1976 im Kunstmuseum Düsseldorf,* ed. Friedrich Heckmanns (Düsseldorf, 1986), 40.

10. Anon., "Die Zeitschrift 'Menschen'," *Menschen: Zeitschrift für neue Kunst* (January 1, 1919): 1.

11. Ludwig Meidner, "An alle Künstler, Dichter, Musiker," *Der Anbruch* (January, 1919): 1.

12. Ibid., emphasis in original. See Weinstein, *Expressionism*, 56–9.

13. "Bolshevism" as understood by many German Expressionists was often an imagined construct, or "image." See Zammito, *Great Debate*.

14. *Lebendige* (Cologne, 1919), woodcut portraits by Anton Räderscheidt, Franz W. Seiwert, Angelika Hoerle, and Peter Abelen.

15. With some notable exceptions, the agitator is usually male. Prominent examples in modern German visual culture of female agitators include the female figure rousing the masses to rebellion in Käthe Kollwitz's *Peasants' War* etching cycle, and, in Weimar cinema, the Maria cyborg in Fritz Lang's film *Metropolis* (an example pointed out to me by Paul Jaskot). Though this essay does not analyze representations of right-wing agitators, they also exist in the work of German avant-garde artists, particularly Dadaists such as Raoul Hausmann, George Grosz, and John Heartfield. A well-known example is Heartfield's 1932 photomontage for the *Arbeiter-Illustrierte-Zeitung* showing Adolf Hitler with the caption: "Adolf the Superman: swallows gold and spouts junk."

16. Editor's note: Because we were unable to secure copyright permission for most of the images discussed in this chapter, web links will be provided when available. *The Orator* can be viewed at http://worldvisitguide.com/oeuvre/photo_ME0000102651.html.

17. Felix Stössinger, "Moderne revolutionäre Kunst," *Freie Welt: Illustrierte Wochenschrift der USPD* (October 17, 1920), 4–5, 8.

18. Ibid., 4.

19. Ibid., 5.

20. Ibid.
21. The final scene climaxes with Friedrich's call for the people to rise up from their misery and the people's response—repeating his words, rising as one, raising their hands, and marching in unison to "revolution! revolution!" Ernst Toller, *Die Wandlung: Das Ringen eines Menschen* (Potsdam, 1919), 94.
22. See Richard Dove, *Revolutionary Socialism in the Work of Ernst Toller* (New York, 1986), 80–82.
23. John Spalek, "Ernst Toller: The Need for a New Estimate" (1966), quoted in Frank Trommler, "Ernst Toller: The Redemptive Power of the Failed Revolutionary" in *German Writers and Politics, 1918-39*, ed. Richard Dove and Stephen Lamb (Houndmills, 1992), 62. Both authors discuss the need for a more measured assessment of Toller.
24. See Wilhelm Hausenstein, "Die Kunst in diesem Augenblick," *Der neue Merkur* (1919/20): 119–37. On the relationship between Expressionist utopianism and radical politics, see Jost Hermand and Frank Trommler, *Die Kultur der Weimarer Republik* (Munich, 1978); Eva Kolinsky, *Engagierter Expressionismus: Politik und Literatur zwischen Weltkrieg und Weimarer Republik* (Stuttgart, 1970).
25. Alfred Kuhn, "Gestern und Morgen" in idem, et al, *Situation 1924: Künstlerische und kulturelle Manifestationen* (Ulm, 1924), 5–6.
26. Ernst Toller in *Quer Durch* (1930), cited in *Ernst Toller: Plays One*, ed. and trans. Alan Pearlman (London, 2000), 121.
27. Anon., "Rückblick und Ausblick," *Klassenkampf* (1924), 1. On the perceived triumph of "classicism" over Dadaism, see L. Zahn, "Dadaismus oder Klassizismus," *Der Ararat: Glossen Skizzen und Notizen zur neuen Kunst* (1920), 50–2.
28. The poster by Pechstein is a monochrome image against a red ground and bears the slogan, "Practice solidarity with Soviet Russia. Remember the 10th anniversary."
29. Stössinger, "Moderne revolutionäre Kunst," 4.
30. Programme of the KAPD (May, 1920), quoted in *Literatur im Klassenkampf: Zur proletarisch-revolutionären Literaturtheorie 1919–1923*, ed. Walter Fähnders and Martin Rector (Frankfurt, 1974), 14, emphasis in original.
31. On the *Kunstlumpdebatte*, see Brigid Doherty, "The Work of Art and the Problem of Politics in Berlin Dada," *October* (Summer, 2003): 73–92; McCloskey, *George Grosz*; Fähnders and Rector, *Literatur*.
32. George Grosz and John Heartfield, "Der Kunstlump," *Der Gegner* (1919/1920), 48–56.
33. Gertrud Alexander, "Herrn John Heartfield und George Grosz," *Rote Fahne* (June 9, 1920), and "Kunst, Vandalismus und Proletariat: Erwiderung," *Rote Fahne* (June 23 and 24, 1920), reprinted in Fähnders and Rector, *Literatur*, 55–7, 60–5.
34. August Thalheimer, "Das Proletariat und die Kunst: Politische Bemerkungen," *Die Rote Fahne* (June 24, 1920), reprinted in ibid., 66.

35. Franz Seiwert, "Das Loch in Rubens Schinken," *Die Aktion* (1920), reprinted in *Der Schritt der einmal getan wurde, wird nicht zurückgenommen: Franz W. Seiwert. Schriften*, ed. Uli Bohnen and Dirk Backes (Berlin, 1978), 16. See also Seiwert, "Tuet Bekenntnis" (1920) in ibid.

36. Anatoli Lunatscharski, *Die Kulturaufgaben der Arbeiterklasse* (Berlin-Wilmersdorf, 1919).

37. Aleksander Bogdanoff, *Die Kunst und das Proletariat* (Leipzig, 1919), 28.

38. Raoul Hausmann, "Puffke propagiert Proletkult," *Die Aktion* (1921), reprinted in Fähnders and Rector, *Literatur*, 119–23.

39. Ibid., 121.

40. Ibid., 123. "Legen Sie Ihr Geld in Dada an!" was the title of a 1919 article in *Der Dada*. The slogan also appears in Dada montages of the period.

41. *Freie Welt: Illustrierte Wochenschrift der USPD* (October 17, 1920): 5.

42. Frommheld, "Politischer Expressionismus," 68.

43. Douglas Kellner, "Expressionism and Rebellion" in *Passion and Rebellion: The Expressionist Heritage*, ed. Stephen E. Bronner and Douglas Kellner (London, 1983), 15.

44. Hubert van den Berg, "Dada Zürich, Anarchismus und Boheme," *Neophilologus* (1987): 583.

45. Anon., "Proletarier und Intellektuelle," *Der Kampfruf: Organ der Allgemeinen Arbeiter-Union* (1924): 3.

46. See http://www.caiaffa.com/IMG/creditos/Opera/conradfelixmuller%28www.caiaffa.com%29.jpg. Rühle was a cofounder of the Spartacus League, the KPD, and later the KAPD. On this painting and a later equally significant image of a communist agitator, Curt Querner's *Der Agitator* (1931), as precedents for images of agitation in the GDR, see Debbie Lewer, "The Agitator and the Legacy of the Avant-garde in the German Democratic Republic: Willi Sitte's Rufer II (Caller II) of 1964," *Art History and Criticism* vol. 3, special issue: *Art and Politics: Case Studies from Eastern Europe* (2007): 62–9.

47. Three examples among many are Felixmüller's woodcut "Revolutionär" ("Revolutionary") (1920), Franz Maria Jansen's woodcut "Aufruhr" ("Uprising") (1920), and Erich Godal's lithograph "Uprising" (1920).

48. Compare the imagery discussed in Sara Ann Sewell's essay in this volume.

49. Sozialdemokratische Partei der Schweiz, *Winke für die Agitation* (Zürich, 1917), 1.

50. Ibid., 2.

51. Vorstand des Deutschen Landarbeiter-Verbandes, *Materialien zur Beurteilung der kommunistischen Agitation unter den Landarbeitern und Kleinbauern* (Berlin, 1919), 10.

52. Dr. Wilhelm Spickernagel, *Die Kunst des Redens: Vortrag, gehalten im Politischen Ausbildungskursus der Deutschen Volkspartei* (Berlin, 1919), 11, emphasis in original.

53. For a comprehensive linguistic analysis of the political speech of the "extreme" Left of the period, see Elizaveta Liphardt, "Aporien der Gerechtigkeit:

Politische Rede der extremen Linken in Deutschland und Russland zwischen 1914 und 1919" (Dissertation, Tübingen, 2005).

54. Ludwig Rubiner, "Die Erneuerung" (originally published 1918/19) in idem, *Künstler bauen Barrikaden: Texte und Manifeste 1908–1919*, ed. Wolfgang Haug (Darmstadt, 1988), 194.

55. For one of the more reflective contemporary critiques of Expressionist individualism described in terms of the pervasive "Ich," see Wilhelm Worringer, "Kritische Gedanken zur neuen Kunst" (1919) in his *Fragen und Gegenfragen: Schriften zum Kunstproblem* (München 1956), 86–105.

56. Raoul Hausmann, "Der deutsche Spiesser ärgert sich," *Der Dada* no. 2 (1919): 2. The "prophet" figure was a long-standing staple of Expressionist art from Emil Nolde to Karl Schmidt-Rottluff to Ernst Barlach and beyond. There was a surfeit of right-wing "prophecies" in and around 1919 in Germany too. See Jost Hermand, *Der alte Traum vom neuen Reich: Völkische Utopien und Nationalsozialismus* (Frankfurt, 1988), 103–7.

57. Huelsenbeck, "Was wollte der Expressionismus?" 38.

58. Ibid.

59. Wieland Herzfelde, *John Heartfield: Leben und Werk* (Dresden, 1971), 25, my emphasis.

60. See Hermand, *Traum*, 104.

61. Max Ernst, *Dada Siegt!*, poster for the *Dada-Vorfrühling* exhibition, Brauhaus Winter, Cologne (1920).

62. Examples can be found particularly in the work of Hausmann and Grosz.

63. Magnus Zeller, "Ein Maler zwischen 30 und 40," *Deutsche Allgemeine Zeitung* (January 1, 1926), reprinted in *Magnus Zeller: Entrückung und Aufruhr*, ed. Dominick Bartmann (Berlin, 2002), 48.

64. This is the case in other Berlin Dada photographs and posters.

65. On these features in international Dada and more widely, see David Hopkins, *Dada's Boys: Masculinity after Duchamp* (New Haven, 2007).

66. Raoul Hausmann, "Eine Flutwelle von Streben nach künstlerischer Kultur geht durch die teutonische Lande," typescript of May 1, 1920, reprinted in *Scharfrichter der bürgerlichen Seele: Raoul Hausmann in Berlin 1900–1933*, ed. Eva Züchner (Ostfildern, 1998), 103–5.

II

Cinema, Radio, and "Mass Culture" in the Weimar Republic: Between Shared Experience and Social Division

Corey Ross

The unique explosion of creativity in Weimar-era Germany has long been a highlight of twentieth century cultural history. From literature to theater, from the visual arts to cutting-edge design, Germany could plausibly lay claim to the most vibrant cultural scene in the world during the 1920s. In some respects, the retrospective brilliance of these artistic feats has cast a peculiar light on the less illustrious popular cultural artifacts of these years. Even if the bulk of films, magazines, and radio shows had little to do with the avant-garde scene, they too are commonly regarded as part of the wider groundswell of cultural change after the First World War. In this view, the combination of a new democratic political system, shorter working hours, technological advances, and the general atmosphere of cultural experimentation encouraged the emergence of a new and more widely shared mass culture.[1]

From classic Weimar cinema to the advent of radio, the 1920s were undoubtedly an era of remarkable innovation in the popular arts. At the same time, the unprecedented circulation of sights and sounds via the mass media suggested not only a gradual displacement of regional cultural particularities but also a flattening of class hierarchies, at least in terms of people's leisure activities. The extent to which this new mass culture actually leveled cultural distinctions and blurred class lines in German society is, however, open to debate. For instance, labor historians have long debated whether commercialized mass culture directly undermined working-class solidarity between the world wars by displacing older forms of leisure sociability with more class-transcendent and individualist pastimes, such as cinema and radio.[2] Yet despite such disagreements, the mass media is generally regarded as a central element of Weimar's cultural modernity, because they supposedly created a more open and level cultural landscape befitting the newly democratized Germany.

Indeed, the notion that the new media was ushering in a new era of cultural standardization was one of the few things on which cultural traditionalists and progressives agreed at the time. It furnished a handy thematic foundation on which to debate the wider virtues or vices of a consumer society in which the "masses" could take part. Given how vehemently these matters were debated during the Weimar years, it is scarcely surprising that historians have often adopted the vocabulary. And given how strongly the Frankfurt School of cultural analysis influenced perceptions of the so-called culture industry since the 1940s—especially but not only in Germany—the persistence of this concept of cultural standardization is less surprising still.[3] But as a basis for historical analysis, the notion of a universal mass culture obscures more than it reveals. For one thing, it suggests an inevitability and straightforwardness about the social and cultural effects of the mass media that simply does not hold up to scrutiny. Perhaps more importantly, it divorces these processes from their actual societal context. After all, historians and contemporaries alike have regarded Weimar Germany as a profoundly divided, even "pillarized" society in which various sociocultural milieus had little to do with one another and common ground was all but impossible to find. Thus the question that confronts us is: how did a supposedly homogenizing mass culture function in such a fragmented society? To what extent did the mass media promote shared experience, and how did this play out amidst the deep social divisions and economic tumult of the interwar years?

By focusing on cinema and radio, the two media that both contemporaries and historians have most closely associated with the cultural changes of Weimar, this chapter seeks to demonstrate how the new forms of media-based culture fitted into the wider framework of social and cultural life.[4] It eschews simple notions of cultural standardization and audience uniformity, looking beyond the contemporary discourse to focus instead on who was seeing or hearing what, and on the specific circumstances in which films and radio programs were created and received. The first section shows how the availability of these media and the constitution of their audiences were profoundly shaped by commercial considerations, technological limitations, and household budgets. The next section surveys how patterns of media use, diverse program offerings, and different audience preferences reflected social distinctions in the Weimar society. The final section considers how the social role of film and radio changed over the course of the Weimar years due both to technological developments and to far-reaching shifts in the social context.

Cost, Availability, and the Shaping of Weimar Audiences

How extensive and socially diverse were radio and film audiences in the Weimar Republic? Although the answer varies significantly between the two media, in both cases their ability to attract users was tightly constrained by a combination of technological, economic, and cultural factors.

Turning first to film, there is no doubt that the Weimar years witnessed rapid growth, even if that increase in number was less explosive than in the take-off years before the war. The number of cinemas nearly doubled from 1919 (2,836 with 980,000 seats) to 1928 (5,267 with 1,876,600 seats). Attendance levels rose accordingly, exceeding 250 million per year by the mid-1920s and 320 million by the end of the decade, which corresponded to around seven annual admissions per adult. Cinema was clearly a booming business in Weimar Germany. The question is where and how it boomed. During the 1920s, the big cities provided the overwhelming bulk of the cinema audience, and the impressive admissions figures can all too easily obscure how remote film was from the lives of many Germans. Although viewed by some contemporaries as a bridge between urban and rural life,[5] the cinema in fact accentuated this gap during the Weimar years. In 1925, over half of all Germans still lived in municipalities with fewer than 10,000 inhabitants, only 2 percent of which (1,462 out of 63,057) had any cinema at all—and most of those were open only two or three nights per week. Most rural and small town people thus had little immediate access to film, despite various projects to promote it in the countryside.[6] And for many farming communities, especially in the east of the country, cinema was completely alien—indeed more so than around the turn of the century, when itinerant operators had been more widespread. Moreover, there were also some cities with surprisingly little cinema capacity. Although commercial centers like Berlin and Leipzig could boast one seat for roughly every thirty inhabitants, the ratio in some of the industrial hubs such as Gelsenkirchen or Mönchen-Gladbach was four to five times lower. Simply put, cinema was far from a universal pastime in Weimar Germany.[7]

How affordable was film for those who did have access to it? In principle, it was easily affordable. The average ticket price after the hyperinflation was around RM 0.80, with some tickets going for as little as RM 0.50. This was well within reach of all but the poorest and represented only a fraction of the price of a theater visit.[8] In practice, however, the austere leisure budgets of most households made even such meager sums quite significant. According to a 1927 survey of household budgets, the average working-class family had only around RM 2.50 left over for entertainments of any kind after purchasing the essentials, and many unskilled households had only RM 1.00. At the most, RM 2.50 meant only four or five cinema tickets per family per month, assuming that none of this money was spent on newspapers, magazines, or any other amusements.[9]

So although the cinema had long possessed a plebeian, even proletarian image, the modest parameters of disposable income meant that it had to rely substantially on the patronage of other, better-off social groups. Civil servants and professionals were undoubtedly well-represented in the cinema audience, even if they tended to spend more on reading material, radio, and theater than the movies. Some contemporaries thus associated the new media above all with the swelling ranks of white collar workers (*Angestellten*), most famously Siegfried Kracauer, who drew a direct connection between what he viewed as the spiritual emptiness of modern office work and the need for compensatory amusement.[10] Survey results in fact show that white-collar households consistently registered the highest proportional expenditure on cinema and radio. Yet as we have just seen, this still did not add up to very many movie tickets, and the idea that cinema formed the basis of an emergent *"Angestelltenkultur"* must therefore be taken with a hefty pinch of salt. In the late 1920s, the average male white-collar worker had only RM 2.69 per month to spend on entertainments of all kinds, while roughly half of all female *Angestellten* could not afford to go to the cinema at all.[11] Although Kracauer's emblematic "little shop girls going to the cinema" might have furnished a potent symbol of the shifts in leisure pursuits and gender roles underway at the time, in reality, most of them could only afford to go to the movies very infrequently.[12]

A similar point can be made about generational assumptions. In the 1920s, most observers also perceived the film audience as overwhelmingly young. This was one of the reasons why Germany's moral guardians became so alarmed about film's putatively corrosive effects on impressionable minds. Again, this perception was not wholly without justification, since from the very beginning of cinema, children and young people had constituted a significant portion of the audience. Youth matinees were commonplace from early on, and surveys always found more interest in film among young age cohorts than among their elders. But whether this had led to a wave of "cinema addiction" (*Kinosucht*)—as many social workers, teachers, and churchmen complained—was another matter entirely. Most young people simply could not afford to go very often. Even in Berlin, the most film-crazy city in Germany, surveys from the early 1930s found that only one-sixth of young people went to the cinema on a regular (weekly) basis, just under half occasionally (monthly), and over a third not at all.[13]

Overall, it seems that the long-standing identification of cinema with youth, the working class, or the "Americanized" flapper was based more on moral panic and educated snobbery than on actual attendance patterns. Even Emilie Altenloh's classic 1913 survey of cinema audiences recognized that the established middle classes—especially men—were well represented among the audience.[14] And as the contemporary film press noted, many cinema regulars were in fact middle-aged people with both the disposable income and the free time to go. (Attendance decreased dramatically among households with small children.[15]) As for the conventional association of cinema with urban life, it seems clear that this perception is absolutely justified, since city dwellers constituted the vast bulk of the interwar audience. In sum, the twin constraints of cost and availability placed considerable limits on the film audience and strongly influenced its social profile.

These factors of cost and availability were even more influential in shaping the early radio audience. Launched in 1923, radio was in many ways regarded as the quintessential "medium of modernity." For many contemporaries, the ability to turn radio waves into sound was nothing short of a miracle, and the idea that listeners as far apart as Freiburg and Königsberg could hear the same thing at precisely the same time was truly astonishing.[16] Again, the figures look impressive. The number of registered wireless sets rose steadily by around 500,000 per year, from one million in 1926 to four million by the end of 1931.[17] Yet for most people, radio remained wholly unaffordable. To understand the form and structure of the early audience, it is necessary to distinguish between the two kinds of sets available: the valve set, which was capable of receiving faint air waves, and the crystal set, which picked up only the much stronger ground waves. Whereas a standard three-valve set cost around RM 300 in the mid-1920s—the entire monthly income of a white-collar clerk or skilled worker—a crystal set (or the newer ground-wave valve receivers available in the later 1920s) could be bought for less than RM 40. Hence the vast majority of sets before 1930 were only capable of receiving ground waves.[18]

This issue of cost was inseparable from the problems of reception, for it was only in the immediate vicinity of a transmitter that ground waves could be received. Transmitters were invariably located near large cities, so inexpensive crystal sets were of no use to the 70 percent of Germans who did not live there.[19] For most German households, adequate reception would have required a three-valve set that a few could afford. It is thus unsurprising that in 1927 over 80 percent of wireless sets were registered within the twenty-one cities where a transmitter was located. Translated into relative listening rates, this meant that around 40 percent of big-city dwellers had radio sets compared to only around 3 percent of those living elsewhere.[20] Like the cinema, radio listening in this period divided rather than united rural and urban culture.[21]

Broadcasting also clearly reflected, and in the process reinforced, the social discrepancies of income and education. The sheer cost of radio listening made it primarily a middle-class activity during the Weimar period. In addition to the onetime purchase price, acquiring the necessary radio license added another RM 2 per month, and the batteries also needed periodic replacement. The average RM 2.50 entertainment budget of middle-earning working-class households barely covered the license fee alone. As late as 1930, entrepreneurial, civil servant, and white-collar households still comprised around two-thirds of the audience, and they were roughly three times more likely to own a set than a working-class household.[22]

Thus in terms of its distribution and social constituency, Weimar-era radio was hardly a widely accessible, socially inclusive "mass" medium. Its audience was even more predominately urban than that of the cinema and was, moreover, starkly middle-class. It was only in the mid- to late 1930s, under the Nazis, that this picture changed substantially due to a combination of technological improvements and that regime's political prioritization of radio. In the meantime, the social composition of the radio audience was also reinforced by the program itself, which did little to popularize the medium among other social groups.

Mass Media and the Social Topography of Taste

Even if the new media were far from universal in Weimar Germany, to what extent did they bridge social and geographic divides among those who regularly used them? This is a difficult question to answer; for if the outer contours of media audiences were bounded above all by cost and availability, a whole range of factors structured their internal composition. Sketching out audience structure is difficult due to the paucity of sources.

As a starting point, it is safe to say that cinemagoers and, to a somewhat lesser extent, radio listeners, in the 1920s and early 1930s were not just seeing and hearing "standardized" fare. Despite the lack of hard survey data, it is still possible to recognize distinctive audiences for certain types of programming that in many ways mirrored the divisions within German society.

One factor that we simply cannot overlook is class. Despite all the current clichés about the "democratic" character of film, Weimar-era cinema seems to have done little to bring the various social strata together. For one thing, different groups tended to go to different cinemas. There were two basic categories at the time: the local neighborhood theaters that catered chiefly to a regular clientele (*Stammpublikum*), and the "cinema palaces" or first-run theaters, invariably located in city centers or at major traffic junctions, which sought to attract a dispersed audience and passers-by (*Laufpublikum*). The overwhelming majority of cinemas in the Weimar era fell under the first category, which continued to account for the bulk of available seats through the 1930s and beyond.[23] Furthermore, the differences within this category were themselves immense, insofar as the local cinemas and their audiences reflected the social makeup of their immediate vicinity. A 1926 series of reports on the myriad "unknown cinemas" in Berlin gives a sense of the spectrum, which ranged from a "clean, quiet, and friendly" little establishment in the West End to the "critical audience" of intellectuals at a cinema in the Wilmersdorferstrasse and all the way to a raucous and smelly flea pit off the Alexanderplatz.[24] Needless to say, these audiences overlapped very little, if at all.

The much larger city center theaters were admittedly somewhat different, as they sought to draw from a much wider radius. But even so, they tended to have a distinctive social profile by dint of their higher ticket prices (usually over RM 1.50, or twice the amount charged in many neighborhood cinemas), to which travel costs also had to be added. Even apart from the issue of cost, such "cinema palaces" were deliberately designed to attract the well-to-do by aping the traditional theater with its plush decor, ushers, and cloakroom fees. According to the cinema operators' journal *Reichsfilmblatt*, the majority of "regular customers" at neighborhood theaters rarely ventured into these central venues unless they were desperate to see a new blockbuster before it was cascaded down to the second-run local cinemas.[25]

One might wonder at this stage how far such differences between individual theaters actually mattered. Given the very practice of cascading films down an established cinematic hierarchy, it is in some ways tempting to dismiss the issue of locality as irrelevant. After all, far-reaching distribution networks meant that a particular film could be screened in any number of theaters. In fact, these differences mattered quite a lot; for in spite of the extensive web of film distribution, it seems clear that the audiences inhabiting the various sorts of cinema were by no means all seeing the same thing. The first scholarly study of film demand in Germany, published in 1928, clearly distinguished between three different markets: the premiere-run theaters, the "cinemas of the middle class," and "workers' theatres." Whereas the most successful pictures in the handful of premiere cinemas tended to be either big budget, German-made films or American blockbusters, American films were relatively unpopular in the "middle class" neighborhood theaters, where run-of-the-mill German productions dominated. In the "workers' theaters," however, westerns and other Hollywood standard fare was remarkably popular—though admittedly the steady stream of nationalistic military films beloved in the "middle class" cinemas also did well here, much to the frustration of socialist activists.[26]

The contemporary film press likewise recognized distinct market segments. In 1928 a journalist for the respected *Berliner Tageblatt* was surprised to discover how unfamiliar he was with the supply of films in the working-class neighborhood of Humboldthain: "[S]ometimes there are films that are not screened at all in the West End."[27] As the journal *Film-Kurier* noted in 1922, operators catering to the "broadest masses of the populace" habitually screened "adventure films and sensation films" and "exciting, gaudy kitsch," whereas those aiming at "the more educated middle class" preferred to show sophisticated dramas and renditions of famous novels.[28] While cultural critics like Siegfried Kracauer were proclaiming the emergence of a new brand of "homogenous metropolitan audience" in the Reich capital, hard-nosed theater operators who made a living by drawing in the locals knew better. As one contemporary observer put it, "Every cinema-quarter actually has its own individual character, and success or failure turns out differently in each case."[29]

Locality was important in another respect as well, for the differences between wealthy and poor areas were overlaid by regional disparities. There were constant mutterings in the film press about taste differences between Berlin and the so-called *Provinz*—the term that was inconsiderately used to refer to the rest of the country. Not only was the *Provinz*—including large cities such as Hannover—supposedly far less interested in American films than the capital, it also chafed at the use of "*berlinerisch*" expressions, which could be utterly incomprehensible to the average Bavarian or Rhenish cinemagoer.[30] Anti-Prussian biases meant that references to "huge successes in Berlin" might prove counterproductive as a means of advertising.[31]

Even apart from regional divergences of taste, the sheer supply of films and the structure of the industry during the silent film era allowed for far greater differences between regional cinema cultures than was possible later on. By the late 1920s, there were over 400 production companies in Germany that together churned out around 180 to 250 features per year. Approximately one-quarter of all German films were made by small firms producing only one per year and around half by firms annually producing two to five films, with large producers such as Ufa and Emelka accounting for the rest.[32] Domestic production alone thus supplied three to five new features per week. And this is only part of the picture, for after the currency stabilization in 1924, German-made productions were outnumbered on the domestic market by the 300 or so foreign-made features imported each year, which brought the average weekly supply of new films up to around ten.[33]

This meant, for one thing, that cinema operators could assemble their programs from a huge palette of available films—hence the marked differences between the offerings in different cinemas noted above. It was quite possible for three or four cinemas to fill their monthly programs without sharing a single film. Moreover, many of the films made by smaller firms cost only around RM 40,000 to 60,000 to produce; such films were designed to provide cheap amusement for the undemanding habitual cinemagoers who liked going to the movies regardless of what was on—as one journalist called them "the regular sheep, so to speak, who fill the first five rows of the provincial cinema."[34] Such modest production costs meant that films could turn a profit even if limited to regional audiences. Indeed, for small firms without a sizeable capital base, it made little sense to compete with the likes of Ufa in the high-risk national or international market, where a single flop could spell bankruptcy. Thus a certain portion of annual production in Germany was never intended for nationwide, let alone international, distribution in the first place. Rather, some films sought to find their audiences closer to home by offering precisely what the big, expensive productions could not: stories or reports of local interest that even Ufa officials admitted "exert a powerful attraction for the public to visit the cinema."[35] Although such locally oriented films (often documentaries, though also longer "milieu films") generally proved unpopular at the national level, this only reinforces the overall point: that the cinema in Weimar Germany was not as culturally homogenizing as is frequently assumed.[36]

In emphasizing the often overlooked importance of class, milieu, and locality to the structure of 1920s moviegoing, one must nevertheless be careful not to underestimate the unprecedented sociocultural reach of what was still a relatively new medium of communication. The block-busters of the 1920s—international hits such as *Ben Hur, Noah's Ark, Anna Karenina, The Gold Rush*—were probably seen by more people from more different backgrounds than anything before, and as such they carried profound social and cultural implications. Filmmakers and critics alike prized Hollywood films in particular for their ability to attract viewers of all colors, creeds, and nationalities.[37] The fact that film audiences reflected the persistent fragmentation of German society does not negate the significance of their very existence, especially the blockbuster audiences that indeed traversed social and geographic boundaries as never before. The point is rather that such megahits were the exceptions that proved the rule. Although these renowned films have understandably attracted the most attention among historians, the vast majority of movies in the 1920s were not seen by a large international audience. What the various audiences saw divided them as much as united them.

Moreover, *how* people saw these films was just as important as the content itself. To borrow an insight from the French sociologist Pierre Bourdieu, even the most widely available goods can still be appropriated in diverse ways by various social groups, thereby reflecting and indeed producing social distinctions in the process.[38] To a great extent, the appropriation of 1920s cinema—again, the most international of all the media at the time—was still by and large channeled through the structures of milieu and neighborhood.

This becomes abundantly clear when we consider the atmosphere and mode of reception in different types of cinemas. The up-market cinema palaces were consciously designed to make the medium of film "legitimate" to a well-heeled, discriminating audience. This generally entailed, among other things, the numbering of seats (with appropriate gradation of ticket prices), the use of ushers, the provision of intervals for purchasing and consuming food or beverages, and the enforcement of closed showings—that is, not allowing general admission between the beginning and end of screening times. Picture quality and musical accompaniment were of a high standard, often involving a professional orchestra of up to thirty members, and patrons were expected to behave in the same quiet and attentive manner as at the traditional theater. In short, the atmosphere in the cinema palaces was formal: "one can't even properly laugh here," remarked a young housemaid in 1925. "You don't dare let out a loud noise because no one else does either."[39]

The average working-class "*Kintopp*" (the oft-used colloquial term for "cinema") could hardly have been more different. Visitors often came and went at all times regardless of advertised screening times, which led to constant problems of overfilling.[40] If there were no seats available, the aisle would suffice until someone left. People often brought along something to eat or drink; frequently smoked in spite of the strict prohibition against it (ventilation was notoriously poor and the flammability of celluloid films increased the risk of fire); and happily chatted away, applauded, or shouted their support for the hero on the screen. Such noise hardly detracted from the show. The captions allowed viewers to follow the plot even in the noisiest theaters, and whatever musical accompaniment was provided—perhaps a string duet or piano—was not much of a loss. Though the films themselves were silent, the cinemas certainly were not. As one visitor to a small Dresden theater remarked in 1928, the "family-like atmosphere" in the auditorium was characterized above all "by the laughter that repeated itself frequently, without inhibition, loudly and clearly, and accompanied by more or less pointless remarks."[41] Overall, *Kintopp* audiences were much more informal, active, and participatory than the reverent viewers in the "refined" theaters, which made for an altogether different cinematic experience.

The manner of presentation only added to the dissimilarity. Whereas the more sophisticated cinemas tended to follow a standard program comprising a feature plus several short films, fleapits often observed what was called the "two-hit system," whereby two feature films (along with any number of shorts) were crammed into a single two-hour screening.[42] This practice may partly have been a hangover from the hodge-podge, vaudeville-style program of early cinema, though for the most part it was simply a competitive measure designed to give the audience more meters of film for their money. The drawback of this practice—though it seems that few *Kintopp*-goers viewed it as such—was that films had to be projected at faster speeds than producers had intended, making captions hard to read and actors' movements jerky. To make matters worse, whatever visual qualities remained at this tempo were further marred by the often poor picture quality resulting from an aging projector and/or worn-out, second-run copy. Taken together, the differences in atmosphere, audience behavior, and film presentation were so vast as to cast doubt on the very idea of "the cinema" as a single, distinct form of popular culture in the interwar period. Even when a *Kintopp* and a posh cinema screened the same film, the resulting shows were so dissimilar that one might question whether audiences were in fact seeing the same thing.[43] In sum, the diverse ways in which various groups actually appropriated the widely shared medium of film clearly reflected the divisions of the German society, generating as much difference as commonality.

This underlying tension between shared experience and social distinction also shaped the development of Weimar radio, albeit in a different way. Although broadcasting, like the cinema, underwent significant growth throughout the 1920s, there were a number of fundamental differences that set it apart from all other media at the time. Like the BBC, German radio was explicitly noncommercial so as to avoid the supposedly chaotic proliferation of privately owned stations in the United States. It is true that private investors were involved in the system from early on, and the regional broadcasters were ostensibly independent concerns. But in practice this was a state-directed system from the outset, centered in the Postal Ministry and the newly created Reich Broadcasting Company (*Reichs-Rundfunk-Gesellschaft mbH*). There were a number of motivations behind this, ranging from democratic concerns about the influence of antirepublican commercial interests to the desire of the Postal Ministry to dispose of license fee revenues. Yet most important was the determination to shelter this promising new medium from the perceived downdraughts of market competition that had so troubled educated elites since before the turn of the century.[44]

One outcome of such concerns was the deliberately decentralized structure of German radio, which was composed of nine broadcasting companies, each operating within a specific region. This federal system was intended not only to avoid political resentments over Berlin/Prussian dominance, but also—unlike the highly centralized BBC—to help protect regional cultures and dialects from the corrosive effects of cultural standardization. Indeed, radio broadcasters were among the foremost proponents of folksy *Heimat* ("homeland") culture, which many hoped would provide an alternative to "Americanized" mass culture.[45] Another outcome of these concerns about market competition was the monopolization of broadcasting within each region, for it meant that radio was not as beholden to audience tastes as the commercially oriented film, publishing, or recording industries. For the architects of Weimar broadcasting, radio was to serve not as just another purveyor of cheap entertainment but rather as a "cultural factor," a bearer of knowledge and spiritual refinement. The first prerequisite was to disengage the medium from the market mechanism, thus liberating it from the tyranny of mediocrity. The efforts of Weimar broadcasters to edify listeners with a diet of demanding high "*Kultur*" were probably the clearest—though by no means only—expression of the interwar tendency to view the media audience as a malleable object in the hands of elites.[46]

Both the content and structure of the radio program clearly reflected this attitude. While cinema operators were busy trying to figure out what their audiences *would* like, radio programmers focused more on what they *should* like. Admittedly, this is not immediately apparent if one considers the proportion of different programming genres. By the end of the 1920s, around half of airtime on most of the nine stations was devoted to music, approximately 15 percent to news and reports, 10 percent to lectures, and a further 10 percent to "target group" broadcasts (often aimed at either children or housewives). Music (and, later on, variety shows) was always recognized as the most popular segment, around one-third of which programming executives classified as "light entertainment" and around one-fifth as either "demanding entertainment" or "musical education."[47] Thus music was the single largest component of the program, and much of it was nominally "light" music. When one considers the program schedule, however, the educational thrust of Weimar broadcasting becomes unmistakable. "Light entertainment" was deliberately broadcast in the morning or at midday, when most people were at work or school. Insofar as contemporary hit music featured at all, it was banished to the late evening slot, often after midnight. The prime time slot between 8 and 10 p.m., when some 80 percent of listeners were tuned in, was thoroughly dominated by the higher things, primarily orchestral music, opera, or "literary education." The only significant break from this pattern came on Saturdays, when cheery fare could be heard in the late afternoon and evening.[48]

Given the popular preference for light entertainment, such programming was hardly a recipe for audience growth. Although it scarcely occurred to programmers to carry out detailed listener surveys in the 1920s—a revealing omission in itself—it was obvious to everyone what most people wanted to hear: "above all, light entertainment music!! But also dance music, marches, variety shows and the occasional operetta and comedy," as one observer put it. What they got instead was "heavy chamber music or great operatic works or boring lectures that barely interest three percent of the listeners."[49] Such impressionistic complaints were broadly confirmed by the first detailed survey, carried out in 1934. This study unsurprisingly found that the most popular segment of the program was light entertainment and dance music, "music that one can sway along to and that helps one forget the monotony, cares and travails of life." Equally unsurprising, the survey revealed that listener tastes, like cinema tastes, were strikingly class-related. Whereas 80 percent of professionals and higher civil servants listened to classical concerts, only 8 percent of unskilled workers and 10 percent of skilled workers did so. These preferences were reversed when it came to dance music, which 41 percent of skilled workers tuned into compared to only 14 percent of professionals and higher civil servants.[50] It thus seems fair to call Weimar broadcasting an essentially "bourgeois" medium, not only in terms of its audience profile but also its programming priorities. Gender and age further divided the audience, and not only via target group broadcasts for children and housewives. An overwhelmingly male audience listened to sport broadcasts, for instance, whereas dance music drew far more women than men and was almost exclusively a preserve of the young.[51]

Weimar broadcasters largely ignored these huge variations in audience preference. Despite their stated goal of molding radio into an instrument of cultural unity that would bring together listeners of all social backgrounds and political camps, this was only ever attempted on the broadcasters' own lofty terms. Education always took precedence over entertainment. For the quintessentially *bildungsbürgerlich* (educated middle class) civil servants and professionals who were in charge of German radio, the aim—not unlike that of social-democratic schemes to educate workers to an appreciation of the finer things—was not to indulge audience tastes but rather to improve them by "gradually but deliberately exposing [the listening public] to higher and greater things."[52]

In the eyes of many broadcasters, there was too much at stake to do otherwise. In view of the fundamental challenge to traditional cultural authority posed by the explosion of commercial entertainments, the state-sponsored market monopoly enjoyed by radio provided an ideal opportunity for the beleaguered *Bildungsbürgertum* to reassert its dwindling claim to cultural leadership. While there was limited scope for preventing the publishing, film, and recording industries from producing heaps of so-called smut and trash, broadcasting was designed to reflect the values and standards of its educated producers. This was why, despite all the criticisms of the unpopular programming and the clear knowledge that it put off many would-be listeners, radio executives prioritized the interests of the privileged few above the wishes of the vast majority. As Karl Christian Führer has argued, the staunchly didactic nature of Weimar radio, its insistence on the centrality of "serious" music and its carefully planned federal structure can hardly have contributed to the creation of a more classless, universal "mass culture" in Germany. As far as its producers were concerned, it actually reflected a deliberate attempt to *prevent* this from happening.[53]

Media, Social Upheaval, and Technical Change

The history of "mass culture" in Weimar Germany, then, is not a tale of powerful new technologies bulldozing their way across the socio-cultural landscape, but rather a complex and contingent story in which social differences and human actions play a key part. The impact of new communications depended crucially on how they were produced—whether nationally or regionally, for a commercial or noncommercial market—and how ordinary users accessed them. Nor was there anything predictable about what happened. This is also a story of continuous change, for the complex interrelationship between technical innovations and cultural practices was, as always, in constant flux. As media technologies evolved, so too did their social and cultural effects. And as the wider social context changed, so too did the role of the media. In both respects, the scale of transformation in Weimar Germany was extraordinary.

Though it might seem counterintuitive, it was precisely during periods of social and economic upheaval that the media made some of their greatest advances. On balance, the crisis that wracked Germany during the years immediately after the First World War probably promoted rather than stifled the growth of entertainments. There was clearly a sizeable increase in demand for amusements during this period; however overblown the contemporary talk of an "amusement addiction" may have been, it was not wholly imaginary. In part, this surge in demand may have reflected, as some have suggested, a desire to make up for lost time after years of wartime austerity. But by and large, it was due to the soaring inflation of the mark. As money lost its value, the virtue of saving gave way to the logic of spending it before it was worthless. In the words of Martin Geyer, "whoever did not consume today would have nothing tomorrow, and what would be available tomorrow was uncertain anyway."[54] Entertainments, unlike many other consumer goods, were in abundant supply even throughout the hyperinflation crisis and thus represented a convenient way to enjoy any discretionary income while it still had value.

It appears that the film industry profited directly from this changed attitude toward money. Cinema furnished not only an outlet for excess income but also a welcome diversion from the chaos and anxiety of the "great disorder."[55] As the contemporary commentator Hans Ostwald remarked, the *Flimmerkiste* (flicks) were "the best narcotic for many thousands who wanted to be transported away from the whirlwind for at least a couple of hours in the evening."[56] For many middle-class Germans who saw their savings and incomes wiped out, the cinema had become the only affordable place to escape. The renowned linguist Victor Klemperer, for instance, confided to his diary in 1922 that cinema had become "a substitute for theatre, opera, concert, and travel."[57] Indeed, it was not the rapid devaluation of the currency but rather its stabilization in 1924 that caused the greater problem for the German film industry. The first half of 1924 saw attendance drop by at least 30 percent (down approximately 10 percent for the year as a whole).[58]

Meanwhile, the inflation crisis also influenced the development of German radio. Although it was only coincidence that the wireless made its debut in October 1923 at the height of the hyperinflation, the timing nonetheless colored perceptions of the medium. The inflation had a devastating effect not only on Germany's prized cultural institutions (especially theaters and concert halls), but also on the educated middle class who frequented them. In these circumstances, it was all the more likely that the new medium of radio should appear to beleaguered elites as an opportunity to reassert their own cultural values and standards.[59]

Far more eventful for broadcasting were the turbulent years of the Depression. Although the timing was once again coincidental in many respects, this too was a period of significant change for the broadcasting industry. By the end of the 1920s, wireless sets were becoming less and less expensive with the development of new valves, and they were also becoming easier to use. By 1929 the standard set could be plugged into a standard electrical wall socket and furthermore came equipped with a loudspeaker instead of cumbersome earphones.[60] Between 1929 and 1933, prices for new sets dropped and performance improved markedly.[61] Although most sets in the early 1930s remained capable of receiving only ground waves, the radius within which this was possible had expanded dramatically with the launch of a new generation of transmitters after 1930, encompassing around 70 percent of the population by the beginning of 1934. For some listeners, this put two or even three regional stations within reach, which offered them a real choice for the first time. And from 1931 onwards, the national *Deutsche Welle* service was also finally receivable throughout the entire Reich, thus providing at least two stations for everyone.[62]

Altogether, the changes that took place during the early 1930s made radio far cheaper, more convenient, and more attractive than in the 1920s. This was reflected in the steady increase in the number of licensed sets from 2.84 million (or 17 percent of households) in 1929 to 4.56 million (25.4 percent of households) in 1933.[63] Although the rate of growth throughout these years remained broadly comparable to that before 1929, it was nonetheless remarkable when compared to the concurrent slump in cinema admissions. Indeed, radio was one of the few segments of the entire German economy that continued to grow during the Depression. It was seemingly unaffected by the squeeze on incomes that hit the other media. The income slump perhaps even aided radio, given the unique economies of scale that radio entertainment could offer large households by entertaining an unlimited number of people for a flat monthly fee.

For all the technological advances of these years, however, neither the program nor the social composition of the radio audience changed very substantially. The audience only slowly became more diverse as it expanded, remaining disproportionately middle class and urban. As late as the mid-1930s, listening rates were still nearly four times higher among civil servants than manual workers. In 1932 only 7.9 percent of rural households had a radio compared to 46 percent in the big cities.[64] And in the meantime the program became only marginally—even grudgingly— less demanding. The improved reception of the largely education-oriented *Deutsche Welle* service made it easier for regional programmers to lighten the tone without necessarily betraying their vaunted cultural mission.[65] There were fewer lectures and slightly more popular music, and new genres such as the variety show also made the rounds. Yet overall, the program was still remarkably stodgy in international comparison, and its educational thrust remained sacrosanct.[66] The first significant change in this respect came under the Nazis, who pragmatically indulged the demand for dance music and light entertainment in their attempt to create a more socially inclusive "national" culture. Ironically, whereas their supposedly liberal Weimar predecessors had consistently placed an emphasis on the classics and folksy *Heimat* music, Nazi radio officials prioritized music that they themselves had previously lambasted as rootless, Americanized "asphalt culture."

If broadcasting made some major advances during the early 1930s, the cinema underwent truly dramatic changes. For it was precisely during the Depression years that films began to speak. The advent of sound film in 1929 signaled a fundamental transformation—both technological and commercial—for the entire film industry. One basic difference was that sound films were many times more expensive to produce than silent films. In order to recoup the costs, they had to reach a far larger audience than the average silent film. This effectively spelled the end for the low-budget, regionally oriented pictures capable of turning a profit within only a small distribution area. The huge financial risks involved in production also spelled the end for most of the small-scale firms, thus concentrating production into fewer and fewer hands and roughly halving the number of films on the market in little over a year.[67] This meant that cinema owners had far less choice than in the 1920s when it came to assembling their programs; and this in turn meant that audiences were more likely to see the same films in their different cinemas.

Moreover, the shrinking supply of films was accompanied by a dramatic convergence in how they were presented. The much-maligned "two-hit system" prevalent among cheaper cinemas came under attack on two fronts. First, projection speeds for sound films could no longer be sped up without making the dialogue unintelligible. In addition, higher rental costs (which reflected higher production costs) made the screening of two talking features for the price of one admission completely unprofitable. At the same time, the soundtrack of a talking film also determined its aural presentation, which had previously been left to the discretion of cinema operators. Given how dissimilar musical accompaniment could be between different types of cinema, this alone amounted to a far-reaching standardization of cinematic practices compared to the silent era. Perhaps most important of all, the introduction of sound film led to a marked shift in audience behavior. The noisy, spontaneous, and participatory mode of reception that characterized thousands of working-class *Kintopps* did not survive the transition to sound. When spoken dialogue replaced captions, silence was required to follow a plot. The upshot was a far more passive and disciplined form of reception broadly comparable to what one found in the more "refined" theaters.[68] Although there were still huge disparities in terms of ventilation, decor, seating comfort, and overall atmosphere, the raft of changes associated with the transition to sound film all tended to erode the differences between various cinemas and render both their programs and presentation techniques more uniform. Simply put, sound film was much more homogenizing in its social implications than silent film was.

The fact that all this happened amidst the social upheaval of the Depression only added to the disruption. While the film industry was itself undergoing far-reaching transformation, its audiences were also being subtly reconfigured by the pressures of unemployment and falling incomes. At the most basic level, the audience became significantly smaller. From a peak of 352.5 million in 1928/9, admissions quickly fell to 290.4 million in 1930/31 before bottoming out at 238.4 million in

1932/3—a fall of almost exactly one-third over just four years.[69] This collapse in revenue could not have come at a worse time for the film industry. From the big producers to the independent cinema operators, every segment was currently making major investments to retool for sound. Although it is hard to establish with any precision, it appears that audiences and attendance patterns were also evolving. For one thing, the novel attractiveness of sound film seems also to have pulled in new viewers who had previously remained indifferent toward silent movies. Moreover, the economic crisis opened up new divisions between the employed and unemployed, since the latter tended to frequent inexpensive matinees and/ or cheap cinemas that were late in converting to sound (some waited for several years). There is also some evidence that the audience was acquiring a more middle-class complexion, as the crisis tended to hit manual wage-earners hardest.[70]

In sum, the film industry was itself undergoing fundamental change at the same time that audience patterns were shifting under the impact of the Depression. As the variety of cinematic production decreased, many of the existing social structures through which film had previously been mediated were breaking down. To be sure, sound-era cinema still accentuated and reproduced social distinctions, and no doubt it continued to do so at least until the advent of television killed off the majority of neighborhood cinemas. But compared to the silent era, it offered its audience a significantly more uniform product than before and also began to draw new groups of viewers into the wider cinema audience.

Conclusion

There was, in Weimar Germany as elsewhere, nothing inevitable or automatic about the effects of mass communication. The role they played in social and cultural life depended very much on the precise nature of their technology, the market structure and regulatory framework, their mode of access, and their relationship to existing traditions and customs. As a result, different media could function in quite dissimilar ways.

In many respects, film and radio during the Weimar period occupied opposite ends of the mass cultural spectrum. Cinema was highly commercialized and thus acutely sensitive to popular demand. Operating in an extremely competitive market, filmmakers had to appeal to as many people as possible by "giving them what they wanted," or at least trying to. Thus the supply of films was exceedingly broad, and this breadth of choice enabled Weimar cinema audiences to be especially active in making their selections from what was on offer. The range of supply and the choices that were made reflected the huge variety of taste and expectations among this diverse audience. In addition, the very manner in which films were shown and consumed also reflected the vast social and cultural differences that partitioned audiences and structured their preferences.

By contrast, Weimar radio, under strict state regulation and protected by a monopolization of supply, tended to be stodgy and highbrow. It was produced for and consumed by a relatively narrow audience. The range of choice available to most listeners in the 1920s—one or two stations that shared roughly similar programming structures—was minute compared to what the cinema offered. Although the dearth of choice was partially based on technical and commercial factors, it was chiefly a result of broadcasters' patriarchal disregard for popular demand. The radio program was thus remarkably monochromatic when set against the complex mosaic of listener preferences. Radio provided rather uniform fare, and in this sense it displayed certain standardizing tendencies that the cinema did not. Yet its very uniformity made it less attractive to a wider, socially diverse audience. This could hardly contrast more starkly with contemporary cinema, which reached a relatively large audience but was characterized by a high degree of differentiation in terms of both its content and manner of consumption. Neither medium was a straightforward conveyor of a homogenous "mass" culture, though for very different reasons.

Contrary to many assumptions about the historical effects of the mass media, the explosion of mass communications since the latter part of the nineteenth century has generally been a process of differentiation rather than standardization. Just as audiences became more complex as they broadened, so too did the variety of material offered to them. Weimar filmmakers recognized far better than broadcasters that the best means of attracting more patrons was to provide more choice. Undoubtedly the new media of cinema and radio were an elemental part of the social fabric in Weimar Germany, and possessed the unique potential to promote a common set of cultural artifacts and experiences shared by a wider range of groups than ever before. Yet the very fact that they had become an integral part of society meant that the social context shaped them as much as the other way around. From this perspective, what is most striking about the new media-based popular culture in the Weimar Republic is not its unbridled "modernity"—that is, its radical break with more traditional conventions, practices, and patterns of social use—but rather the extent to which it was still bounded by older structures of locality and milieu.

It would be unsatisfactory, however, simply to reverse the conventional wisdom by identifying the growth of the media with audience fragmentation instead of homogenization. The expansion of communications *did* overlay—and over the long term, helped erode—many regional and class-based cultural distinctions. The point is rather that this relationship was not static but shifted significantly over time as a result of commercial, technical, and social change. There always existed a tension in the media of Weimar Germany between the forces of commonality and difference, audience integration, and fragmentation. And as the transition from silent to sound film demonstrates especially vividly, this balance— and thus the social role of the medium itself—could tip quite rapidly.

We can most clearly discern such shifts during the periods of greatest social upheaval—first in the inflation crisis of the early 1920s, which witnessed the launch of radio amidst a supposed wave of "pleasure addiction" (*Vergnügungssucht*); and secondly during the Depression. In the early 1930s, not only did films begin to talk, but radio also became more widely available, and the social framework itself began to buckle under the strain of the crisis. Popular entertainments have a way of flourishing in the bleakest circumstances. Perhaps precisely because of all the fun, color, and cheer they peddle, they often have their greatest impact in times of turbulence. Insofar as there was ever a "golden age" of media expansion and audience convergence in the Weimar Republic, it came not in the interlude of relative stability from 1924–29, but rather during the traumatic birth and death phases of the Republic.

Notes

1. See, for example, Detlev Peukert, *The Weimar Republic* (London, 1991), 164–77; Peter Alter, ed., *Im Banne der Metropolen: Berlin und London in den zwanziger Jahren* (Göttingen, 1993); Kaspar Maase, *Grenzenloses Vergnügen: Der Aufstieg der Massenkultur 1850–1970* (Frankfurt, 1997); Eric Weitz, *Weimar Germany* (Princeton, 2007), 207–50. The term "mass culture" is used here as a neutral shorthand for popular commercialized culture, without pejorative connotation.

2. See Peter Lösche and Franz Walter, "Zur Organisationskultur der sozialdemokratischen Arbeiterbewegung in der Weimarer Republik: Niedergang der Klassenkultur oder solidargemeinschaftlicher Höhepunkt?," *Geschichte und Gesellschaft* (1989): 511–36; Hartmann Wunderer, "Noch einmal: Niedergang der Klassenkultur oder solidargemeinschaftlicher Höhepunkt?," *Geschichte und Gesellschaft* (1992): 88–93.

3. Max Horkheimer and Theodor Adorno, *Dialectic of Enlightenment*, transl. John Cumming (London, 1973, orig. 1947).

4. It is worth noting that in the 1920s, neither film nor radio were as widely used as the popular press, which had grown explosively between the 1880s

and 1910s. Yet precisely because the press had become so established by the Weimar years, it was the glamour of the rapidly expanding cinema and the sheer novelty of the radio that most captivated contemporaries and that most significantly reshaped the cultural landscape of the interwar period.

5. See Daniela Münkel, "'Der Rundfunk geht auf die Dörfer': Der Einzug der Massenmedien auf dem Lande von den zwanziger bis zu den sechziger Jahren" in *Der lange Abschied vom Agrarland" Agrarpolitik, Landwirtschaft und ländliche Gesellschaft zwischen Weimar und Bonn*, ed. Daniela Münkel (Göttingen, 2000), 180–81.

6. See, for example, Friedrich Lembke, *Jedem Dorf sein Kino!* (Berlin, 1930). Such projects were developed by agricultural organizations keen to make rural living more attractive in order to mitigate the problem of migration to the cities.

7. Above figures from Alexander Jason, *Handbuch der Filmwirtschaft, Jahrgang 1930* (Berlin, 1930), 61, 69, and *Der Film in Ziffern und Zahlen (1895–1925)* (Berlin, 1925), 74.

8. Jason, *Film*, 79.

9. Statistisches Reichsamt, *Die Lebenshaltung von 2000 Arbeiter-, Angestellten- und Beamtenhaushaltungen; Erhebungen von Wirtschaftsrechnungen im Deutschen Reich vom Jahre 1927/28* in *Einzelschriften zur Statistik des Deutschen Reichs*, no. 22 (Berlin, 1932), 57.

10. Siegfried Kracauer, *Die Angestellten* (Allensbach, 1959, orig. 1930), 90.

11. Susanne Suhr, *Die weiblichen Angestellten: Arbeits- und Lebensverhältnisse* (Berlin, 1930), 45; Otto Suhr, *Die Lebenshaltung der Angestellten: Untersuchungen auf Grund statistischer Erhebungen des Allgemeinen freien Angestelltenbundes* (Berlin, 1928), 22–23; Statistisches Reichsamt, *Lebenshaltung*, 57.

12. Siegfried Kracauer, "Die kleinen Ladenmädchen gehen ins Kino" (1927) in his *Das Ornament der Masse* (Frankfurt, 1977), 279–94. See also Henri Band, *Mittelschichten und Massenkultur: Siegfried Kracauers publizistische Auseinandersetzung mit der populären Kultur und der Kultur der Mittelschichten in der Weimarer Republik* (Berlin, 1999).

13. Alois Funk, *Film und Jugend: Eine Untersuchung über die psychischen Wirkungen des Films im Leben der Jugendlichen* (Munich, 1934), 48.

14. Emilie Altenloh, *Zur Soziologie des Kino: Die Kino-Unternehmung und die sozialen Schichten ihrer Besucher* (Jena, 1914), 79, 91–92.

15. Eg, "Wenn man vor dem Kino steht," *Film-Kurier* (hereafter cited as *FK*) (February 10, 1926): 1; Statistisches Reichsamt, *Lebenshaltung*, 75, 104, 157, 190.

16. See Carsten Lenk, *Die Erscheinung des Rundfunks: Einführung und Nutzung eines neuen Mediums 1923–1932* (Opladen, 1997), 74–79.

17. Figures and above quote from Karl Christian Führer, "A Medium of Modernity? Broadcasting in Weimar Germany, 1923–1932," *Journal of Modern History* (1997): 731.

18. Figures from *Radio-Händler* (hereafter cited as *RH*) (7 Apr. 1931): 316; Konrad Dussel, *Deutsche Rundfunkgeschichte* (Konstanz, 2004), 41; Führer, "Medium," 735.

19. This area was initially very small, amounting to only 1.4 percent of the territory of the Reich in 1927. Führer, "Medium," 736.

20. Lertes, "Rundfunk aufs Land!" in *Radio-Almanach 1927*, ed. Rudolf Lothar and Adolf Ihring (Berlin, 1927), 69–74.

21. High costs meant that the rural audience in this period was largely drawn from village elites–pastors, estate owners, teachers, etc. See Florian Cebulla, *Rundfunk und ländliche Gesellschaft 1924–1945* (Göttingen, 2004), 65–67.

22. Führer, "Medium," 738.

23. Jürgen Spiker, *Film und Kapital: Der Weg der deutschen Filmwirtschaft zum nationalsozialistischen Einheitskonzern* (Berlin, 1975), 137–38.

24. "Das unbekannte Kino," *FK* (October 30, 1926): supplement.

25. "Wie man's macht," *Reichsfilmblatt* (hereafter cited as *RFB*) (March 10, 1928): 10–11; Erbus, "Das Kino des guten Films," *RFB* (October 4, 1924): 18–20.

26. Irmalotte Guttmann, *Über die Nachfrage auf dem Filmmarkt in Deutschland* (Berlin, 1928); "Wie man's macht," *RFB* (March 10, 1928): 10–11; Hans Bauer, "Statistik der Geschmacksverirrung," *Der Abend, Spätausgabe des "Vorwärts"* (May 25, 1928): 3; "'Klassenbewusste' Kinobesucher," *FK* (December 12, 1925): supplement 2.

27. Hanns Horkheimer, "Badstrasse 58," *Berliner Tageblatt* (July 1, 1928), cited in Wolfgang Mühl-Benninghaus, *Das Ringen um den Tonfilm: Strategien der Elektro- und der Filmindustrie in den 20er und 30er Jahren* (Düsseldorf, 1999), 59.

28. J. Blochert, "Gibt es einen internationalen Durchschnittsgeschmack?," *FK* (April 25, 1922): 3.

29. Quotes from Siegfried Kracauer, "Kult der Zerstreuung" (1926) in *Ornament*, 313; "Der Kinobesuch an den '4 Sonntagen'," *FK* (December 27, 1930): 1.

30. Ernst Rehse, "Amerika in der 'Provinz,'" *FK* (November 14, 1925): 4; Walter Jerven, "In Münchener Kinos erlauscht," *FK* (December 27, 1928): 3.

31. "Das rheinländische Publikum: Eine unsachgemässe Betrachtung," *FK* (June 11, 1924): 1.

32. Figures from Paul Monaco, *Cinema and Society: France and Germany During the Twenties* (New York, 1976), 29.

33. Jason, *Handbuch*, 51.

34. "Die wahre Krise: Das Fiasko des 'Mittelfilms,'" *FK* (October 22, 1926): 1.

35. Bundesarchiv Berlin, R/109I/5370: Ufa-Palast Erfurt to Theaterverwaltung Berlin (February 22, 1932).

36. Lynn Abrams, "From Control to Commercialization: The Triumph of Mass Entertainment in Germany 1900–1925?," *German History* (1990): 288. On the supply of regionally oriented films, see also Karl Führer, "Auf dem Weg zur

'Massenkultur'? Kino und Rundfunk in der Weimarer Republik," *Historische Zeitschrift* (1996): 758–60.

37. See Thomas Saunders, *Hollywood in Berlin: American Cinema and Weimar Germany* (Berkeley, 1994); Victoria de Grazia, "Mass Culture and Sovereignty: The American Challenge to European Cinemas," *Journal of Modern History* (1989), 53–87, and *Irresistible Empire: America's Advance through Twentieth-Century Europe* (Cambridge, MA, 2005); Joseph Garnacz, "Hollywood in Germany: Die Rolle des amerikanischen Films in Deutschland 1925–1990" in *Der deutsche Film*, ed. Uli Jung (Trier, 1993), 167–97.

38. Pierre Bourdieu, *Distinction: A Social Critique of the Judgement of Taste* (London, 1984), and *The Logic of Practice* (Cambridge, 1990), 52–65.

39. "Kinobesucher: Das Dienstmädchen sagt...," *FK* (October 10, 1925): 9.

40. Staatsarchiv Hamburg, Gen IX F19a; Landesarchiv Berlin, A Pr. Br. Rep. 030, Tit. 74, Nr. 1384.

41. "Ein Besuch im Kleinkino," *FK* (May 26, 1928): supplement.

42. See, generally, H. Bingel, "Der Vorführer an das Publikum," *FK* (October 30, 1926): supplement; F. Henseleit, "Das notwendige Uebel: Zum Thema Zweischlagersystem," *RFB* (November 19, 1927): 14; "Unerfreuliches aus der Provinz," *RFB* (September 24, 1927): 20.

43. Some contemporaries indeed questioned this, e.g. Stefan Fingal, "Grossfilm im Kleinkino," *FK* (March 10, 1925): 2.

44. See Winfried Lerg, *Rundfunkpolitik in der Weimarer Republik* (Munich, 1980).

45. Adelheid von Saldern, "*Volk* and *Heimat* Culture in Radio Broadcasting during the Period of Transition from Weimar to Nazi Germany," *Journal of Modern History* (2004): 319–20.

46. See Jürgen Reulecke, "'Veredelung der Volkserholung' und 'edle Geselligkeit'" in *Sozialgeschichte der Freizeit*, ed. Gerhard Huck (Wuppertal, 1982), 141–60; Adelheid von Saldern, "Massenfreizeitkultur im Visier: Ein Beitrag zu den Deutungs- und Einwirkungsversuchen während der Weimarer Republik," *Archiv für Sozialgeschichte* (1993): 21–58; Georg Bollenbeck, *Tradition, Avant-Garde, Reaktion: Deutsche Kontroversen um die kulturelle Moderne* (Frankfurt, 1999); Kaspar Maase, "Schund und Schönheit: Ordnungen des Vergnügens" in *Schund und Schönheit: Populäre Kultur um 1900*, ed. Wolfgang Kaschuba and Kaspar Maase (Cologne, 2001), 9–28.

47. Renate Schumacher, "Programmstruktur und Tagesablauf der Hörer" in *Programmgeschichte des Hörfunks in der Weimarer Republik, Bd. 1*, ed. Joachim-Felix Leonhard (Munich, 1997), 383; Führer, "Medium," 751.

48. Schumacher, "Programmstruktur," 344–51, 364–66, 412–13.

49. E. Rellseg, "Zur Programmefrage!," *Radio-Zeitschrift* (July 10, 1930): 582–84.

50. Quotes and figures from Werner Hensel and Erich Kessler, *1000 Hörer antworten: Eine Marktstudie* (Berlin, 1935), 53–54. See also G. Thann, "Von der sozialen Bedeutung des Rundfunks," *Soziale Praxis* (March 28, 1935): 377–82.

51. Gerhard Eckert, *Der Rundfunk als Führungsmittel* (Berlin, 1941), 203. Although this study is based on surveys from the late 1930s, the overall pattern was similar in the Weimar era. See also Kate Lacey, *Feminine Frequencies: Gender, German Radio, and the Public Sphere, 1923–1945* (Ann Arbor, 1997).

52. Carl Hagemann, "Die künstlerisch-kulturelle Zielsetzung des deutschen Rundfunks" (1928), reprinted in *Aus meinem Archiv: Probleme des Rundfunks*, ed. Hans Bredow (Heidelberg, 1950), 235. On bridging social and political divides, see Hermann Schubotz, "Politik und Rundfunk" (1930) in ibid., 170.

53. Führer, "Medium," 753.

54. Martin Geyer, *Verkehrte Welt: Revolution, Inflation und Moderne: München, 1914–1924* (Göttingen, 1998), 266. In this sense, Bernd Widdig's argument that the inflation intensified ongoing modernization processes in the realm of elite culture can also be applied to popular culture. Bernd Widdig, *Culture and Inflation in Weimar Germany* (Berkeley, 2001).

55. Gerald Feldman, *The Great Disorder: Politics, Economics, and Society in the German Inflation, 1914–1924* (Oxford, 1993).

56. Hans Ostwald, *Sittengeschichte der Inflation* (Berlin, 1931), 208.

57. Victor Klemperer, *Leben sammeln, nicht fragen wozu und warum: Tagebücher 1918–1924*, vol. 1 (Berlin, 1996), 626–27.

58. These box office woes were compounded by the need to face a renewal of foreign imports. Figures from H. Bräutigam, "Die Krisis im Lichtspielgewerbe," *FK* (July 19, 1924): 1–2; "Rund um die Woche," *FK* (November 17, 1924): 1.

59. Even contemporaries noted this link, e.g. Fritz Kohl, "Schädigt der Rundfunk andere Kultureinrichtungen?" (1930) in Bredow, *Aus meinem Archiv*, 117-21. See also Führer, "Medium," 753.

60. See "Zur Entwicklung des Rundfunks in Deutschland," *RH* 6 (January 2, 1929): 30.

61. Over these years reception selectivity roughly doubled and amplification capacity increased twenty-fold. "Radio im Jahre 1933," *RH* (January 10, 1934): 20.

62. Figures from Lerg, *Rundfunkpolitik*, 305–10, 357, 370–71.

63. *Rundfunkarchiv* (October, 1941): 413.

64. Figures from Uta Schmidt, "Radioaneignung" in *Zuhören und Gehörtwerden 1: Radio im Nationalsozialismus. Zwischen Lenkung und Ablenkung*, ed. Inge Marssolek and Adelheid v. Saldern (Tübingen, 1998), 262–63, 266–67; Führer, "Medium," 737.

65. Ludwig Stoffels, "Sendeplätze für Kunst und Unterhaltung" in Leonhard, *Programmgeschichte*, 649.

66. Edgar Lersch and Helmut Schanze, eds., *Die Idee des Radios: Von den Anfängen in Europa und den USA bis 1933* (Konstanz, 2004); Konrad Dussel, "Deutsches Radio, deutsche Kultur: Hörfunkprogramme als Indikatoren

kulturellen Wandels," *Archiv für Sozialgeschichte* (2001): 124–26. For a contemporary, if somewhat earlier, international comparison, see Heinz Engel, "Völkerpsychologie und Rundfunk" in *Radio-Almanach 1926*, ed. Rudolf Lothar and Adolf Ihring (Berlin, 1926), 49–54.

67. Alexander Jason, ed., *Handbuch des Films 1935/36* (Berlin, 1935), 105; Gerhard Paschke, *Der deutsche Tonfilmmarkt* (Berlin, 1935), 127; "Eine Abstimmung gegen zwei Schlager," *FK* (September 7, 1931): 1.

68. See the comments in "Die Revolte des Publikums," *FK* (January 30, 1931): 1.

69. Jason, *Handbuch 1935/36*, 161.

70. See Paschke, *Tonfilmmarkt*, 40–41; Mühl-Benninghaus, *Ringen*, 199; C. Riechmann, "Tonfilm und Kinogeschäft," *RFB* (June 7, 1930): 2; "Das Kino sieht neue Besucher," *FK* (January 12, 1931): 1.

III

BLUE ANGEL, BROWN CULTURE:
THE POLITICS OF FILM RECEPTION
IN GÖTTINGEN

David Imhoof

The *Blue Angel* opened in the town of Göttingen to a sold-out crowd on June 17, 1930. Like most viewers, Heinz Koch, the leading cultural critic at Göttingen's largest newspaper, could hardly contain his excitement. His review made clear that advertisements, which promoted the film as "Germany's greatest sound film" and "the greatest artistic achievement of the season," were not hyperbole. Koch wrote that the film served as nothing less than "an eternal mirror" on the human condition, one that showed "ecce homo."[1] Overall in 1930, cinema's role in German society reflected a great deal about a nation in turmoil. Reichstag battles over films on the Great War, the spread of sound technology, intensified scrutiny of film by censorship bodies, and greater anxiety about the role of American culture made movies front-page news in Germany. That year, too, violent political agitation and elections across the nation marked a major watershed in the politics of the Weimar Republic.

Much has been written about *The Blue Angel* as an icon of Weimar German cinema and culture, an important advancement in sound film, and the vehicle that launched Marlene Dietrich as Germany's greatest international movie star. This film does, in fact, illuminate many of the artistic and technical accomplishments of Weimar cinema, as well as the relationship between American and German film industries. The film's content—the legs, the songs, the decadent nightclub setting, and especially the iconic imagery of Dietrich—has become shorthand for "Weimar culture." And film scholars, beginning with Siegfried Kracauer in 1947, have made great use of the movie as political allegory.[2] My goal here, though, is to study *The Blue Angel* as a vehicle for understanding the role of cinema in Germans' daily lives.

The process by which this film became a part of cultural life in the mid-sized university town of Göttingen illuminates the complex relationship in Weimar Germany between national production and local consumption, and between political ideology and everyday cultural life. In this case, that process occurred in two steps. First, national reviews of the Berlin premiere in local newspapers contextualized the film's appearance, creating a set of ideas that shaped Göttingers' consideration of the film. Second, local reviews built upon these ideas to emphasize features of the film that reinforced the conservative political ideologies, which were becoming increasingly popular in Göttingen. The special attention paid by local reviewers from across the political spectrum to the danger of strong female sexuality in *The Blue Angel* pointed toward the need for male authority. These interpretations came in the wake of a major right-wing victory in local elections; they coincided with the creation of the authoritarian Brüning government in Berlin and were articulated in the midst of a vitriolic political campaign for Reichstag elections in the fall. Local cultural purveyors guided discussions about *The Blue Angel* in ways that paralleled some of the "solutions" to political problems that the Nazis and other right-wing parties were advocating.

More generally, my analysis indicates that both national and local ideas influenced the Göttingers' experience of mass culture. This chapter offers a microcosm of how mass culture became a part of Germans' lives. The individuals, institutions, and ideas may have been unique to Göttingen, but they point to the fact that all Germans experienced mass culture locally, in their towns, neighborhoods, and streets. This study moves away from Berlin as center of cultural production and explains the role local contexts played in consumption. The reception of *The Blue Angel* in Göttingen shows that local experiences and assumptions mediated the impact of German mass culture.

Film and the Weimar Republic

As the chapters in this book demonstrate, Germans in the 1920s produced a torrent of creative activity. The better-known and longer-lasting examples often employed new structures and ideas, explored liberal morality, promoted tolerance, experimented with new technology, and rejected past assumptions about culture. Cinema encapsulated the artistic tension between individual expression and mass consumer culture that characterized this era.

More than merely reflecting political change, cinema directly impacted Weimar German politics for four main reasons. First, this form of mass culture represented a common experience that paralleled and spoke to mass political behavior. For instance, movies about the Great War, especially Lewis Milestone's 1930 *All Quiet on the Western Front*, proved that mass culture could have explosive political results all the way up to the Reichstag.[3] For those on the Left, mass politics and, to a lesser extent, mass culture gave voice to average people, while those on the Right viewed mass behavior as an expression of a racially defined *Volk*.[4]

Second, gendered readings of mass culture by a variety of commentators reflected both a narrowly constructed view of what women should do in public life and the recognition that their very presence denoted real change in Germany after the Great War. Right-wing politicians characterized mass culture and politics as "feminine" and thus susceptible to emotion rather than guided by reason.[5] Even left-wing male critics sometimes echoed this gendered presumption about mass culture. These groups sometimes shared a cultural conservatism, manifested in gendered beliefs about mass culture, which shaped perceptions about the participatory politics of Germany's first democracy.

A third reason for film's political impact was the fact that its great popularity made it an irresistible means of communication and propaganda dissemination. The German government had already enlisted cinema to garner support during the Great War. The Universum Film AG (or Ufa) film corporation, Germany's greatest film studio and the one that produced *The Blue Angel*, grew out of a wedding of public and private funds in 1917 to generate bellicose propaganda.

Finally, cinema highlighted the broad impact of American mass culture. Austrian-Polish filmmaker Otto Preminger quipped to fellow *émigrés* whom he heard speaking Hungarian in the 1930s, "Don't you people know you're in Hollywood? Speak German."[6] But especially in the 1920s, the influence was greater in the other direction. In fact, Hollywood shaped the kinds of movies made in Germany, their distribution, and popular discussions about them, as well as how Germans related to consumer mass culture generally, the growth of German democracy, and the development of German fascism.[7]

By the late 1920s, many conservative elites in Germany had realized that mass culture could be an effective means by which to reinforce their ideas.[8] Similarly, some leftist intellectuals such as Walter Benjamin, Bertolt Brecht, and Siegfried Kracauer wanted to use film to democratize Germany but lacked the means and will to do so extensively.[9] With financial resources and control of mass media, right-wing capitalists like Alfred Hugenberg thus wielded greater influence over the ways that Germans thought about movies.

The 1920 Motion Picture Law aided those conservative interests. It grew out of politicians' moral panic at the rash of films with explicitly sexual and violent content that popped up in Germany after the new republican government lifted censorship in late 1918. As the first systematic expression of national cinema regulation, this law shaped film production and consumption until after World War II. With support from almost every political party, it preserved established moral values, the business status quo, and the policing methods of Imperial Germany.[10] A censorship board in either Berlin or Munich viewed every domestic and foreign film before release and banned movies that could "endanger public order or security, injure, abuse, or morally offend religious sensibilities, [or] endanger German prestige or Germany's reputation with foreign states."[11] Despite these broad powers, no more than two percent of films made in the 1920s were banned each year, often fewer than one percent.[12] Although censorship tightened a little for potentially critical films in the early 1930s, the vast majority of German films faced no censorship during this era.[13]

Becoming *The Blue Angel*

The Blue Angel is based on Heinrich Mann's 1905 novel *Professor Unrat*. It concerns the unlikely seduction of an academic high school teacher, Professor Immanuel Rath (played by Emil Jannings), by a traveling nightclub singer named Rosa Fröhlich or "Lola Lola" (Marlene Dietrich). Jannings and Ufa producer Erich Pommer asked the American (Austrian-born) Josef von Sternberg to direct the project. Sternberg's direction and the film's dual release in German and English made *The Blue Angel* a German-American hybrid creation.[14]

With some assistance from novelist and playwright Carl Zuckmayer, playwright and screenwriter Karl Vollmoeller, and screenwriter Robert Liebmann, Sternberg altered Mann's *Professor Unrat* to create *The Blue Angel*. In both narratives, Rath follows his students to the seedy nightclub, The Blue Angel, located in an unnamed port town, to stop their visits. Once there, however, he encounters Lola, who enchants him with a mixture of respect for his position, raunchy chanson, and sexual innuendo. Rath eventually finds himself in her dressing room and sleeps with her. Afterwards, his morals compel him to marry Lola, at which point his peers force him to surrender his elite academic position. Unlike the protagonist of Mann's book, the film version of the "professor" slowly self-destructs as he is forced to play the fool, first in Lola's traveling troupe and then ultimately in their relationship. His final humiliation comes when he must appear at The Blue Angel on stage as a clown. There, Lola reveals her new romantic interest for the company's strongman (Hans Albers). Rath goes berserk and tries to strangle her. He then stumbles down a haunted and snowy street, while Lola basks in adoration on stage. Rath finally dies broken-hearted in his old classroom.

The movie version minimizes Mann's social critique, in which Rath continues his tyrannical control of others by starting a casino and brothel with Lola to smite the town citizens who stripped him of his professorial authority. In the film, Sternberg makes Rath into a more sympathetic and tragic character, focusing greater attention on Lola's sexual power by modeling her character after Lulu in Frank Wedekind's plays *Earth Spirit* (1895) and *Pandora's Box* (1904).[15] After seeing the film, Heinrich Mann fully approved the "free adaptation" of his novel, despite the variances.[16]

The Blue Angel highlights the intersection between Marlene Dietrich's rise to stardom and the function of sex in the cinema.[17] Just as adoration for Lola eventually kills Rath, Dietrich ultimately superseded Jannings as star. She received only 25,000 Marks for the film, compared to his 200,000, but this role and her collaboration with Sternberg began a string of successful American films in the 1930s that made her an icon and, for a while, the highest paid actress in Hollywood.[18] Elizabeth Bronfen argues that both Dietrich's allure and that of her characters come from a tense synthesis of threat and satisfaction, voyeurism and exhibitionism.[19] Even this analysis underscores the importance of the male gaze and concerns in Weimar Germany about women's social roles and sexuality.

Shot between November 1929 and January 1930, *The Blue Angel* passed the censorship board in March 1930, earning an "artistic" label, presumably in part because of Sternberg's innovative use of sound. In addition to clear dialogue and good sound effects, the movie's setting in a nightclub made music an integral part of the story. Rath, for instance, falls for Lola when she sings "Head to Toe, I'm Ready for Love" ("*Ich bin von Kopf bis Fuss aus Liebe eingestellt*") and trains a spotlight on him.[20] This scene works well because Sternberg weds sight and sound to illustrate Lola's capture of Rath. This and three more hit songs by composer Friedrich Holländer, as well as featured performances by the famous jazz combo the Weintraub Syncopators, greatly expanded the reach of the film's sound.

The Blue Angel premiered in Berlin on April 1, 1930 and broke all records on its first run. Hailing it as "the first artistic sound film," national reviewers especially marveled at how well the dialogue and music fit into the film, unlike many of the first talkies' jarring and sometimes painful noises.[21] With few exceptions, reviews of the Berlin premiere also enthused over the adaptation of Mann's novel and the performances of Jannings and Dietrich. In the *Berliner Börsen-Courier*, leftist intellectual and literary critic Herbert Ihering proclaimed that "for the first time one can speak about poetry and sound film."[22] The liberal journalist Wolf Zucker praised the technical achievement and claimed that he was almost ready "to name *The Blue Angel* the best German film."[23] Other arbiters of high culture, such as Kurt Pinthus, noted that *The Blue Angel* had advanced sound film and cinema generally, at last distinguishing it from theater.[24] Finally, film had become a total work of art (to borrow a phrase from composer Richard Wagner) and, beginning with *The Blue Angel*, was a new kind of mass culture.

Lola in Göttingen

Sabine Hake calls writing about cinema "a focal point for problems in modern mass society," arguing that "discourses on film functioned simultaneously as symptom and cause for the crisis of bourgeois culture, and they contributed to the negotiation of social and political differences by alternately providing an instrument and a projection screen."[25] Göttingen critics only began writing reviews in the later 1920s, before which most coverage was mainly ballyhoo. Beginning in 1927, however, a string of great movies—F. W. Murnau's *Faust*, Fred Niblo's *Ben Hur*, and Fritz Lang's *Metropolis*—convinced Göttingen critics to take film more seriously. As a result, movie reviews, articles about stars, and writing on the industry dramatically expanded in Göttingen's papers. Grafting greater coverage onto previous promotional efforts, these local cultural arbiters served as important advocates for cinema's expanded role in Göttingen's cultural life. They also reflected the generally conservative politics of this city's media and, especially in the later 1920s, its government.[26]

Located south of Hanover, Göttingen was a historically important trading and administrative city for the Kingdom of Hanover and then Prussia. The George August University, which opened in 1737, defined the city as a provincial intellectual center. With a population of about 45,000 in 1930,

Göttingen was large enough to boast a wide variety of cultural offerings, especially because of its well-regarded university. Yet it was small enough to reveal the finer workings of local cultural practices. In the years following the Great War, the many pensioners, military personnel, students, professors, and bureaucrats in Göttingen helped make it a socially and politically conservative town.[27] Cultural arbiters, in particular newspaper critics and cinema owners, reflected this social and political conservatism. Top city officials, who passed and enforced laws controlling cultural activities, remained much the same in personnel and perspective from before World War I through the end of World War II.

Göttingen's conservative political atmosphere shaped cultural activities and the ways in which they were discussed in the media. City leaders, for instance, viewed the expansion of leisure activities, especially cinema, with some apprehension. The 1920 Motion Picture Law enabled local governments to use taxation to encourage the showing of some films over others. Politicians and newspaper critics in Göttingen generally favored historical dramas, documentaries, and films based on classical literature, rather than the popular musicals, melodramas, comedies, and mysteries that dominated the silver screen during these years. Civic leaders used tax regulations to modify ticket prices, which impacted their revenue and the profitability of individual films. *The Blue Angel*'s "artistic" rating made it eligible for a slight tax discount throughout Germany. We do not know the ticket prices for the Göttingen screenings, but the theater owner could have either lowered the prices slightly or, more likely, kept them at normal rates, in order to earn larger profits from the popular film. Especially since they printed reviews of national premieres before the film played in Göttingen, local newspapers helped frame the way Göttingers viewed and discussed cinema. The media generally promoted cinema as a benefit for the local economy and civic prestige, favoring positivist interpretations of films' meanings over potential social critiques. The generally conservative slant of most papers in town often minimized the social critique of some Weimar-era films.

Together, these forces reinforced Göttingen's rightward political drift in the 1920s and early 1930s. The Göttingen Magistracy, the highest elected body in the city and the group responsible for regulating cinema, remained very stable from the 1910s to 1930s. Its general approval of nationalism (in cinema and in government) helped legitimize the lower Town Council's move toward the right that began in the mid-1920s. The citizens of Göttingen were increasingly attracted to the solutions offered by Hitler's National Socialist Party in the Weimar era. Because the Nazis blamed the democratic system itself for Germany's woes, they actively sought "solutions" outside of the existing political system and looked for cultural life to change Germany. Indeed, one Nazi leader in Göttingen in the mid-1920s proclaimed that "politics doesn't belong in the town hall," expressing the desire to avoid messy democratic political wrangling and to seek political rejuvenation through culture.[28]

This political and cultural context shaped the local meanings given to Sternberg's film. *The Blue Angel*'s Berlin premiere in April 1930 received almost as much coverage in Göttingen's press as its showing in the smaller town two months later. Extensive praise from Berlin raised expectations about the film, sharpened the focus on certain qualities, and made the characters and story into immediate icons. Just three days after *The Blue Angel*'s premiere, the Berlin writer Adolf Stein wrote in the *Göttinger Tageblatt* about the film's meaning. He praised the technological accomplishment and claimed that sound film was emerging from its "childhood sickness." Written under the *nom de plum* "Rumpelstilzchen," Stein's column "Berlin Pot-Pourri" had run in the *Tageblatt* since 1924, describing daily life in the capital from a personal perspective, sometimes with irony and humor. Politically, Stein pushed a rabidly nationalist and occasionally anti-Semitic point of view that fit well with the *Tageblatt*'s editorial slant. His thoughts were often the first impressions that people in Göttingen had about a new film, movie star, or development in the film industry. Stein wrote about the advance of film technology in *The Blue Angel* and, somewhat disdainfully, about the role of "sex appeal" (a new English language import that most reviews used). In this review, he contrasted the "delicate" and limited function of "sex appeal" in a war film of the same time, *The Last Company*, with the "most plebeian form" used in *The Blue Angel*, the sole redeeming quality of which was to serve as the catalyst for Rath's "tragic end." For Stein, "sex appeal" served only to illuminate the leading man's downfall and display Dietrich's "impressive beauty." Like other reviewers, Stein found "Lola-Lulu-Pandora" scary yet enticing.[29] Of course, Sternberg portrayed Lola's character this way. But like other conservative reviewers, Stein viewed female sexuality as just a tool for male character development and therefore treated the film as a misogynist cautionary tale.

Another national review in the *Tageblatt* by "Dr. F.K." concentrated more on technical and artistic progress, naming *The Blue Angel* "the first artistic sound film," one that could garner an international audience (which it did). Less focused on sexual power than Stein, "Dr. F.K." praised the entire cast's skills.[30] A national piece in the more liberal *Göttinger*

Zeitung confessed that many critics entered *The Blue Angel* screening in Berlin thinking, "Oh, God, here comes another sound film!" but were quickly taken by "heart-pounding enthusiasm" that continued to the closing credits. Like Stein, this author centered on Rath's downfall, arguing that Lola "betrayed" him and turned him into a "monstrosity."[31]

The most fascinating use of *The Blue Angel*'s national reception in Göttingen newspapers, though, was in the Social Democratic newspaper *Volksblatt*. This paper published no national review of the film but used its visual imagery in a political cartoon to comment on national politics in April 1930.[32] The cartoon "The Black-White-Red Angel" (Figure 3.1), mockingly imagines "a new Ufa sound film with Hugenberg in the Jannings

Der schwarzweißrote Engel.
Ein neuer Ufa-Tonfilm mit Hugenberg in der Jannings-Rolle.

Der Abstieg eines gutbürgerlichen Politikers, der den Verführungskünsten der Regierungskokotte Lola Banderola erliegt, zum parlamentarischen Hanswurst wird ergreifend geschildert.

Figure 3.1   From the Göttingen *Volksblatt* (April 9, 1930). Courtesy of Stadtarchiv Göttingen.

role." Here Lola's seductive power was likened to that of the authoritarian Brüning government, which President Hindenburg had appointed without elections the month before. By casting Alfred Hugenberg, the right-wing head of the German National People's Party (DNVP) who ran Ufa, in the tragic role of Rath, the cartoon implied that authoritarianism (symbolized by the reactionary, monarchical colors of black, red, and white) could even ruin conservatives. The caption described "the fall of a solidly middle-class politician, finished by the seductive arts of the coquettish government of Lola Banderola, and movingly playing the parliamentary clown."

Just as Stein feared Lola's "sex appeal," this Social Democratic cartoon warned against the emotional appeal of authoritarianism at a time when democratic institutions were struggling with little success to solve mounting problems. The cartoon demonstrated *The Blue Angel*'s immediate currency in Göttingen. It showed that observers on the Left and Right agreed that the concept of powerful sexual femininity was a threat itself, and it acted as a metaphor for social and political trends they deemed dangerous.

As the *Volksblatt* cartoon indicated, the months around *The Blue Angel*'s run in Göttingen were some of the most fraught during the Republic's turbulent history, setting precedents that would enable the Nazi destruction of democracy three years later. By 1930 Hitler's party controlled Göttingen's government. National Socialism had first flourished in Göttingen in the early 1920s among university students, who believed their privileged positions to be under siege in the Weimar Republic. They used nationalism and anti-Semitism to attack their professors and society as a whole. The Nazis began to attract broader support in Göttingen by the mid-1920s due to disillusionment with an economic and political system that seemed unable to secure "order" as many in Göttingen understood it.[33] As elsewhere in Germany, the "floating" middle-class vote in Göttingen increasingly favored nationalist parties that questioned the validity of the entire Weimar republican "system."[34] Starting in 1927, growing debt and other financial problems further weakened Göttingen's governing coalition of Social Democrats and centrist liberal parties. After intense and vitriolic campaigns, the May 1929 City Council elections gave a Nazi-led right-wing coalition an absolute majority.[35]

The worldwide Depression prompted by the American stock market crash in October 1929 only worsened the economic and political crisis in Germany. By the time *The Blue Angel* arrived in Göttingen, the right-wing coalition elected to the City Council the year before had fallen apart, and the National Socialist Party had emerged as the ideological and political leader. In the Reichstag election three months after the film's local debut, almost 38 percent of Göttingen voters supported the Nazi Party, more than twice the party's 18.2 percent national vote. And the DNVP, the other major national right-wing party, claimed over 20 percent of the Göttingen vote, giving the right wing nearly 60 percent of the town's support.[36]

Sternberg's film also came to Göttingen in the midst of intense discussions in local newspapers about the spread of sound films and the relationship between German movie stars and Hollywood. Ernst Heidelberg's new, grandiose Capitol Theater, which hosted *The Blue Angel*, raised the visibility of these issues. The Capitol opened on October 2, 1929 with 820 plush seats, two roomy levels, art-deco interior, classical-modernist exterior, bold pink neon accents, and a one million Mark price tag. A very distinguished crowd of political, educational, and cultural leaders gathered for the opening. The *Göttinger Tageblatt* and *Zeitung* devoted full pages to the event. One reporter in the *Zeitung* concluded that this modern "big-city movie theater" would take up Göttingen's "great cultural obligation" and fulfill "a cultural mission in our city."[37] Participants and reporters that night considered the advance of sound films across Germany, which had dominated cinema writing since 1928.[38] The Cinema Association's leader and the university's representative denounced "talkies" as nothing more than evidence of "an American need for sensation."[39] Göttingen's other theater magnate, Fritz Hoffmann, managed to install sound facilities first at his Central Theater and premiered the city's first sound film on April 1, 1930. Whatever questions critics and industry people may have had about sound and its future, the *Göttinger Zeitung*'s chief cultural critic, Max Maass, immediately dismissed that very day by declaring that, "[S]ilent film is dead. Only sound film has a future now."[40]

The Blue Angel opened in Göttingen at Heidelberg's Capitol Theater on June 17, 1930. Extra chairs had to be brought in to accommodate the overflow crowd at the glitzy premiere. In Berlin, conservatives like Adolf Stein and the Nazi press had questioned the film's value. In Göttingen, however, only the Social Democratic *Volksblatt* was somewhat disappointed, chiefly because Sternberg's story minimized the social critique in Mann's novel. The middle-class press was swept away by the movie's artistry and stars. All the local reviewers commented on the intense anticipation in Göttingen about the film's arrival. The *Volksblatt* reported hearing the question, "When is *The Blue Angel* coming?" in the weeks before it played in Göttingen.[41] Max Maass wrote in the *Göttinger Zeitung* that people waited with "knowing excitement" for the local premiere of this movie, which "the entire press has almost universally described as the best sound film to date."[42] The ten-week lag between the movie's national premiere and its arrival in Göttingen was about the norm at this time. Especially for a major film like *The Blue Angel*, this waiting period helped to establish a ritual of moviegoing in Göttingen that began with the hype and excitement surrounding the Berlin premiere, followed by a period of anticipation, and ended with the local consumption and discussion of the film. Heidelberg's new theater, now fitted with sound projection facilities, heightened Göttingers' interest in *The Blue Angel*. Heinz Koch exclaimed in the *Tageblatt* that, "The expectations with which one looked forward to this most successful and tragic German sound film in Göttingen were not disappointed."[43]

Local response to *The Blue Angel* generally focused on the same features that national reviews had—sound quality, literary value, and the sexually charged performances of Jannings and Dietrich. But Göttingen reviewers connected each of these three points to ideas and events in this town, and they offered interpretations of *The Blue Angel* that generally reinforced conservative political trends.

First, reviews celebrated the technical quality and impact of sound in *The Blue Angel*. The Tourist Association's weekly publication, *Göttinger Leben*, had already offered readers in April detailed descriptions and diagrams of how the new sound projection apparatus worked. All *The Blue Angel* reviews in June played upon this familiarity and the expectations that national critics had raised about the superior sound quality in Sternberg's picture. By June, in fact, the *Volksblatt* could already compare *The Blue Angel*'s sound in Heidelberg's theater with that of the popular recording of Holländer's hit songs from the film. The *Volksblatt* critic applauded the movie's "highest economy in picture, gestures, word and sound."[44] The *Niedersächsische Morgenpost* reviewer likewise wrote that "[t]he high quality and effectiveness of this sound film lies in the connection of accomplished acting performance and technological progress."[45] In the *Göttinger Zeitung*, Max Maass stressed that the effective marriage of music and dialogue represented a "step forward in sound film."[46]

Media emphasis on the technical quality of this first "artistic sound film" helped make it into an instant classic, as critics realized immediately that Sternberg had accomplished something distinctive and path-breaking. By stressing the importance of sound and music, Göttingen reviewers also reinforced the idea that *The Blue Angel* offered a moral lesson.

Friedrich Holländer's "Head to Toe, I'm Ready for Love" became a big hit in Germany, but 1930 audiences would still have known better the traditional song "Always practice Truth and Honesty" (*Üb immer Treu und Redlichkeit*) that Holländer uses for the opening, closing, and throughout the film to represent humility and industry, in contrast to the potential destruction in Lola's siren song.[47]

Music in fact makes the film's final point. After Rath's humiliation on the Blue Angel stage, Lola sings "Head to Toe, I'm Ready for Love" alone. She looks contemptuously at the audience, adding visual power to her lines "Men flock around me like moths to a flame/And if their wings burn, I know I'm not to blame." After stumbling back to his old classroom desk and former source of power, Rath dies while the "Always Practice Truth and Humility" chimes play to end the film. The contrast between the two songs—"sex appeal" vs. traditional morality—determines *The Blue Angel*'s narrative. Göttingen reviewers amplified the seductive quality of mass culture in the film's sound and music and thus underscored the notion that women controlling their own sexuality threatened traditional, male-controlled morality. Conservative critics like Heinz Koch had in fact trumpeted cinema's technical marvel for some time, echoing other right-wing intellectuals' appreciation of technology.[48]

Second, Göttingen's critics crafted a context for Sternberg's film that emphasized their conservative, misogynist readings. Heinz Koch in the *Tageblatt* stressed Janning's proven skill at portraying tragic characters, as he had in F.W. Murnau's *The Last Laugh* (1924) and Victor Fleming's *The Way of All Flesh* (1927). Koch also mentioned the origins of Lola's character in Wedekind's plays.[49] The *Niedersächsische Morgenpost* review likewise called her "a genuine Lulu type."[50] Local critics also discussed the film's adaptation of Mann's *Professor Unrat* as a way to drive home their interpretations of the film's meaning. Koch applauded the changes as a way to "fulfill the strongest dramatic impulses" of the novel, while the *Morgenpost* review called the director's adaptation "something unique." Maass in the *Zeitung* addressed in some detail the changes to Mann's original novel. The filmed Rath was simpler, more innocent, and more sympathetic, he argued, so his fall from professor to clown was more tragic and his story more human.[51]

The Social Democratic paper offered a different take on the film's free use of Mann's book. Echoing leftist Berlin critic Siegfried Kracauer, the *Volksblatt* reviewer argued that the movie "weakens the psychological dignity" of the original story. "One would have done better," the reviewer maintained, "to follow the novel more closely."[52] In the book, Mann critiques Imperial Germans' obsession with status by having Rath destroy himself *and* his community in order to avenge his lost prestige. While the *Volksblatt* lauded the film's characters, acting, and sound, it nevertheless stressed that sex-driven mass culture muted the potential social critique in *The Blue Angel*. The film does portray the erosion of Rath's authority, even beyond his seduction by Lola. His status, for example, never means much to the patrons of the Blue Angel, who laugh at him throughout the film. But Social Democrats remained ambivalent about the power of consumer leisure activities—those shown in the film and the act of going to this movie—to effect social change. In a sense, therefore, the Social Democratic reviewer interpreted the film more conservatively than those writing in the middle-class newspapers, believing that Mann's high cultural text could challenge traditional, middle-class authority better than this mass cultural version.

Finally, reviewers' responses to the link between sex and power in the film tended toward the conservative. Reviews in the two largest newspapers took their vision of the film's meaning from the perspective of Rath, celebrating Jannings' tragic performance. Maass wrote that the actor brought the "right format" to expressing the "Gestalt" of this story.[53] Koch agreed that Jannings' acting "is just as deep as it is broad." Jannings was at his best, Koch maintained, when portraying "cleverer people."[54] In a portrait appearing in the Göttingen Tourist Agency's publication, Jannings seemed to draw similar connections between his own personality and those of his characters. "I love German people," he said, "with their depth and their dreamy souls that one often describes as difficult."[55] While Koch was dismayed by the way in which Lola used her "sex appeal" to destroy Jannings' good professor, he wrote that Rath's fall in *The Blue Angel* "opens the deepest and darkest shafts of the human spiritual and emotional labyrinth."[56] The *Morgenpost* review agreed: "One must see the Professor Unrat by Emil Jannings, his supremely detailed, human reflection of the soul's collapse into madness."[57]

All the reviews pointed to Dietrich's portrayal of the sexually empowered Lola as the seductive cause of Rath's revealing destruction. None noted, by contrast, that Rath was petty, infantile, and domineering, the kind of overblown character ripe for a fall. Critics across Germany expected much from the top-billed Jannings but were almost universally amazed by Dietrich's performance. Even the *Volksblatt* reviewer in Göttingen, who disapproved of Stenberg's story, admitted that "the real surprise of the film, though, is Marlene Dietrich as Lola. The interplay of the two [Jannings and Dietrich] one simply must experience."[58] For the *Morgenpost*, Dietrich's "masterly performance" "fit perfectly" with Jannings as Rath.[59] In the *Zeitung* Max Maass wrote that Dietrich played Lola as

> a little animal full of lasciviousness, common yet in her own way charming, a whore [*Dirne*], who shows some heart here and there yet comes out of a somewhat coarse milieu, a hussy [*Luder*], who lives in the present, seeking pleasure—but always on her own terms—and wants nothing more than to be what she is. One simply cannot be angry with this little creature with such an attractive appearance: that's just how she is.[60]

For Heinz Koch, the entire story and the film's effect turned on Lola's sexual prowess and her ability to undermine education, sensibility, caution, and emotional distance—in short, bourgeois masculinity. He claimed that in this film, it is the "maddening aura of a little blonde beast's sex appeal that makes the great man into a little man." Koch used vaguely Freudian language to describe the transformative power of Lola's sexuality: in Rath "another self grows, one that sleeps deep in his soul and is set free by the stirring eroticism of a Lulu." The tragedy at the heart of *The Blue Angel*, Koch wrote, was Rath's final realization "that he has sacrificed his life for belief in a whore."[61] Unlike the liberation he experiences in Mann's novel, Rath's freedom through sexuality proves to be his undoing. In this way, interpretations by Göttingen critics amplified the misogyny inherent in Sternberg's film.

"Like Moths to a Flame": Gender, Mass Culture, and Politics

"Falling in Love Again" became Dietrich's signature song for decades, forever connecting her status as international siren to *The Blue Angel*. The cool yet powerful sexuality of that song, which frames Rath's downfall, figured prominently in many reviewers' interpretations of the film's meaning. More generally, the emphasis placed in national and local reviews on Lola/Dietrich's sex appeal points to the importance of male perspectives in shaping discourses about cinema. Gendered assumptions about *The Blue Angel* in reviews illuminated the ways in which reception of this film fueled conservative politics. Koch especially drew universal lessons from his viewing of *The Blue Angel*. He concluded that the film's tragic story proclaimed: "ecce homo." This perspective reveals his gendered vision of what constituted human strength and weakness.

In fact, Koch defined "humanity" itself through the male character of Rath and contrasted it with the feminine sexuality that could destroy it. Koch certainly granted Lola considerable authority in *The Blue Angel*; like most reviewers, he clearly relished her performance. But he found the film, finally, to be a conservative "human tragedy" about "a brainless, unconcerned instinctual creature of the dangerous-ingenuous type, whose influence works directly upon intellectual, ivory-towered men like Professor Rath in a vague yet destructive manner." For Maass, too, Rath was a tragic man, who made too much of his love for Lola. Lola was, on the other hand, a "little animal" who "doesn't take love too seriously." Koch and Maass had some months earlier similarly commended G.W. Pabst's *Pandora's Box*, based on Wedekind's 1895 play of the same name. Koch called that 1929 film an "unmoral moral piece" in which men's experience with Lulu (played by the "young, insanely beautiful" Louise Brooks) landed them in the "hell of human tragedy." For Koch, these experiences of sexual destruction, like Rath's in *The Blue Angel*, acted as a "mirror on the deepest chasms of the soul."[62] Maass also praised Brooks' performance, "in which dwells all the bodily charms of woman with the face of the Madonna."[63] These important local critics thus strengthened their own interpretive function by situating reviews of *The Blue Angel* into their larger body of work on mass culture in Göttingen.

Patrice Petro argues that views of Weimar German cinema—then and now—have partly resulted from the male viewing perspective that almost completely dominated writing on cinema during that era. That male perspective, however, did not necessarily prevent women (or men) from reading films differently.[64] For instance, some who saw *The Blue Angel* might have viewed Lola as liberating or Rath as stifling. Cultural leaders in Göttingen did not unilaterally form readers' definitions about cinema or a specific film. However, local media and established cultural arbiters did influence discourses about cinema in Göttingen. Political reporting and editorializing in local newspapers helped contextualize the implications of their writing on cinema. For example, Koch mentioned Dietrich's departure to America in his review of *The Blue Angel*, echoing concerns about Garbo's earlier defection to Hollywood. Germans were at this time coming to terms with the authoritarian Brüning government, which Hindenburg had appointed partly in response to the constitutional crisis caused by the USA's Young Plan for Germany's war reparations payment. Koch's *Göttinger Tageblatt* vehemently condemned the American plan and used the crisis to question democracy's efficacy. In such a volatile situation, discussions about Hollywood's control over "German" movie stars[65] or about the dangerous power of female "sex appeal" could bolster political parties seeking to solve pressing problems with nationalism and authoritarian politics.

Göttingen's reviews of *The Blue Angel* emphasized conservative interpretations of the film as morality tale, not as path to liberation. They did not commend Lola as an example of female strength, nor did reviewers draw moviegoers' attention to the critique of status still present in the story of Rath's downfall. Instead, most Göttingen reviews highlighted the technical wonder of consumer mass culture, the tragically "human" portrayal of a "great man" destroyed by a "blond beast," and the distracting sex appeal of movie stars. Only the *Volksblatt* review mentioned that Mann's social commentary was absent from the film. None of the reviews even hinted that Lola's powerful and self-controlled sexuality promoted a form of liberation. Whether revealing costumes, coquettishness, and suggestive songs were the best tools for female emancipation in the interwar era is another question. But Lola is clearly a woman in charge of her own sexuality in ways that male reviewers found both frightening and appealing. Koch and Maass wrote off any of Lola's potential authority by calling her a whore and a hussy. This "brainless Lulu type" therefore stood in contrast to the "cleverer" professor whose status was conferred by education, wealth, and gender.

For more conservative reviewers, Lola's (and Dietrich's) appropriation of male voyeurism pointed to the danger of strong female sexuality. They viewed *The Blue Angel* as a warning to viewers about men losing control. Given Sternberg's dictatorial control of his films and of Dietrich, these interpretations draw on the misogyny that was clearly a part of this movie.[66] The *Volksblatt* commentator, who sought signs of liberation in the film, nevertheless viewed Lola as a dual threat. Like writers in more conservative papers, this author recognized the destructive power of Lola's sexuality. But he also conflated Lola with mass culture generally. The "sex appeal" of the character, movie star, and mass-produced film undermined the progressive power of Mann's original novel. In other words, the seductive qualities of movie stars, and of mass culture more generally, convinced commentators across the political spectrum that strong, sexual femininity was dangerous.[67] This broad reading of the film as psychosexual tragedy gave viewers a compelling image of why men should control the public sphere at a time when conservatives evoked gendered definitions of mass culture and politics to decry democracy.[68]

In sum, at the very moment that the Nazi Party and the Brüning government were asking Germans to repudiate democracy and trust instead the authority of one man (Hitler, Hindenburg, or Brüning), most Göttingen reviewers were pushing interpretations of the era's most popular film that implied the need to shore up men's control of sexuality, morality, and the public sphere. Peter Jelavich has recently pointed to 1930 as the moment "Weimar culture" died, because it failed to stand up to the Right's attack on democracy and freedom that year.[69] Conflicts over filmed versions of the Great War (especially *All Quiet on the Western Front*), for instance, racked Göttingen and also helped strengthen Nazi ideas.[70] The popularity of *The Blue Angel*, its technical accomplishments, and its conservative use of "sex appeal" made it an effective vehicle for advocating some of the same antifeminist ideas that Nazis were using to attack the Weimar Republic.

We cannot know the degree to which reviews of *The Blue Angel* informed the views of people in Göttingen about the film, much less their political behavior. Still, the generally conservative, misogynist interpretations of the film provided powerful parallels in mass culture to the rhetoric and political agenda of popular right-wing political parties. As a reflection of and potential catalyst for political change, therefore, *The Blue Angel* played an important role in cinema's politicization in Göttingen. And while specific contexts would have in turn shaped the role the film played elsewhere, this analysis makes clear that popular and provocative movies could act as an important medium through which Germans considered politics.

"Falling in Love Again": Conclusions and Afterlife

In his 1947 book *From Caligari to Hitler: A Psychological History of the German Film*, Siegfried Kracauer expanded on his 1930 review of *The Blue Angel* with the benefit of hindsight. He argued that the film appealed to viewers because Lola "was a new incarnation of sex" and because Germans identified with the emotionally immature Rath who "needed" sadistic control.[71] Kracauer's explanation of why Germans accepted Nazi "totalitarianism" also began with this male perspective of Rath's domination.[72] Despite his very different agenda from Göttingen's conservatives of 1930, Kracauer in 1947 made similar assumptions about *The Blue Angel*. Indeed, his political allies in the Social Democratic *Volksblatt* had done much the same in 1930. Göttingen reviewers of all political persuasions described the film as a display of dangerous female sexuality, and the implication was that men should remain in control. As an incarnation of the sexually empowered "New Woman," Lola clearly threatened many men. Antifeminist fears of strong women served to boost support for the Nazis and other conservative parties.[73] The fact that a movie helped make this political point indirectly through attractive consumer culture further reinforced the tendency among those on the Right to seek solutions outside the republic's democratic mechanisms.

This chapter has focused on the ways in which gendered readings of *The Blue Angel* strengthened conservative politics. But the kind of analysis I have offered also points to other conclusions about this movie's impact on images of women, the function of new technology in daily life, the significance of sound film, or identification with movie stars. Contemporary responses to *The Blue Angel* reflected, above all, the complexity of exchange between local, national, and international culture in Weimar Germany. Reactions to the film in Berlin partially shaped those in Göttingen. At the same time, the local political atmosphere, social organization, and individuals influenced responses to *The Blue Angel* in the Göttingen press. Viewers in Göttingen, in turn, absorbed a mixture of all these elements and then saw the movie (or thought about it) through their own personal filter. Thus integrated, *The Blue Angel* finally became a part of local syntax for discussing cinema. References to the film in Göttingen newspapers continued to surface into the 1930s, and the film remained critics' benchmark for cinematic quality, star power, and depth.[74]

In his 1965 autobiography, Josef von Sternberg claimed that when Adolf Hitler "became Lord High Executioner," he ordered the destruction of the negative and all but one copy of the *The Blue Angel*. "Curiously enough," writes Sternberg, "I learned form a reliable source (that is, if an intimate of the Hitler circle can be called reliable) that he viewed this remaining copy repeatedly and that it was his favorite film."[75] Probably apocryphal, this story nonetheless points to the lasting (if bizarre) impact of *The Blue Angel*. The official Third Reich machinery may have deemed the film's imagery dangerous, but if Sternberg's claim is true, Hitler understood (and perhaps relished) the cautionary tale that conservative reviews in Göttingen noted. Scholars continue to mine *The Blue Angel* to understand the role of sexism, sadism, "sex appeal," fetishism, voyeurism, emotional domination, emancipation, and even colonialism in cinema. Together with Sternberg's tale about the power of his film even over Hitler himself, these analyses make *The Blue Angel* ever more iconic. And my local study suggests another level of meaning. Local critical reception of this popular film articulated ideas about male control of society that resonated with National Socialism at a critical moment in the history of the Weimar Republic. At the very least, this resonance added discursive support to Nazism's growing popularity in Göttingen. That legacy should not overburden Sternberg's film. Rather, it shows that Nazi ideas could also draw strength from mass culture, even from a film that stood, above all, on great legs.

Notes

1. *Göttinger Tageblatt* (hereafter *GT*) (June 18, 1930).
2. Siegfried Kracauer, *From Caligari to Hitler: A Psychological History of the German Film* (Princeton, 1971, orig. 1947), 215–18; Peter Baxter, "On the Naked Thighs of Miss Dietrich," *Wide Angle* (1978): 18–25; John Blair, "Colonialism in Josef von Sternberg's *Der Blaue Engel*," *West Virginia University Philological Papers* (Fall, 2003): 53–61; Erica Carter, *Dietrich's Ghosts: The Sublime and the Beautiful in Third Reich Film* (London, 2004), 136–45; Elisabeth Bronfen, "Seductive Departures of Marlene Dietrich: Exile and Stardom in 'The Blue Angel,'" *New German Critique* (Spring/Summer, 2003): 9–31; Stephen Lamb, "Woman's Nature? Images of Women in *The Blue Angel, Pandora's Box, Kuhle Wampe* and *Girls in Uniform*" in *Visions of the "Neue Frau": Women and the Visual Arts in Weimar Germany*, ed. Marsha Meskimmon and Shearer West (Aldershot, 1995), 124–42; Judith Mayne, "Marlene Dietrich, *The Blue Angel*, and Female Performance" in *Seduction and Theory: Readings of Gender, Representation, and Rhetoric*, ed. Dianne Hunter (Urbana, 1989), 28–46; Heidi Faletti, "The Doomed Moralist in The Blue Angel and Lola" in *National Traditions in Motion Pictures*, ed. Douglas Radcliff-Umstead (Kent, 1985), 80–4.
3. Modris Eksteins, "War, Memory, and Politics: The Fate of the Film *All Quiet on the Western Front*," *Central European History* (1980): 60–82; Jerold Simmons, "Film and International Politics: The Banning of *All Quiet on the Western Front* in Germany and Austria, 1930–1931," *The Historian* (1989): 40–60.
4. The fact that both groups invoked the same term—the *Volk*—points to the power of these ideas.
5. Eve Rosenhaft, "Women, Gender, and the Limits of Political History in the Age of 'Mass Politics'" in *Elections, Mass Politics and Social Change in Modern Germany*, ed. James Retallack and Larry Eugene Jones (Cambridge, 1992), 149–73.
6. Cited in Joseph Horowitz, *Artists in Exile: How Refugees from Twentieth-Century War and Revolution Transformed the American Performing Arts* (New York, 2008), 298.
7. Thomas Saunders, *Hollywood in Berlin: American Cinema and Weimar Germany* (Berkeley, 1994).
8. Adelheid von Saldern, "'Kunst für's Volk': Vom Kulturkonservatismus zur nationalsozialistischen Kulturpolitik" in *Das Gedächtnis der Bilder: Ästhetik und Nationalsozialismus*, ed. Harald Welzer (Tübingen, 1995),

45–104, and "Massenfreizeitkultur im Visier: Ein Beitrag zu den Deutungs- und Entwirkungsversuchen während der Weimarer Republik," *Archiv für Sozialgeschichte* (1993): 21–58.

9. Bruce Murray, *Film and The German Left in the Weimar Republic* (Austin, 1990); Theodore Rippey, *"Kuhle Wampe* and the Problem of Corporal Culture," *Cinema Journal* (2007): 3–25; John Willet, *Art and Politics in the Weimar Period* (New York, 1978), 145–9, 206–8.

10. Saunders, *Hollywood*, 26–8.

11. Lichtspielgesetz of May 12, 1920, *Reichs-Gesetzblatt* (1920): 953.

12. Paul Monaco, *Cinema and Society: France and Germany in the Twenties* (New York, 1976), 59.

13. See Peter Jelavich, *Berlin Alexanderplatz: Radio, Film, and the Death of Weimar Culture* (Berkeley, 2006); Helmut Korte, *Der Spielfilm und das Ende der Weimarer Republik* (Göttingen, 1998); Jan-Peter Barbian, "Filme mit Lücken: Die Lichtspielzensur in der Weimarer Republik" in *Der deutsche Film: Aspekte seiner Geschichte von den Anfängen bis zur Gegenwart*, ed. Uli Jung (Trier, 1993), 51–78.

14. Gertrud Koch, "Between Two Worlds: Von Sternberg's *The Blue Angel* (1930)" in *German Film and Literature: Adaptations and Transformations*, ed. Eric Rentschler (New York, 1986), 60–72; Bronfen, "Seductive Departures."

15. Josef von Sternberg, *Fun in a Chinese Laundry* (New York, 1965), 230.

16. Heinrich Mann, "Der Blaue Engel wird mir vorgeführt," *Berliner Börsen-Courier* (March 30, 1930).

17. Scholars have used the relationship between Lola and Rath to study this nexus. See David Davidson, "From Virgin to Dynamo: The 'Amoral Woman' in European Cinema," *Cinema Journal* (Autumn, 1981): 31–49; Richard McCormick, "From 'Caligari' to Dietrich: Sexual, Social, and Cinematic Discourses in Weimar Film," *Signs* (Spring, 1993): 640–68.

18. Werner Sudendorf, *Marlene Dietrich* (Berlin, 1980), 68, 71–2.

19. Bronfen, "Seductive Depatures," 26–30. See also E. Ann Kaplan, *Women and Film* (London, 1983), 49–59.

20. The song is called "Falling in Love Again" in its English version, which had new lyrics by Sammy Lerner. It became a popular and oft-recorded jazz standard.

21. *GT* (April 7, 1930); *Göttinger Zeitung* (hereafter *GZ*) (April 14, 1930).

22. Herbert Ihering, *Berliner Börsen-Courier* (April 2, 1930).

23. Wolf Zucker, *Die Literarische Welt* (April 11, 1930).

24. Kurt Pinthus, *Das Tagebuch* (April 5, 1930).

25. Sabine Hake, *The Cinema's Third Machine: Writing on Film in Germany, 1907–1933* (Lincoln, 1993), xi.

26. Throughout the Weimar years, Göttingen boasted four daily newspapers. The *Göttinger Tageblatt*, which controlled at least a quarter of the town's circula- tion, generally espoused a nationalist, right-wing ideology, offering early sup- port for Hitler's party. The cautiously liberal *Göttinger Zeitung* captured about

17 percent of local readership. The probusiness *Niedersächsische Morgenpost*'s reach was somewhere between that of the *Tageblatt* and *Zeitung* but paid less attention to culture. The *Volksblatt* supported the Social Democratic Party and represented a steady oppositional voice with about 20 percent of local circulation. Eckhard Sürig, *Göttinger Zeitungen* (Göttingen, 1985), 17–20, 39–55.

27. Adelheid von Saldern, "Göttingen im Kaiserreich" in *Göttingen: Geschichte einer Universitätsstadt, Band 3*, ed. Rudolf von Thadden and Günter Trittel (Göttingen, 1999), 14–56, and "Zur Entwicklung der Parteien in Göttingen während der Weimarer Republik," *Göttinger Jahrbuch* (1971): 171.

28. Stadtarchiv Göttingen, AHR III A F 5, Nr. 13, cited in Fritz Hasselhorn, "Göttingen 1917/18–1933" in Thadden and Trittel, *Göttingen*, 91.

29. *GT* (April 5, 1930).

30. *GT* (April 7, 1930).

31. *GZ* (April 17, 1930).

32. *Volksblatt* (hereafter *VB*) (April 9, 1930).

33. Barbara Marshall, "The Political Development of German University Towns in the Weimar Republic: Göttingen and Münster, 1918-1933" (Dissertation, University of London, 1972), 201.

34. Thomas Childers, *The Nazi Voter* (Chapel Hill, 1983); Fritz Hasselhorn, *Wie wählte Göttingen: Wahlverhalten und die soziale Basis der Parteien in Göttingen 1924–1933* (Göttingen, 1983).

35. Marshall, "Political Development," xvi, 227–81, and 321–34.

36. David Imhoof, "Guns, Opera, and Movies: Local Culture in Interwar Germany, Göttingen 1919–1938" (Dissertation, University of Texas, 2000), 18.

37. *GZ* (October 3, 1929).

38. *GT* (April 18, 1929, July 28, 1929, and January 8, 1930).

39. *GT* (October 3, 1929).

40. *GZ* (April 1, 1930). See also *GT* (April 1 and 4, 1930); *GZ* (April 5 1930); *Göttinger Leben* (April 1, 1930); *VB* (April 5, 1930); *Niedersächsische Morgenpost* (hereafter *NM*) (April 5, 1930).

41. *VB* (June 19, 1930).

42. *GZ* (June 18, 1930).

43. *GT* (June 18, 1930).

44. *VB* (June 19, 1930).

45. *NM* (June 19, 1930).

46. *GZ* (June 18, 1930).

47. Friedrich Holländer, "Die Musik in Tonfilm," *Reichsfilmblatt* (May 10, 1930). Mozart had used the melody in *The Magic Flute* (1791) to signify the innocence of Papageno in that character's famous aria, "The Bird Catcher." Simon Richter, "The Return of the Queen of the Night: Joseph von Sternberg's *Der blaue Engel* and *Die Zauberflöte*," *German Life and Letters* (2007): 171–85.

48. Jeffrey Herf, *Reactionary Modernism: Technology, Culture, and Politics in Weimar and the Third Reich* (Cambridge, 1984).

49. *GT* (June 18, 1930).

50. *NM* (June 19, 1930).
51. *GZ* (June 18, 1930).
52. *VB* (June 19, 1930). Kracauer's Berlin review raised similar concerns. *Die Neue Rundschau* (June, 1930): 861–63.
53. *GZ* (June 18, 1930).
54. *GT* (June 18, 1930).
55. *Göttinger Leben* (January 1, 1929).
56. *GT* (June 18, 1930).
57. *NM* (June 19, 1930).
58. *VB* (June 19, 1930).
59. *NM* (June 19, 1930).
60. *GZ* (June 18, 1930).
61. *GT* (June 18, 1930).
62. *GT* (October 17, 1929).
63. *GZ* (October 17, 1929).
64. Patrice Petro, *Joyless Streets: Women and Melodramatic Representation in Weimar Germany* (Princeton, 1989).
65. Greta Garbo was Swedish, but people often assumed her to be German.
66. Sternberg, who claimed that Dietrich had once given him a photograph signed "I'm nothing without you," wrote of Dietrich's performance in *The Blue Angel*: "I then put her into the crucible of my conception, blended her image to correspond with mine, and, pouring lights on her until the alchemy was complete, proceeded with the [screen] test. She came to life and responded to my instructions with an ease I had never before encountered…Her remarkable vitality had been channeled." Sternberg, *Fun*, 226, 237.
67. Klaus Theweleit, *Male Fantasies*, trans. Stephen Conwa (Minneapolis, 1987–1989, two vols.), and Renate Bridenthal, Atina Grossman, and Marion Kaplan, eds., *When Biology Became Destiny: Women in Weimar and Nazi Germany* (New York, 1984) remain touchstones for studying the ways in which men in Weimar Germany viewed women and female sexuality as threats. See also Katharina von Ankum, ed., *Women in the Metropolis: Gender and Modernity in Weimar Culture* (Berkeley, 1997); Vibeke Petersen, *Women and Modernity in Weimar Germany* (New York, 2001).
68. Andreas Huyssen, "Mass Culture as Woman: Modernism's Other" in *Studies in Entertainment*, ed. Tania Modelski (Bloomington, 1986), 188-207; Rosenhaft, "Women."
69. Jelavich, *Berlin Alexanderplatz*.
70. David Imhoof, "Culture Wars and the Local Screen: The Meaning of World War I Films in One German City around 1930" in *Why We Fought: America's Wars in Film and History*, ed. Peter Rollins and John O'Connor (Lexington, 2008), 175–95.
71. Kracauer, *Caligari*, 217.
72. A number of scholars have critiqued Kracauer's assumptions, especially his gendered readings. See the *New German Critique* issue devoted to Kracauer,

72 / DAVID IMHOOF

volume 54 (1991); Mike Budd, ed., *The Cabinet of Dr. Caligari: Texts, Contexts, Histories* (New Brunswick, 1990); Petro, *Joyless Streets*.

73. Julia Sneeringer, *Winning Women's Votes: Propaganda and Politics in Weimar Germany* (Chapel Hill, 2002), 119–218.

74. *GT* (October 11–12 and October 17, 1930); *GZ* (July 21, 1932); *GT* (January 17, 1935).

75. Sternberg, *Fun*, 49.

IV

MIDDLE-CLASS HEROES: ANTI-NATIONALISM IN THE POPULAR ADVENTURE FILMS OF THE WEIMAR REPUBLIC

Ofer Ashkenazi

Scholars traditionally read Weimar film as a symptomatic manifestation of national traditions, longings, and fears. Siegfried Kracauer's seminal work of 1947, *From Caligari to Hitler*, identified postwar German film with the three major paradigms customarily associated with Weimar culture as a whole: ominous anticipation of the rise of Nazism, inability to come to terms with the traumatic experiences of World War I, and dispassionate escapism in the face of contemporary crises.[1] While present-day scholars reject Kracauer's focus on the "German soul" and its psychotic pathology, they often share his perception of the essential role of films in the formation of postwar German nationalism.[2]

This chapter suggests an alternative framework for the interpretation of Weimar film. In noting the transnational nature of filmmaking in postwar Germany and the circumstances that shaped Weimar cinema, I highlight a major tendency in Weimar popular film that has been frequently disregarded—that is, the progressive-liberal, antinationalist portrayal of the struggle of middle-class individuals for freedom and justice in the constantly transforming cities of postwar Europe.[3]

At first glance, Weimar adventure films seem at odds with this emphasis on an antinationalist, liberal worldview. Scholars have repeatedly linked this extremely popular genre to nationalist sentiments, to a longing for the lost colonial empire, and even to racist tendencies.[4] I will argue, however, that these films deliberately shift the spotlight from the national to the individual, in particular to the urban middle-class individual, who was the subject of the "modernity crisis" of the Great War and its aftermath.[5] Focusing on Joe May's eight episode film *Mistress of the World* (*Die Herrin der Welt*, 1919/1920) I will show the development of the visual imagery and narrative patterns that governed popular Weimar adventure films. I will then briefly demonstrate the presence of these elements, as well as their revisions, in films of the late 1920s and early 1930s. While the later films continued to explore the different aspects of the modern urban experience, they lacked the earlier zeal for social reform. Nonetheless, the visualization of the mysterious journeys in these films continued to reject, and even to ridicule, the longing for national glory, as well as the notions of inherent difference between members of different national communities.

Exotic Journeys and Outlandish Foreigners in Weimar Adventure Films

Between the end of World War I and the collapse of the Weimar Republic, more than 170 German films depicted journeys to unknown lands and encounters with exotic foreigners, both in (pseudo-) documentary productions (known as *Kulturfilme*) and in popular feature films.[6] Highlighting the sizeable budget and the visual sensations they offered, Weimar critics, politicians, and filmmakers perceived the exotic adventure films as examples of both the potential and the menace of contemporary cinema and of its political and educational influences. Joe May's *Mistress of the World*, for instance, was screened in the Reichstag in February 1920, during a discussion of "the meaning of film" that sought to expose Weimar politicians to the substantial role of film in modern society.[7] A few weeks later, the liberal film-magazine *Der Film Kurier* depicted *Mistress of the World* as signifying one of the two possible future trajectories of German cinema, alongside the celebrated *The Cabinet of Dr. Caligari* (*Das Kabinett des Dr. Caligari*, directed by Robert Wiene, 1920).[8] This flattering comparison, however, also reveals the reason for the comparative neglect of this genre by post–World War II scholars; for while historians and film scholars praised *Caligari* for its stylistic innovations and intellectual flair, they deemed adventure films an unsophisticated combination of suspenseful narrative and second-rate visual attraction.

Noting their poor aesthetic standards, Siegfried Kracauer found these films to be of "secondary importance."[9] Admitting their popularity, he associated these films with escapist and nationalist sentiments that governed "the average German" during Weimar. According to this argument, adventure films attracted enthusiastic moviegoers because they provided the "fantasy of a prisoner"—that is, the German spectator—whose jail-house was "the mutilated, blockaded fatherland."[10] The relationship that Kracauer emphasized between adventure films and the grave sociopolitical conditions of postwar Germany should not be overlooked. Nevertheless, a closer examination suggests that the visual imagery, narrative patterns, and popularity of these films were more closely related to a transnational frame-work of modern urban experience than to nationalist compensations.

The imagery of Weimar adventure films is undeniably rooted in a cultural tradition that celebrated the supremacy of (white) Western civilization, something that had long been manifested in various modern media from the journals of great European explorers to the adventure literature of the nineteenth century.[11] Weimar-era cinematic depictions of foreigners were also influenced by another racist tradition, the early twentieth century *Völkeranschauen* ("Display of Peoples"), which exhibited "genuine" tribesmen and women in their "indigenous environment."[12] Weimar filmmakers were often inspired by prewar novels and exhibitions, but they tended to incorporate them into a considerably different ideological context. In fact, Weimar adventure films showed less interest in the colonization of exotic realms or in the encounters between representatives of different ethnic groups or "peoples." Instead, they sought to portray the encounter of a bourgeois city dweller with a culture in which reason and freedom were annulled, either by tyrannical rulers or by lawless anarchy.

Similar to other popular cinematic genres of the early 1920s such as detective and war films, adventure films attracted their audience with the promise to reveal a reality that was normally invisible to the bourgeois urbanite. The apparent popular desire to experience the invisible aspects of modern reality instigated the ethos of realism attached to Weimar adventure films. In order to strengthen their case for realism, German filmmakers highlighted the "scientific research" that preceded the production, as well as the employment of academic experts (anthropologists, ethnography scientists, etc.).[13] The quest for realist images of the "Orient" was repeatedly addressed in the German film magazines of the early 1920s. Weimar newspapers eagerly reported the numerous changes of shooting locations, the employment of academic researchers, and the building of extravagant settings, in order to demonstrate the filmmakers' perfectionist fervor for "authenticity."[14] Even Chancellor Friedrich Ebert amusingly acknowledged the renowned "realist" aspirations of the filmmakers during his 1922 visit to Babelsberg Studios. Stepping onto the set, Ebert greeted the Indian prince "as one head of a country to another," sarcastically replaying an outdated colonial encounter with the "natives."[15]

Nevertheless, as Weimar filmmakers repeatedly explained, their commitment to authenticity was limited to a particular notion of realism. A 1922 article in *Film-Kurier*, for instance, was dedicated to the conventional nature of realism in adventure films. According to leading filmmakers such as Joe May and Paul Leni, a "realist image" of the filmed foreigners and their landscapes reflected the spectators' expectations, not the actual foreign reality. In addition, Weimar filmmakers sought to expose the "essence" of the distant continent and its inhabitants—that is, the meaning of their social practices and beliefs, rather than the actual reality in a particular land.[16] Corresponding to this approach, the marketing of adventure films tended to blur the exact destinations of the journeys and the particular identities of the foreigners encountered by the protagonists. In the early 1920s, the plot descriptions in the official film program guides that spectators received in the theater lobby were often devoid of specific historical background or references to particular places. Thus Joe May's *The Indian Tomb* (*Das Indische Grabmal*, 1921) was situated in India, but the film was generally advertised as a portrayal of "the fantastic, enigmatic world of the orient."[17] Likewise, advertisements for Robert Reinert's *Opium* (1919) described the events as taking place in two different locations interchangeably—either in "India" or "China"—and both were depicted as "the homeland of opium."[18]

Weimar reviewers were similarly not certain of the specific locations of the filmed adventures, and they tended to disregard the differences between specific nations and cultures.[19] But the vague location of the films did not damage their credibility. As Ludwig Brauner's review of May's *The Indian Tomb* suggested, adventure films could have a ludicrous "fairytale style" and nonetheless capture the "soul of India."[20] Adventure films were mainly expected to display a "foreign" worldview, rather than to depict a particular foreign country. The filmed exotic sphere was supposed to evoke a sense of otherness, of unfamiliarity, of a place ruled by entirely foreign powers and laws, inhabited by peoples whose behaviors and beliefs could not be comprehended within the spectators' cultural context.[21]

Weimar adventure films thus showed an awareness of the conventional nature of realism combined with an obsessive search for the invisible essence of the foreigners, and for the notion of absolute otherness. As such, they provide a unique viewpoint on popular trends in Weimar identity discourse and on common perceptions of the "objective" differences between "Us" and "Them." This basic dichotomy is highlighted in recent studies of Weimar adventure films. Emphasizing the ongoing constructions of differences between the protagonist and his or her native adversaries, these studies explore the films' efforts to envisage a homogeneous national community with distinctive, superior qualities.[22]

My analysis of *Mistress of the World* challenges such interpretations, however. It demonstrates how the identity of the protagonist took form in relation to the city, not to the nation-state, and how it was constructed around particular worldviews and values, rather than nationality or race. Encounters with foreign cultures in these films are not intended to demonstrate the superiority of Western civilization, but rather they show the faults of an illiberal system of law and order. These faults appear in the modern city as well as in the exotic lands, but they can only be remedied within an urban sphere. Consequently, more than a nationalist reaction to war trauma, the exotic landscapes and cultures shown in Weimar films are symbolic warnings against the decay of liberal bourgeois society in the urban centers of postwar Germany.

A Liberal Daydream: *Mistress of the World* and Early Weimar Adventure Films

Premiering only a few months after the end of World War I, Joe May's *Mistress of the World* introduced to German spectators a sensational fable of adventurous revenge, carried out by a humiliated protagonist who travels around the globe in pursuit of power and fame.[23] Maud Gregaards, the female protagonist, is an innocent victim of an elaborate scheme, planned and carried out by her fiancé, which has resulted in her imprisonment and the loss of her child. After her release from prison she sets out to avenge her misfortunes. In order to finance her revenge, Maud leaves the city and looks for the legendary treasure of the Queen of Sheba, hidden in the lost African city, Ophir. *Mistress of the World*, a series of eight two-hour films made over the course of two years, portrays a circular journey in search of the treasure, from the modern European city to China, Africa, North America, and back home. The experiences during the journey change Maud's worldview and ambition. Upon her homecoming, with gold and fame, she declares her new vocation: now, instead of revenge, she will struggle for fundamental social reform, seeking "to bring a new dawn to humanity."[24]

German newspapers depicted *Mistress of the World* as one of the most important cinematic events of the early Weimar Republic. Contemporary reports emphasized the extravagant production that employed thousand of extras. Readers of the film magazines were repeatedly informed about the hundreds of temples, palaces, and houses, as well as the cities and villages, which were built for the production in a studio near Berlin.

The main motifs and visual attractions of *Mistress of the World* can also be found in many of the German adventure films of the time. More importantly, this film illustrates the characteristics and boundaries of the identity discourse developed in such films. May's film provides a detailed depiction of identity formation, the process through which the protagonist differentiates herself from her surroundings and becomes an independent, powerful individual. A series of encounters with the inhabitants of the foreign lands transforms her from a passive victim of modernity—similar to the primitive natives she encounters—to its master.

The temptation to read this film as an allegory of German national-ist sentiments is strong. Indeed, Maud's victimization by an international conspiracy, as well as her rebirth as a vigorous and admired power, reflect fundamental elements in post–World War I German nationalism. But this interpretation would be misleading for several reasons. First, similar to the protagonists of most early adventure films, Maud is not German, and there is nothing typically German, or stereotypically German, in her portrayal. The film's program guide describes her as Danish. However, aside for her light-colored hair, there is hardly any sign of this identity, either in her conduct or in her environment. This apparent indifference to national dis-tinctiveness confused the reviewers of the film series. While some review-ers repeated the program guide's portrayal of Maud as a Danish heroine, others presented divergent interpretations, labeling her "a German educa-tor," "an American 'girl'," or simply "the little blond woman."[25] Unlike current scholars, Weimar conservatives easily recognized the antination-alist sentiments promoted by protagonists like Maud. "We must admit," warned Otto Riebiecke in 1921, that most successful local adventure films "have no connection to anything German."[26] Highlighting the inability to identify the protagonists, their worldviews, and their behavior with any national particularities, Riebiecke's criticism also evoked the heteroge-neous and the flexible nature of identity in these films (Figure 4.1).

Indeed, May's film series undermines the fundamental conviction of nationalism—the presumption of "inevitable shared destiny, a natural fact that determines morals and loyalties."[27] During the film, the premise of this innate nature of identity is repeatedly contested by various identity conversions. Throughout her quest in distant lands, Maud gathers around her a group of foreigners who identify with her purpose and help her to fight her way back to Europe with the treasure. The members of Maud's community change their loyalty from their tribe, family, or gods to Maud and her destiny. This conversion of the natives generally occurs after they identify with her sense of justice and her worldview. For instance, a young

Figure 4.1 Maud and her Chinese companion fight together against the Chinese mob in *Mistress of the World*.
Source: Stiftung Deutsche Kinemathek.

African tribesman disobeys the words of his father, the tribe's leader, and disregarding the imperatives of the tribe's cult, he joins Maud and protects her when his peers attacks her convoy.

Unlike her enemies, Maud willingly approves of these conversions, which turn out to be essential to her cause. A similarly favorable approach to identity conversion is apparent in many early adventure films, in which the inborn identity of the characters does not predetermine their beliefs, activities, and sense of belonging.[28] Notably, these films do not replace a nationalist belief in a fixed, inborn identity, with an imperialist zeal to "civilize" the "savages." Maud does not seek to educate the "savages" in order to make them loyal subjects of a superior empire (and certainly not subject of an imagined German empire). She is indifferent to their inborn identity because, as I will argue below, she struggles to overthrow the existing hegemony together with its imperialist and nationalist biases.

Complementing the ability to choose between different communities and alternative identities is the concept of a hybrid identity. The success of the protagonist of *Mistress of the World* is often contingent upon the recognition of multilayered, multifaceted identity, which combines cultural, social, and ethnic aspects of personality. Maud's first companion is Dr. Kien-Lung, a Chinese man who has been educated in Europe. Played by Henri Sze, himself a Chinese actor who married a European woman, Kien-Lung is a foreigner in his fatherland. He cannot identify with the local superstitions or with the racist rage against the Europeans, and he resents both the lack of efficient law enforcement and the lack of compassion toward the weak.[29] Torn between two cultural traditions, Kien-Lung is a natural companion to Maud who functions as an essential link to the local customs, language, and expectations. After Kien-Lung saves her from a brothel (she has been kidnapped upon arrival to China and taken there), Maud meets another "hybrid" character, the local Danish consul. He seems to be an ideal "Aryan" type, with light-colored skin and a tall and muscular body, whose strength suggests racial supremacy. (He defeats dozens of Chinese warriors with his bare hands.) In the third episode of *Mistress of the World*, however, his Jewish identity is revealed, and this discovery saves the day. Because of his multilayered identity, he alone is able to speak with the Rabbi of the ancient, now ruined, Jewish community in Manchuria, the last person to know where the treasure is hidden.[30]

Recurrent dismissal of the idea of inborn, fixed identity in adventure films reflected various sentiments and needs of the filmmakers. Weimar filmmakers' avoidance of identifying their protagonists as Germans was partly a marketing strategy based on an awareness of the widespread resentment of German nationalism in postwar Western Europe.[31] Nevertheless, it seems that these filmmakers were not only trying to blur the German identity of the protagonists, but also to detach them from *any* national context and to envisage them as heroes of an alternative transnational community. Apparently this tendency was influenced by the personal experiences of leading filmmakers in Weimar popular cinema. For instance, as a Jewish immigrant in Berlin, Joe May (born Julius Otto Mandl) was sensitive to the threats of chauvinism and racism; and he sought both to promote a notion of hybrid identity and to emphasize its constructive contribution to the community. In any case, the critics of these films did not find them particularly "Jewish" in essence, and the marketing aspect was similarly disregarded.

Instead of portraying them as manifestations of a specific identity, German or Jewish, Weimar reviewers depicted adventure film heroes as the embodiment of transnational characteristics and frequently as the personifications of European values and worldviews.[32] The program guide for the second episode left little room for misunderstanding about Maud's genuine identity, stating that her homeland, her *Heimat*, was not Denmark, but "old Europe."[33] This *Heimat* of "old Europe" is the place she leaves behind at the beginning of the series, and the place she returns to at the end of her journey.

The identification of Maud's *Heimat* as "Europe" associates her identity with a particular aspect of European modernity. *Heimat* is a concept that has long held significance in German culture. Incorporating various aspects of modern and premodern imagery, the notion of *Heimat* signified a harmonious existence. The environment of the *Heimat* and the relationships between members of the community were supposed to shape the identity of the people who inhabited it.[34] Present-day scholars emphasize the multifaceted historical role of *Heimat* sentiments in the formation of national, regional, and class identities.[35] They have shown that far from simply embodying premodern, reactionary fantasies of rural harmony, *Heimat* concepts and images have been an important aspect of the adjustment to life in a modern, increasingly urbanized environment. The case of *Mistress of the World* reinforces this scholarly view of the *Heimat* concept. Maud's *Heimat* is the city, and her nostalgic longing is directed at this landscape, at a lost urban paradise. While her nationality is obscured, she is clearly a city dweller. And her passions, anxieties, and goals are formulated within an urban setting that includes the bourgeois apartment, the university, the local tavern, the operetta concert hall, the archive, the courthouse, and the jail.

Her journeys around the globe further emphasize that Maud comes from a modern city and not a state. The foreign territories she explores are mostly alternative formations of cities. At the heart of "Africa" lies the city of Ophir, which has been detached for thousands of years from civilization and still maintains age-old religious practices. "America" is an ultramodern city with its skyscrapers, mass media, and mass consumerism. Even in "China" the emphasis is on the urban environment, rather than the national. "China" is portrayed as a realm governed by a powerful criminal organization that exploits the city and dominates its everyday entertainments (including the erotic entertainment performed in the "club" in which the kidnapped Maud is held). The program guide also describes China not as a state or an empire, but as "the city of four million people."[36]

The encounter with the "Other" takes shape as the venture of a middle-class city dweller into a variety of imaginary cities, which in turn represent possible alternatives to the urban modernity of Europe. Maud's ambition to initiate social reform at the end of her journey is also linked to the urban surrounding, her *Heimat*. The ailments of this particular realm (forgery, blackmail, and false imprisonment) have prompted her to set off on an adventurous journey, and an urgent need to heal the urban *Heimat* has brought her back.

As the left-wing magazine *Die Lichtbild-Bühne* ironically remarked, instead of embodying a nationalist fantasy of glory, Maud represents the quest of the urban bourgeoisie to rule the world.[37] These "fantasies of the bourgeois class" were screened in a period of ominous crisis and growing insecurity among Germany's urban middle class. Mounting inflation, political violence in the streets, and the prospect of increasing unemployment had a profound influence on daily experience in German cities during the 1920s. The essential beliefs and social practices of the prewar bourgeoisie began to fade in the face of the new, unprecedented challenges. Reflecting on the current crisis, postwar German adventure films evoke nostalgic yearning for a lost bourgeois bliss. They portray a reality in which the war never occurred and middle-class characters—architects, engineers, physicians, civil servants, and athletes—enjoy security and prosperity.[38]

Nonetheless, this nostalgia was rather limited, for the early adventure films soon revealed how fragile and misleading this dream was. *Mistress of the World* depicts a shift of the city from an urban paradise to a bourgeois nightmare. At the beginning of her adventures (shown as flashback scenes in the second film in the series), Maud lives with her parents in a comfortable city dwelling. She is a young, promising student, who innocently trusts the social, political, and legal authorities. This fantasy life is brutally shattered by her unjust imprisonment and the death of her parents. In other Weimar adventure films, harmonious bourgeois existence is frequently visualized in terms of secure privacy, and the annihilation of this ideal realm is caused by the invasion of foreigners, or of foreign objects, into the private apartment. Joe May's *Indian Tomb*, for example, depicts the master of a Hindu cult penetrating the European bourgeois apartment; Fritz Lang's *The Spiders* (*Die Spinnen*, 1919) places Asian gang warriors in the protagonist's home. In Robert Reinert's *Opium*, the incursion by "oriental" elements is revealed in the presence of opium, and the sexual hallucinations it causes, within European domestic settings.

Mistress of the World begins with a stereotypical image of the European bourgeois family. The father, who is depicted in the film as an old school civil servant, sits in the living room with his daughter and peacefully helps her study for the university finals. This safe haven is devastated when Maud's fiancé asks her to translate a Chinese document. The mysterious

Figure 4.2 The Indian hermit enters the bourgeois private sphere in *The Indian Tomb,* bringing chaos to the urban environment.
Source: Stiftung Deutsche Kinemathek.

document changes her life forever. Soon she realizes that her secure existence has been a masquerade. Her father, she learns, was blackmailed into stealing the document from the archive, and the villain who forced him to do this shameful deed was her charming fiancé (who is actually married to another woman). Instead of punishing the con artist, the legal authorities find Maud guilty of treason. In sending her to prison for many years, they take away not only her freedom and her newborn child, but also her belief in the just nature of modern social institutions. Consequently, when she is released, she leaves modernity behind and begins a search for justice on premodern continents.

As *Mistress of the World* exemplifies, the collapse of the private sphere and the deviation from harmonious monogamy in early adventure films constitute an initial stage in a process of decay, leading toward a loss of reason and order in the urban surrounding. The loss of privacy is the main theme in the second episode of May's film. This episode depicts the formation and disintegration of Maud's two private spheres—her family's apartment, where she lives with her caring parents, and the new suburban house that she shares with her fiancé. At first these two apartments seem to provide an ideal combination of middle-class tradition (the parents' dwelling) and modern optimism (the suburban house). But by the end of this episode, it is clear that an untroubled sense of progress and security is no longer part of the urban experience. As she steps out of the prison, Maud finds that her parents' apartment has been sold and the furniture piled up on the street; and the lover's house is deserted with the entrance blocked, as if no one had ever lived there.

The protagonists of adventure films set out to exotic destinations in order to regain what they lost in their cities. Their journey is a necessary phase in the construction of a better bourgeois society, one that would restore the sense of security that prevailed before the crisis. Thus even though the Great War is absent from Weimar adventure films, they portray the journey of a protagonist who has gone through experiences that, just like the war, shattered their former knowledge and beliefs. *Mistress of the World* emphasizes the similarity to posttraumatic syndrome caused by the war, displaying experiences within the lost urban paradise as flashbacks to Maud's dreamlike "past." Again, these images of an idyllic past do not articulate nostalgia for national grandeur or longing for Germany's lost colonies. Rather, they mourn the loss of the social practices and the worldviews that characterized the European middle class in the pre–World War I era. Symbolically experiencing the collapse of the nineteenth-century bourgeois order, Maud's journey expresses the urgent desire to establish a new liberal society from its ruins. Maud, like the protagonists of most Weimar adventure films, journeys to a distant land because she cannot endure the new conditions in the city. Such filmic heroes must find a way to revise them, first through personal revenge and then through a commitment to social reform.

Differentiating themselves from people in the exotic lands, the protagonists of early adventure films demonstrate the favored qualities of the desired new social order. The mystical Orient offers various law and order authorities with diverse understandings of justice; the protagonists examine these legal practices, experience their implications, and struggle against them. From the first scenes, it is evident that the exotic sphere is governed by passions, hallucinations, and meditative trances. In many adventure films, the Orient is presented as the origin of hallucinogenic drugs and as a realm that corresponds to the (sexual) fantasies and desires of the European (male) protagonist. In Reinert's *Opium*, for instance, the drug's origins lie in the exotic Asian landscape, and the fantasies of the Europeans who use the drug are a mixture of "Indian" rites, scenery, and erotic motifs. The foreign rulers of these exotic spheres embody the "extremely emotional nature of the Orient" or, as one reviewer asserted, "the fanatical cruelty of the Asian."[39] Such rulers are often driven by jealousy and seek revenge for their misfortunes (commonly related to women, gold, or the gods). Their followers behave in similar ways, irrationally sacrificing their lives for religious causes, sexual passions, or uncontrolled greed.[40]

Maud's journey introduces various types of "native" behavior that exhibit this kind of jealousy or revenge. She starts her adventures in China, the place of "secret pleasures and secret sin," where "opium is smoked."[41] The setting of busy waterfront streets, where brothels and opium dens are intermingled, demonstrates the linkage between narcotic fantasies and sexual exploitation in the early adventure films. And irrational behavior in China expands beyond drug users. Other inhabitants of the Chinese city are willing to sacrifice their lives for small sums of money, or to show their complete submission to the will of the local mafia leader. Similar practices are evident in Africa. There Maud encounters a nomadic tribe, whose members' irrational anxieties are exploited by a local witch doctor. The members of the tribe fear and obey him, and they join his stubborn fight against Maud, despite the tragic results of such senseless struggle (the fight ends with the death of the chieftain's son). After leaving the wounded tribe behind, Maud arrives at the city of Ophir, where the treasure is buried. The city dwellers worship Maud as a goddess. Their behavioral code is one of cruel slavery and complete obedience to primitive cultic rules. Eventually, these rules prevent the inhabitants from taking precaution against encroaching danger, and they perish in a devastating earthquake. Maud, who uses the latest technology to call for help, is rescued in the last moment by an American expedition and flees to the new continent.

Landing in an ultramodern city, she notices a similar pattern of cult-worship in America; here it is directed at celebrities. Maud's life story is promptly filmed, and she becomes a revered superstar. The Americans' irrational nature is further revealed by their childish, violent behavior. Maud finds herself in the middle of a conflict between two newspaper publishers, who seek to exploit her sensational biography for financial gain. When one of the publishers realizes that his rival had the upper hand, he destroys his own office in a fit of rage and sits with an infantile smile on the ruins, as the intertitle announces "Hannibal over Carthage." These irrational settings and practices form the context from which Maud must differentiate herself.

In an environment controlled by ancient cults and rites, adventure film protagonists are markedly secular. They do not counter the native cults with Judeo-Christian mythology or rites; instead, they answer the mythological interpretation of reality through the "gods" of reason and technology. Maud counters the cult of Ophir with an American engineer, who finds a way to transmit an S.O.S. signal and thereby launches a rescue expedition. Similar scenes are found in other German adventure films, in which the protagonists exploit the latest technology (airplanes, air balloons, sailing ships), to save the lives of the natives when their gods fail to appear. Unlike the German adventure fables of the nineteenth century, whose protagonists vow Christian supremacy, in Weimar adventure films religious sentiments signify the denigration of reason and its tragic outcome.[42]

Thus these protagonists repeatedly highlight the reign of reason over passion. Maud's journey begins as a revenge mission, similar in character to many of the "natives" in these films. But in the process of differentiating herself from her surroundings, her quest is reshaped into an attempt to improve the human condition. Her passion for revenge thus gives way to a rational acknowledgment that the source of her mistreatment lies not in the deeds of a specific villain, but rather in a society that has lost its ability to distinguish right from wrong. Reason alone, however, will not suffice to shape the mentality of the new society. Reflecting on the first episode of *Mistress of the World*, the reviewer in the *Illustrierte Filmwoche* noted that a purely rational society already exists in China—the Chinese "thinking machine is based on logic, on heartless measuring, with no mistakes."[43] Maud and her friends are different, the reviewer concludes, because they mix reason with compassion. In other words, they favor modern culture's *reasonableness* over purely "objective" rationality.

Alongside the absence of reasonableness, technological progress, and compassion, the foreign lands also lack any sense of privacy and intimacy. Unfulfilled longing for a private sphere is another central theme of Maud's exotic journey. When Maud arrives in China, members of a local crime organization kidnap her to a brothel and order her to exhibit her body to the gazes of local men. In Africa, the native tribesmen are constantly watching her through the holes in her tent. When she gains the status of a goddess in Ophir, her private room is located in the city's temple, where the communal rites are celebrated. The least private setting of all is America. This ultramodern realm is governed by the two newspaper publishers, each of whom races to reveal more private details about the new celebrity, Maud. All of the people around her are actually their agents, hired to spy on her and disclose her most intimate secrets to the readers. Maud, who has left her European city because she was denied a private sphere, realizes that neither the premodern nor ultramodern cultures of the world answer her initial need for privacy. The collapse of the European private sphere cannot be remedied by adopting premodern, or ultramodern, social practices and morality, because these discard such liberal notions as reason and privacy. As *Mistress of the World* demonstrates, the reconstruction of privacy and intimacy requires a homecoming, back to the European city.

In *Mistress of the World*, however, the restoration of privacy presupposes a thorough social reform. The quest for privacy is thus complemented in this film by the quest for a better law and order system, one that would employ reason and compassion to bring about justice. Maud's journey enables her to experience various *illiberal* perceptions of law and order, with all their appalling faults. The legal authorities in the lands she visits follow two forms of social order, which often intertwine: tyranny and anarchy. Tyranny dominates the African tribe, and "justice" is the whim of the tribe's leader. This chieftain is himself guided by irrational fears of gods and nature, which are in turn cultivated by the witch doctor who "advises" him. This system is fragile, and it subsides upon the encounter with modern culture, morals, and technology. Maud's visit causes an inevitable uproar against this system, which leads to the senseless deaths of many. Religious sentiments also determine law and punishment in the city of Ophir, where ancient traditions and prophetical imperatives facilitate the enslavement of thousands of people to the rites of the local goddess. And in America, what is "real" is determined by the newspaper publishers, regardless of what really happens. The newspapers recount Maud's life story to make her an international celebrity; and in order to increase sales, they "enhance" her biography. This farce culminates in a movie based on her story. Intriguingly, the publisher who makes the movie recognizes that Maud's actual behavior is not "realistic" enough and should be elaborated in order to convince the spectators. America lacks both objective procedures to discern the truth and the authority that could dictate such procedures.

The impression of chaotic law enforcement in foreign lands is intensified in a Chinese courtroom scene following the murder of Kien-Lung's father by the mafia. The film seems purposely to juxtapose this scene with the earlier sequence of a European courtroom procedure. Maud's trial in Europe has declared an innocent woman guilty, mainly because the judges confused real evidence with speculation.[44] The second trial, in China, is different from the European version in two main respects: the layout of the courtroom and the action of the judges. Unlike the European court, the Chinese do not have a clear spatial division within the courtroom to distinguish between the judges, the prosecutor, the accused, and the audience. The architecture of the European court isolates each of these functions in a convoluted arrangement of stairs, banisters, and podiums. The Chinese court is a wide hall with the judges standing next to one wall, the accused standing within a painted circle, and the audience spread throughout the room, occasionally stepping into the circle to argue for and against the case. This arrangement breeds a chaotic procedure. Moreover, the architecture of the courthouse parallels judicial incompetence. During the trial, Maud learns that the Chinese authorities have no method or power to decide who tells the truth and who lies. There is no police force and no agency for criminal investigation, so Maud and Kien-Lung—due to their "European education"—are asked to conduct a private investigation and provide the court with evidence that would implicate the head of the mafia as the murderer. Required to build a case against the murderous Chinese mafia, Maud realizes that efficient, European style law enforcement is a crucial condition for forming a just society.

Throughout her journeys, Maud begins each episode as the victim of an unjust legal system, and in the end she overcomes the shortcomings of that system. Her triumph in each episode brings her closer to her destination. But in the process, the destination itself also undergoes a transformation. Her experiences in the wilderness and her encounters with foreign cultures transform her from an avenger to a reformist. Differentiating herself from the exotic surrounding, she herself undergoes a transformation, one that sparks a desire to make her *Heimat* different from everything she encounters, including the "old European" society that put her behind bars in the first place. This is the reason why Karl Figdor, the author of the novel that inspired the film, stated that, "[N]o film has ever been made out of such idealism."[45] "Idealism" here has a specific meaning in relation to a specific social and intellectual framework—that of the liberal urban middle class and its struggle to transcend the ruins of its prewar ethos, desires, and hopes.

Bourgeois Heroism in the Age of Liberal Pessimism: Late Weimar Adventure Films

In his *From Caligari to Hitler*, Siegfried Kracauer argued that Weimar films reflected the "psychological tendencies" of the Germans and revealed their attraction to "tyranny and chaos."[46] However, the German adventure films of early Weimar offered a popular fantasy of liberal urbanites who were aware of the threat of tyranny and chaos and tried to surmount its lure. In an endeavor to resurrect a liberal society that would cherish individual freedom and social justice, they warned against the abolition of the private in favor of the powerful masses (the *Volk* or the class). Notwithstanding certain important amendments, German adventure films of the late 1920s and early 1930s were still influenced by the ideas, and the visualizations thereof, found in *Mistress of the World*. Encounters with exotic foreigners continued to stir German spectators' imagination, even though after 1924 extravagant productions of sensational films became less lucrative. Such encounters were now frequent in the abundant urban melodramas and domestic comedies of that time. In films such as *Heaven on Earth* (1927), *The Other Side of the Street* (1929), and *The Living Corpse* (1929), the natives (Africans, Americans, and Gypsies) were represented as the irrational element of modern urbanism.[47] Although the foreigners in these films were depicted as an inherent part of the modern city, they were restricted to a particular realm, the nightclub, in a way that enabled the portrayal of the bourgeois apartment as a sanctuary of intimacy and security.

Figure 4.3   Scene from *Spies*.
Source: Stiftung Deutsche Kinemathek.

These popular melodramas and comedies adapted the narrative pattern of adventure films to the urban setting, while continuing to campaign for a society based on reason and compassion.[48] However, there was an important shift in their contemplation of identity conversion and hybrid identities. As signifiers of the menacing, irrational facet of modernity, the foreigners in these films remain detached from the bourgeois dwelling, residing solely in the eternal twilight zone of the club. When this restriction is disregarded and foreigners appear in other parts of the city, for example in Fritz Lang's *Spies* (*Spione*, 1927), the city leadership deteriorates quickly into anarchy, leading to chaotic murders, an inability to differentiate the criminals from the authorities, and the collapse of the city infrastructure. In Lang's apocalyptic urban vision, the vicious murderer is also a secret police agent, a manager of the bank, and a stage performer. Together with an Asian criminal organization, he commits several mysterious murders that paralyze the law and order authorities of the city.

Cinematic journeys to exotic lands in the late 1920s adopted the new tendency to reject multifaceted identities and conversions. For instance, in the 1926 film *The White Geisha* (*Die weisse Gaischa*, directed by Karl Heiland and Valdemar Andersen), a European engineer travels to Asia in order to purchase potentially lucrative mines. There he falls in love with a local geisha. This situation is similar to that presented in Fritz Lang's 1919 film *Harakiri*, in which passionate exotic romance challenges the protagonist to reconsider the unsatisfying relationships with his European fiancée. In the later film, however, the geisha turns out to be merely a European girl in disguise, a middle-class adventurer who has lost her money in a casino sting operation. Her only way to repay her debt is to assist the engineer hero's adversaries in their efforts to sabotage his purchase of the mines. Even the adversary, Williams, is a modern Western investor, not the native ruler or priest of an ancient cult as found in earlier adventure films. Asia therefore becomes a playground for the modern European, while the native presence is secondary and limited to assisting Europeans. Correspondingly, the oriental city in *The White Geisha* is no longer an amalgam of extravagant palaces, expressionistically stylized alleys, and underground labyrinths, but rather a modern international port town, an urban center with wide streets, automobiles, cranes, and large ships.

Several destructive elements that had been associated with the exotic lands in earlier adventure films were jettisoned in the later 1920s. First, by contrast to the earlier films, the European protagonist is no longer passionately attracted to the oriental female, nor is the native male is attracted to the powerful white woman. The indifference of *The White Geisha*'s protagonist to the female foreigner's appeal is revealed in a narcotic hallucination scene. Given the opium pipe, the engineer experiences sexual fantasies that are unmistakably similar to the ones experienced by the protagonist in the 1919 film *Opium*. The object of his fascination, however, is reversed. While the naked girls in *Opium*'s fantasy perform a pagan rite in an exotic landscape, the girls envisioned in *The White Geisha* are European, and they are dancing in the modern city's night club. When the protagonist in the later film first encounters the "geisha," he shows indifference to oriental charms. He does eventually fall for her, just as his vicious rival Williams has intended—but only after he realizes she is European.

These differences notwithstanding, *The White Geisha* preserves the main theme of the earlier adventure films, namely, the quest of the bourgeois protagonist for an authentic existence within the modern city. Travel to distant lands both discloses the faults of modern urbanity and facilitates their "corrections" by the protagonist when he returns home. The journey to China and Japan enables the hero to experience genuine intimacy (with the fake geisha). His experiences on the foreign continent—becoming the totally unwitting victim of a powerful criminal organization, undergoing drug-induced fantasies—only emphasize his submissive personality, which has already become clear in the early scenes set in Europe, in which he agrees to marry his employer's shallow-minded daughter. However, while the adventures in Asia expose and underline his weaknesses, the exotic setting also empowers him and enables him to discover his "real self." Upon his return to Europe, he confronts his employer for the first time and marries the woman he genuinely loves. Thus, in a way similar to the earlier adventure films, the longing for individual freedom and authentic existence in the modern city is encoded in *The White Geisha* in terms of a journey to unknown terrains. This journey provides the protagonist, as well as the film's audience, with intimate knowledge of his genuine desires, fears, and hopes.

Similar patterns surfaced on the German screen also in the early sound films of 1930–1932. However, the urgent cry of liberal filmmakers for a reform of contemporary bourgeois society seems in these late Weimar films to give way to desperation or indifference. An example is the 1932 film *Peter Voss, Who Stole Millions* (*Peter Voss, der Millionendieb*) by the Jewish filmmaker E. A. Dupont. As in the early 1920s adventure films, the protagonist is anxious to leave the city and travel to distant lands. Peter Voss is the trustee of a bank who is faced with bankruptcy at the time of a world economic crisis. In order to save the bank, he conspires with the bank manager to give the impression that he robbed the (empty) safe and escaped with the money. Unfortunately for the conspirators, two stubborn people—a police detective and the manager's daughter who is unaware of the scheme—go after Voss and the alleged fortune he robbed. The rest of the film recounts the adventurous hunt for Voss and his last-minute escapes, which take him from Berlin to Marseilles and continue in colonial Morocco.

While Dupont reiterates key motifs of the early adventure films, representing similar hopes and anxieties, the gravity of these themes seems to fade. As one reviewer remarked, *Peter Voss* shares the sense of crisis that initiated earlier adventure films, but the film omits the sense of urgency, staging the journey as a dismissive parody.[49] Nevertheless, Dupont carefully constructs his film around the theme of the origins and "authenticity" of identity. Exploiting the new opportunities offered by sound, he uses spoken dialogue in different languages early in the film in order to emphasize the allegedly "objective" differences between nations. Soon thereafter, however, he mocks these nationalist stereotypes. As he travels across the Mediterranean, Voss takes advantage of such common stereotypes in order to deceive his adversaries and escape. He assumes different national identities, using accents and vocabulary in the same way he wears costumes and, at one point, a faked, Hitleresque mustache. Like earlier films, therefore, *Peter Voss* rejects the concept of inherent national identity that determines the individual's appearance, behavior, and worldview. Voss is a city dweller, a product of modern urbanism, and he manipulates this environment to outwit his creditors. But unlike the earlier adventurous protagonists, Peter Voss does not return to his city at the end of his adventures. Instead, he remains in North Africa, joining his true (European) lover in the exotic terrain. He simply lacks the capability, and the will, to return home and instigate a social change.[50]

Conclusion

From *Mistress of the World* to *Peter Voss*, Weimar adventure films portrayed a series of encounters with exotic foreigners as a way to address the anxieties of the liberal middle class. The protagonists of these films are "middle-class heroes," city dwellers who have witnessed the collapse of nineteenth-century bourgeois society during World War I and its turbulent aftermath. They are not representatives of a particular nation or race, nor do they endeavor to reconstitute a lost empire. Rather, they are typical bourgeois urbanites, who suffer from the loss of security and intimacy and mourn the deterioration of the liberal ethos. The anxieties they embody revolve around unjust authorities, the dangerous appeal of mysticism and irrational convictions, and fears of absolute rulers and social chaos. The journeys in these films enable the protagonists, and with them the audience, to consider various alternatives to the liberal social order—and to realize just how menacing such alternatives are. The heroes also learn about the advantages of conversion from one community to another, in a way that highlights the presence of multilayered, or hybrid, identities.

Intriguingly, these films thrived in an age of radical nationalism and illiberal political extremism. Their success at the box office suggests that their liberal, transnational worldview was not considered exceptional or intimidating for urban audiences or for most of the reviewers. Facing the threats of political radicalism, these films propagated an alternative ideal of community: a transnational community of middle-class urbanites, who would share similar experiences and similar liberal convictions. In this respect, Weimar adventure films were not only a product of the traumatic experiences of the recent past, but also an attempt to envision a better, postnationalist future.

Notes

1. Siegfried Kracauer, *From Caligari to Hitler: A Psychological History of German Film* (Princeton, 1966, orig. 1947).

2. For instance, Bernadette Kester, *Film Front Weimar: Representation of the First World War in German Films of the Weimar Period (1919–1933)* (Amsterdam, 2003); Garth Montgomery, "'Realistic' War Films in Weimar Germany: Entertainment as Education," *Historical Journal of Film, Radio and Television* (1989): 115–33; Anton Kaes, *Shell Shock Cinema: Weimar Cinema and the Wounds of War* (Princeton, 2009).

3. This approach is compatible with recent research on the role of urban modernism and transnational worldviews in Weimar films, e.g., Marc Silberman, "What is German in the German Cinema?," *Film History* (1996): 297–315; Thomas Saunders, "History in the Making: Weimar Cinema and National Identity" in *Reframing the Past: The Historiography of German Cinema and Television*, eds. Bruce Murray and Chris Wickham (Carbondale, IL, 1992), 42–67.

4. Gaia Banks, "Imagining the Other and Staging the Self: German National Identity and the Weimar Exotic Adventure Film (1918–1924)" (Dissertation, University of California at Irvine, 1996), 43–9.

5. Detlev J.K. Peukert, *The Weimar Republic* (New York, 1992); Moritz Föllmer and Rudiger Graf, ed., *Die "Krise" der Weimarer Republik: Zur Kritik eines Deutungsmuster* (Frankfurt am Main, 2005).

6. Jörg Schöning, "Rund um den Erdball" in *Triviale Tropen: Exotische Reise- und Abenteuerfilme aus Deutschland 1919-1939*, ed. Jörg Schöning (München, 1997), 195–206.

7. Frank, "Der Bedeutung der Filmindustrie," *Film-Kurier* (February 27, 1920).

8. M., "Caligari oder Herrin der Welt? Prunkfilm oder expressionistischer Film," *Film-Kurier* (March 9, 1920).

9. Kracauer, *Caligari*, 56–7. This post–World War II assessment echoes a widespread perception during the late 1920s. Adventure film directors struggled to be taken seriously as artists, e.g., Harry Piel, "Regisseur—nicht Sensationdarsteller," *Beiblatt zum Film Kurier* (January 5, 1928).

10. Kracauer, *Caligari*, 57.

11. Klaus Wyborny, "Lieder der Erde: Eine Reise um den Horizont" in Schöning, *Tropen*, 9, 12; Sander Gilman, *On Blackness Without Blacks: Essays on the Image of the Black in Germany* (Boston, 1982), 119–20.

12. Hilke Thode-Arora, "Herbeigeholte Ferne: Völkerschauen als Vorläufer Exotisierender Abenteuerfilme" in Schöning, *Tropen*, 19–33.

13. Fritz Lang, for instance, hired the famous ethnographer Heinrich Umlauf as a "consultant" for his film *The Spiders* (*Die Spinnen*, 1920). The advertisement of the film *White Woman Among Cannibals* (*Eine Weisse unter Kannibalen*, 1921) emphasized the fact that the director, Hans Schomburgk, was himself "a scientist, expert for Africa." *Film Kurier* (October 31, 1921). The realistic, "scientific" representation of exotic cultures and scenery in adventure films was also perceived as evidence for the uniqueness of the contemporary German film industry and its superior quality in comparison with its American counterparts. Gerhard Koch, *Franz Osten's Indian Silent Films* (Delhi, 1983), 16–17.

14. Irene Stratenwerth, "Joe May: Familiendrama in mehreren Aufzügen" in *Pioniere in Celluloid: Juden in der frühen Filmwelt*, ed. Irene Stratenwerth and Hermann Simon (Berlin, 2004), 41; Patrick McGilligan, *Fritz Lang: The Nature of the Beast* (New York, 1997), 65, 96.

15. Current scholars have highlighted this visit and argue that it manifested German longing for a colonial empire. According to the reports of the people on the set, however, Ebert and the players were ridiculing the situation, mocking both the filmmakers' pretensions of realism and the pathos of pre-war colonialism. Anonymous, "Reichspresident Ebert†," *Die Lichtbild-Bühne* (March 2, 1925).

16. Anonymous, "Glashaus oder Afrika? Soll Man im Atelier oder in der Natur Freilicht-Aufnahmen drehen?," *B.Z. am Mittag* (June 16, 1922).

17. Other advertisements shied away from any particularities, situating the plot in the vague "lands of vice." Various ads for this film are found in the Deutsche Kinemathek-Archiv, Berlin (SDK-SGA), folder 4509.

18. SDK-SGA folder 4509: advertisement in the film journal *Die Lichtbild-Bühne* (February 1919).

19. Reviewers depicted the main battle in Lang's *Spiders* as taking place in Inca and Maya temples interchangeably. The difference between the cultures was not deemed relevant to the realist nature of the film.

20. Ludwig Brauner, "Berlin Filmneuheiten," *Der Kinematograph* (October 23, 1921).

21. Egon Jacobson, "Neuheit auf dem Berliner Filmmarkte," *Der Kinomatograph* (February 5, 1919); SDK-SGA folder 4627: Karl Figdor, "Herrin der Welt," *Illustrierte Film-Kurier* (1919).

22. For instance, Wolfgang Kabatek, *Imagerie des Anderen im Weimarer Kino* (Bielefeld, 2003).

23. Joe May is credited for "artistic supervision" (*künstlerische Oberleitung*) in these films. The directors were Joseph Klein (episodes 1–6) and Uwe Kraft (7–8). Weimar film reviewers, however, tended to identify *Mistress of the World* as May's film, highlighting his influence on the whole series.

24. SDK-SGA, folders 4632/4633.

25. The aforementioned descriptions were also cited in various advertisements of the film. SDK-SGA, folder 4627.

26. Otto Riebiecke, "Der Nationale Film: Eine Forderung an die deutsche Filmindustrie," *Deutsche Allgemeine Zeitung* (October 2, 1921).

27. Ulf Hedetoft, *Signs of Nations: Studies on The Political Semiotics of the Self and Other in Contemporary European Nationalism* (Aldershof, 1995), 26.

28. Fritz Lang's *Spiders* provides a typical example for this tendency. A female priest of the Maya cult deserts her temple and her sacred underground dwelling, relocating to the modern city with her Western rescuer and lover. She is soon domesticated, adjusting to modern ways of life, beliefs, and ideals.

29. The reviewers of the film asserted that Sze actually "played himself" in the film. Podehl, "Herrin der Welt, 1. Teil: Die Freundin des gelben Mannes," *Der Film* 49 (1919).

30. This episode in now lost. The details cited above are taken from the program guide and from film reviews cited below.

31. Helmut Regel, "Der Schwarze und sein 'Bwana': Das Afrika-Bild im deutschen Film" in Schöning, *Tropen*, 65; Banks, *Imagining*, 82.

32. Ludwig Brauner, "Berlin Filmneuheiten," *Kinematograph* (October 23, 1921).

33. SDK-SGA, folder 4629.

34. Alon Confino, "The Nation as Local Metaphor: Heimat National Memory and the German Empire, 1871–1918," *History and Memory* (Spring/Summer, 1993): 42–86; Bernhard Waldenfels, "Heimat in der Fremde" in *Heimat: Analysen, Themen, Perspektiven*, eds. Will Cremer and Ansgar Klein (Bonn, 1990), 109–21.

35. Celia Applegate, *A Nation of Provincials: The German Idea of Heimat* (Berkeley, 1990); John A. Williams, *Turning to Nature in Germany: Hiking, Nudism and Conservation, 1900–1940* (Stanford, 2007).

36. SDK-SGA, folder 4628: Karl Figdor, "Herrin der Welt," *Illustrierte Film-Kurier* 8 (1919).

37. Anonymous, "Der teuerste Film," *Lichtbild-Bühne* (November 15, 1919).

38. For example, the protagonist of *Indian Tomb* is an architect; the protagonist in *Opium* is a physician; Maud's father is a civil servant in *Mistress of the World*; and the protagonist of *The Spiders* participates in boat races. On the decline in bourgeois values, see Bernd Weisbrod, "The Crisis of Bourgeois Society in Interwar Germany" in *Fascist Italy and Nazi Germany*, ed. Richard Bessel (Cambridge, 1996), 23–39.

39. Ludwig Brauner, "Berlin Filmneuheiten," *Der Kinematograph* (October 23, 1921); Bernhard Schulze, "Land des Grauens und der Wunder: Indien im deutschen Kino" in Schöning, *Tropen*, 75.

40. The occurrences in the South American temple in *The Spiders* are typical for this genre. While the Mexican gang members who invade the temple are blinded by the local treasures and fight each other for a share of the loot, the local tribesmen are frantically waiting for their gods to protect them and thus fail to face the danger. Both parties perish in a flood that inundates the treasure caves.

41. Anonymous, "Die Herrin der Welt," *Illustrierte Filmwoche* (December 7, 1919).

42. The protagonist in Karl May's *Old Surehand* identifies himself as "a proud German" and then praises the supremacy of Christianity. Adventure film protagonists shy away from both national and religious identifications.

43. Anon., "Herrin der Welt."

44. A thorough investigation of Maud's crime would have pointed to the real criminal, her fiancé, but the judges were reluctant to investigate further and accepted the speculative framing of Maud as "common sense." Joe May was interested in this fault of modern legal procedure in other films he made during these years. The theme is most prevalent in *Tragedy of Love* (*Tragödie der Liebe*, 1923), which focuses on a tragedy caused by judges' inability to differentiate evidence from speculative testimonies.

45. SDK-SGA, folder 4627: Karl Figdor, "Herrin der Welt," *Illustrierte Film-Kurier* (1919).

46. Kracauer, *Caligari to Hitler*, 6.

47. *Heaven on Earth* (*Der Himmel auf Erden*, 1927), an urban comedy directed by Reinhold Schönzel, is about a conservative man who inherits an infamous nightclub. Leo Mittler's melodrama, *The Other Side of the Street* (*Jenseits der Strasse*, 1929), portrays the encounter of a careless bourgeois man with the homeless, prostitutes, and outlaws of the poorer neighborhoods. Fiodor Ozep's *The Living Corpse* (*Der Lebende Leichnam*, 1929) portrays the misfortune of a man who fakes his own death in order to release himself from the irrational laws of the church.

48. Ofer Ashkenazi, *A Walk Into the Night: Reason and Identity in Weimar Film* (Tel Aviv, 2010).

49. Fritz Olimsky, "Peter Voss, Der Millionendieb," *Berlin Börsen-Zeitung* (March 26, 1932).

50. Intriguingly, the "natives" in his new dwelling place do not talk at all, or they shout and scream unintelligibly. This is the only environment in which he can be an individual, by speaking comprehensibly and thereby differentiating himself from his surroundings.

V

EXOTIC ATTRACTIONS AND IMPERIALIST FANTASIES IN WEIMAR YOUTH LITERATURE

Luke Springman

Imperialism garnered relatively little attention in Weimar politics, although imperial fantasies abounded in the popular imagination. The Second Empire had acquired colonies relatively late in the nineteenth century and had never developed a coherent policy on imperialist matters.[1] Only after the Berlin Conference of 1884–1885 did Germany obtain colonial territory, mostly in Africa: German East Africa (comprising present-day parts of mainland Tanzania, Rwanda, and Burundi), German South West Africa (present-day Namibia), Cameroon, and Togo. A little over three decades later, the Treaty of Versailles stripped Germany of all territorial claims in Africa and elsewhere. After 1918, the former colonies became marginal in German national politics, and the topic arose mostly in negotiations surrounding war reparations.[2]

Weimar popular culture—fiction, film, and advertising—portrayed Africa as an excitingly strange place, but it was more than just an exotic playground. While political realities during the Weimar Republic barred Germany from colonial expansion, new empires emerged in enduring cultural fantasies. Seemingly innocuous stories for children about Germans in Africa propagated a role for Germany as a bearer of civilized culture, a dispenser of prosperity, and a catalyst of order, even though Germany's record of colonial brutality challenged such claims.[3] In colonialist children's literature, the younger generation of the Weimar Republic could understand themselves as the most reasonable stewards for the development of "primitive" cultures. The disparate texts analyzed in this chapter demonstrate that Weimar's multilayered colonial discourse reflected a complicated consensus that Germany was still entitled to colonies.

Colonialist youth literature relied on a consistent set of assumptions. As a case in point, an exhibition about the former German colonies took place in Stuttgart in 1929. The author of a review article in the conservative boys' magazine *Der gute Kamerad* stated the threefold purpose of the event: to display the powerful achievements of "German determination and energy" and belie the criticisms of Germany's enemies; to demonstrate that bountiful colonies were vital for the future of Germany's economy, culture, and existence as a nation; and to "hammer into the soul" of youth the necessity of colonies for Germany.[4] This review summarized essential premises of Weimar juvenile literature regarding Africa—that is, Germany had been the most beneficent among the European colonial masters, and the German nation had to expand outside of continental Europe in order to survive.

Numerous Weimar adventure stories and novels for young people set in Africa fostered the idea that Germans' struggles and achievements could have created a paradise in their colonies, if only the competing European powers had not "disgracefully" deprived them of their "rightful" dominions. Novels such as Friedrich Wilhelm Mader's *Am Kilimanjaro* (*On Mount Kilimanjaro*, 1927) and Josef Viera's *Kampf um Wild-Süd* (*Battle for the Wild South*, 1929) bore unmistakable revanchist attitudes in their fictional portrayals of Germans fighting a guerilla war against the British in German East Africa during World War I. While Weimar colonial literature did not display the cold brutality against Africans, which had been the hallmark of Wilhelmine African adventures, much of it aligned with reactionary ideology.[5]

Rather than dwell on blatant nationalism and racism in Weimar colonial adventure stories for youth, however, this chapter reveals inherent complexities in the ways that Germans regarded both Africa and themselves during the Weimar Republic. Three works from different genres—a memoir of the African campaign in World War I, a written travelogue, and an illustrated children's magazine—reflect a greater diversity of popular beliefs and cultural ideals in Weimar Germany than does the dominant genre of the adventure story. The following discussion treats these three texts as cultural artifacts that can contribute to our knowledge about colonialist discourse in postcolonial Weimar. In these documents, cultural projections express an *imagined* racial and cultural intercourse between Germans and black Africans.[6] Setting such imaginings in stark relief, juvenile literature idealizes and simplifies depictions to clarify its message. Despite differences between them, the three textual examples analyzed here had in common one key message for young people, which remained unchanged from the Wilhelmine era: Germans possessed cultural and technological advantages that entitled them to control African resources.

The three texts under scrutiny are Paul von Lettow-Vorbeck's World War I memoir *Heia Safari!* (1920); Colin Ross' travelogue *Mit Kamera, Kind und Kegel durch Afrika* (*With Camera, Kith, and Kin Through Africa*, 1928); and a selection of illustrations from the popular children's magazine *Der heitere Fridolin* (*Merry Fridolin*, 1921–1928). *Heia Safari!* and *Mit Kamera* are especially representative of an attitude of colonial superiority. Lettow-Vorbeck uses the story of his legendary East Africa campaign during World War I to inspire his young readers to seek new lives in Africa and thus to "heal the sick Fatherland."[7] Colin Ross also supports imperialist ambitions, although he emphasizes exotic tourism rather than colonial settlement. His account of a voyage from the Transvaal region of South Africa to Kenya in 1927 tells how his wife, teenage daughter, and three-year-old son adapt to privation and danger. For Ross, adaptation means staging events among black Africans that conform to his (and to his German audience's) notion of exotic encounters. Ross and Lettow-Vorbeck engage young people through adventure, report untold wealth in natural resources, and seek to foster a pioneering spirit. Africans appear as servants and savages, and thus as a resource to be domesticated, much as Germans tamed African landscapes through their railways and farms in order to make peoples and lands ordered and productive.

Photographs, drawings, and maps in Lettow-Vorbeck's memoir and in Ross' travelogue added texture to their descriptions. In children's magazines such as *Der heitere Fridolin*, visual imagery was primary, and texts usually supplemented the illustrations as captions or descriptions of the pictures. Pictorials from children's magazines extended the spectrum of Weimar myths about exotic lands. During its run from 1921 to 1929, the popular children's magazine *Der heitere Fridolin* featured a wealth of photographs and illustrations on African themes. Alongside educational pieces, the journal featured silly low-brow entertainment, usually taking the form of cartoons that deployed stereotypical caricatures of Africans. At times, however, the humor in these caricatures lies in *self-reflections* of the young reader's own world imposed on an imagined "primitive" context. And *Der heitere Fridolin* never refers directly to German settlement in Africa. Only in the larger context of the magazine's most common theme, modern technology, does the association with colonialism emerge. This text sent the message that the future of colonial power lay in transportation and communication. By implication, Germany would reassert itself in Africa through commercial dominance rather than political or military supremacy.

Paladin of Germany: Lettow-Vorbeck and *Heia Safari!*

On March 2, 1919 General Paul von Lettow-Vorbeck, on horseback, triumphantly led his few surviving troops through Berlin's Brandenburg Gate. Throngs cheered the military hero whose guerilla campaigns had bogged down hundreds of thousands of enemy soldiers in East Africa during the war. Lettow-Vorbeck soon went on to lead an armed militia against the Spartacist uprising in Hamburg, and he supported the Kapp Putsch in Berlin in 1920. These events led to his dismissal from the Reichswehr. Nevertheless, his fame as the undefeated general secured his reputation as a German hero. Because he had remained unvanquished in Africa against overwhelming odds, he became living proof for reactionaries that Germany had been defeated at home and not on the front lines.[8]

Lettow-Vorbeck preserved his own legend by publishing two memoirs in 1920: *Meine Erinnerungen aus Ostafrika* (*My Recollections from East Africa*), and a version for young people, *Heia Safari! Deutschlands Kampf in Ostafrika* (*Heia Safari! Germany's Campaign in East Africa*). Both were bestsellers throughout the Weimar period. In the latter book, Lettow-Vorbeck encouraged young readers to seek their fortunes in Africa, and he used his celebrity status throughout the Weimar years to advocate for regaining Germany's former colonial possessions in Africa. His memoir suggested that, above all, deep mutual esteem between Germans and Africans legitimated future recolonization.

Lettow-Vorbeck wanted thousands of Germans to settle in East Africa and to prosper by developing its resources. In *Heia Safari!* he describes the richness of East Africa and promotes its potential for German settlement. Before 1914, according to the author, only eight million Africans and 6,000 Europeans dwelled in a land twice as large as Germany. Abundant, desirable land was available for the taking. Many parts of "German" Africa, such as the Uluguru Mountains, offered splendid vistas; German settlements, parks, and gardens conjured up a feeling of home.[9] Moreover, the settlements had yielded a variety of agricultural goods for export,[10] supporting the argument put forth by Germany's colonial lobby that colonies offered a solution to economic turmoil.[11] Lettow-Vorbeck predicts that settlers would become largely independent of industrial supplies from Germany, as demonstrated in the way that East Africa had already produced numerous nonfood agricultural products: textiles, tires from rubber, motor fuel from coconut oil (called "trebol," a type of bio-diesel), and soap. During four years of continuous marching, Lettow-Vorbeck's troops had readily supplied themselves from native crops, livestock, and game. During lulls in fighting, German soldiers, African soldiers (*Askaris*), and support groups (carriers and family members) had all lived in relative comfort.[12]

Recent historical research has cast doubt on the real economic value that African colonies held for Germany.[13] Yet facts were irrelevant to the colonial longings that permeated the popular and political discussion of Africa. Lettow-Vorbeck, addressing his young readers directly as "my dear German youth," instructed them that America did not represent the land of their yearning. Instead, land awaited them in distant Africa. Young Germans should colonize Africa so that "Germanness" would expand in this "great, beautiful world."[14] Lettow-Vorbeck was propagating the exotic as an intimate locale, implying that the next generation would be able to appropriate *their* African space as Germans (unlike the Germans in the United States, who had lost their identity and become "Americanized").

Lettow-Vorbeck asserted throughout his book that the Germans' right to colonize rested upon their ability to initiate and foster cooperation and mutual respect with Africans. He saw his campaign against the British forces as having proved that the German character was adaptable, able to thrive in an East African colony under extreme conditions. In reality, the Germans had relied greatly on the Africans in adjusting to unfamiliar and changing conditions. Lettow-Vorbeck estimated that white civil servants and military personnel ideally needed eleven to fifteen porters each.[15] He admitted also that, in general, Europeans required a large number of African servants in all their endeavors, whether conducting a military campaign or running a plantation.[16] Anecdotes that highlighted the unwavering loyalty between Germans and hired African laborers and soldiers allowed Lettow-Vorbeck to affirm German honor and integrity. He insists repeatedly that Africans would always welcome Germans back. Germans had earned devotion and respect, because unlike the other colonial powers, they had treated Africans the same as Europeans, practicing the customs and learning the language of their African servants and soldiers.[17] He maintains, too, that African soldiers were usually not mere mercenaries; *Askaris* under German command had proved every bit as devoted to the distant *Vaterland* as any loyal German. At one point, he waxes maudlin with the tale of the young *Askari* recruit who died gratified to have sacrificed his life in the service of the German Emperor.[18] Lettow-Vorbeck contends that the pure chivalry of the Germans in their conduct of war and in colonial relations had won for them the admiration and loyalty of *Askaris* and African servants, who recognized a nobility of national character that they did not perceive among the English.[19]

Lettow-Vorbeck had indeed performed many acts of gallantry toward the *Askaris* and other Africans who served under his command. But he was also ruthless against his enemies. In *Heia Safari!* war appears as a game to be scored according to the number of casualties. Lettow-Vorbeck indulges in a gruesome propensity to describe slaughter as great sport. At one point, he describes having trains dynamited with an eye to maximizing death, followed by a sprightly march through the bush to a festive meal at camp.[20] These juxtapositions between bloody encounters and celebrations were likely fascinating for some young German readers. Lettow-Vorbeck appeared in his book as an adventure hero, whose righteousness justified brutal violence.

Lettow-Vorbeck's *Heia Safari!* expressed the conservative premises that Germans had ruled their colonies as the most beneficent among colonial lords and that Germany's future depended on the reacquisition of colonies. The author appealed to his young readers in part through persistent reminders of natural abundance in a spacious unsettled land, where native Africans welcomed, admired, and respected Germans. Yet it was ultimately the adventures and heroics—literary constructs—that drove this narrative. Contemporary readers of Lettow-Vorbeck no doubt had on their bookshelves Karl May, who was perhaps the most popular German author of all time and certainly the most popular author among boys during the Weimar Republic. Lettow-Vorbeck's memoir incorporated key elements of May's fanciful adventures in far-flung exotic lands, including a German hero who contends against overpowering forces conspiring for power; foes who appear as one-dimensional, faceless Others; loyal natives who ally with the hero on the basis of shared nobility of character; and a continual chain of fighting and narrow escapes to fuel the suspense. Like May, Lettow-Vorbeck cultivated his own legend. The general portrayed himself as the unbeatable German, a living version of May's stock heroes Old Shatterhand and Kara ben Nemsi.[21] His memoirs, and indeed Weimar colonial consciousness itself, must be understood in the context of the pulp fiction that was increasingly commonplace at the time.

Although stereotypes obscure reality, it is possible to recover some of the underlying complexity from the flat conventions in Lettow-Vorbeck's story. Whatever racist projections appear in *Heia Safari!* or in Weimar literature in general, images of black Africans were not uniform, nor were Germans always oppressive. In a different context, Susanne Zantop notes in Karl May the sympathetic interaction of cultural strangers when Old Shatterhand first meets Winnetou: "Unlike Spanish or British colonizers, Germans—May's fiction suggests—were/are able to establish a relationship of mutual recognition and collaboration with American Indians." According to Zantop, "caricatured notions of the Other" prevent a nuanced understanding of colonial relations.[22] Zantop's observation applies to Lettow-Vorbeck and his *Askari* comrades. Despite his bravado, Lettow-Vorbeck viewed himself as desiring acceptance and integration among Africans. For the present analysis, however, he provides a useful example of a Wilhelmine colonial master in contrast to the postcolonial tourist-explorer Colin Ross.

Snapshots from Marvelous Africa: Colin Ross and *Mit Kamera, Kind und Kegel durch Afrika*

As a journalist and documentary filmmaker, Colin Ross was one of the most prolific and well-known exotic travelers of the Weimar period. His reports, books, and films shaped Germans' understanding of colonial relations; and for young readers, he opened exotic realms as Germany's leading "boy scout" explorer.[23] In 1929 Ross's children's book *Mit Kamera Kind und Kegel durch Afrika* earned a "warmest recommendation" from Germany's foremost pedagogical journal, *Die Jugendschriften-Warte* (*Children's Literary Observer*). The same review recommended Ross's far more detailed *Die erwachende Sphinx* (*The Awakening Sphinx*, 1927) for school libraries as a companion volume, so that teachers could inform themselves about the world-political context of *Mit Kamera*.[24] While this earlier volume for adults provided the underlying historical dimension and ideological perspective, these matters would have interfered with the entertaining adventure of the children's book.

Die erwachende Sphinx contains two main ideas. First, Ross asserts that the African continent would rise in the coming century to become an immense economic and political power, with Egypt acting as the intersection between Africa and Europe. Second, he advances a vision of a United Europe, for which the annexation of the African continent would be necessary to compete globally in the future with the Soviet Union and the United States. Ross goes so far as to imagine a collaborative system of European governance for the entire Sub-Saharan region, writing that, "The ideal thing would be to make Africa a single common colony for a future Pan-Europe."[25] Ross, a patriotic German, did not see his Eurafrican solution as compromising Germany's status, but rather as enhancing it. After all, according to Ross,

Germany had been the most successful among the European colonizing nations in Africa, and therefore Germans would naturally assume a prominent role in the future administration of colonized realms.

When writing for children, Ross avoided overt political commentary. Instead, *Mit Kamera, Kind und Kegel durch Afrika* dramatized future interaction among cultures through the microcosm of a German family—father, mother, preteen daughter, and toddler son—that successfully undertook exotic travels. In the introduction, Ross notes the deep insights about the world that his daughter had gained from previous schooling in Bolivia, Rhodesia, and Cairo; and he avers that the good and courageous behavior of his three-year-old son among wild animals and "wild" Africans demonstrated that exposure to strange and challenging things at the earliest age built strong character. By implication, cultivating open-minded adaptability ennobles the individual and the nation.

Ross's depiction of his own tolerance and progressive attitudes does not conceal his true prejudices. For both Ross and Lettow-Vorbeck, Africa represented hope for Germany's future generations, and a "Germanized" Africa would be as much of a *Heimat* as their own homeland in Europe. The chapters in *Sphinx* on former German East Africa, in particular, outline arguments for the legitimacy and necessity of Germans settling there. Ross remarks repeatedly how hospitable East Africa would become once Germans planted gardens, plied their trades, and once again proved that Germany was by far the most competent of any nation to colonize.[26] Imperial competence, Ross claims, was still evident in the 1920s, because natives in the former German East Africa still extended greater service, admiration, and respect to Germans than to any other Europeans. Ross concludes that Germans would come to Africa, whether under German administration or not, and would thrive better than they had before World War I. Indeed, he notes that the German population was once again growing in East Africa.[27] He did not, however, regard future relations with Africans as mutually beneficial. For example, he proposes that indispensable "black labor" would in the future sometimes require severe discipline, to the point of forced conscription of laborers, but this was a task that the proven and still palpable boon of German civilization justified.[28] The reader gains a sense of Ross's condescension toward native African servants in *Mit Kamera*, when for example he complains about the unreliability of the native Africans hired to carry supplies for white people.[29] Both of Ross's books express greater distrust and fear of native Africans than did Lettow-Vorbeck, who with few exceptions claimed to admire the tenacity and stamina of his carriers and servants.

In *Mit Kamera*, Ross renders his African experiences less menacing, and even enticing, by portraying his family, especially his three-year-old son, as fully adapted to the "savage" environment and able to engage with white and black African people alike. For example, a lion cub, rescued from a hunt after the mother was killed, frightens a black African child (whom the mother "raised to be a coward"), but Ross' small son delightfully plays with the cub as if it were a house pet.[30] African tribesmen, whom Ross depicts as ominous and threatening, appear to his son as harmless performers in a strange and fascinating carnival.[31] Ross promotes colonial consciousness by conveying to his young readers that the harsh climate, dangerous animals, and potentially malevolent native peoples did not represent an insurmountable deterrent to their planned tour. On the contrary, in Ross's view, European children were not as predisposed to the anxieties of exotic environments as were adults. They suffered neither distress nor privations and even reveled in uncanny encounters. Photographs illustrating the family's travels in Africa contributed much to the romance. An image of the family at its mining camp bears the caption "There is no place like home"; and under the photograph of three-year-old Ralph-Colin playing with the lion cub appear the words "youth belongs with youth." The father undermines the sentimentality of the children's experiences, however, by dramatizing the arduous labor, dangerous hunts for lions and elephants, and perceived physical threats from grotesque, violent, and unrestrained natives.

The passage describing Ross's experiences with Africans in a tribal village contains the most glaring representation of the "Black Other" in terms of sexualized violence. After prospecting for gold in the Transvaal and then hunting lions and elephants, Ross guides his family to the limits of "primitive" civilization. He desires immediate contact with one of the few supposedly untouched "Negro peoples" (*Negervölker*) on Lake Victoria and enters the realm of the "naked Kavirondos."[32] Ross wishes to film and to photograph the spectacle of tribal festivities, but he recoils in shock and disgust at the unexpected "grotesqueness" of the Kavirondos' behavior. His first attempt to film women dancing fails in the chaos of a small throng of naked "old disgusting hags," whom he describes as mostly drunk and wild as they encircle him from all sides and "lunged at him with their saggy breasts" during their crude dance. Ross's black guide has the women whipped to drive them away, whereupon Ross demands that the women come back and perform their dance "properly" for the camera, instructing that two young "naked little witches" be placed in front—whereupon "in ecstasy, the young and old women then threw their bodies at me." Before he can shoot, men arrive in face and body paint, costumed so that they appear to have "lost all resemblance to humans," and stop Ross from taking photographs.[33] Here he confronts the Africa that he needed to subdue. He ultimately exercises mastery over the "primitives" through his photographs, which all portray gentle harmony, in stark contrast to the frenetic savagery he recounts in the text.

Ross later obtains his desired images, and in doing so, figuratively takes possession of wild African terrain. After his attempt to film the Kavirondo women performing an authentic dance has failed because he found it too weird and chaotic, he bribes the chief to stage a spectacular warriors' funeral celebration. This account suggests that Ross felt the need to exercise control when in Africa, because his family was living detached from an environment in which they could function coherently. Ross adapted to their displacement by orchestrating the behavior of the "aliens." The book further describes how Ross succeeds in filming an inauthentic funeral rite, whereby warriors wearing elaborate costumes ride in on bulls, perform a pageant, and pose throughout for the camera. Through his management of the natives, Ross himself performs a theatrical feat, deftly maneuvering his family through what he describes as a set of bizarre experiences. Thus, he is able to demonstrate skills of power and control over the encounter with "anticipated unknowns."[34]

In his *Mit Kamera, Kind und Kegel durch Afrika*, Colin Ross symbolically conquers terrain in Africa by manipulating the "natives" into performing for his camera. By staging events, he casts the German as master of the most strange and forbidding people and conditions. Moreover, when he exhibits his children in pictures as peacefully integrated among fearsome black Africans, Ross transforms fear into "wonder."[35] Through film, Ross claims African domain by stamping it with the mark of his camera, which he uses as an instrument of imaginary control. Hence, the family outing through the African wilderness in *Mit Kamera, Kind und Kegel* represents an act of colonization no less crucial to the German imperial imagination than the programmatic writings such as those Ross presented in *Die erwachende Sphinx*.

In order to cultivate a sense of wonder regarding Africa, especially among young people, Ross created a written journal of alienation at complete odds with his photographic journal of harmony. He used pictures in *Mit Kamera* to resolve the turmoil expressed in the narrative. Ross choreographed his family's African journey so that he could bring back to Germany visual marvels in film and photographs, having fabricated images that conformed to his preconceptions of Africa. The author written account, however, betrays the charming appeal of his family's adventures, especially in his blunt hostility toward Africans.

Fridolin's Africa

While photographs and illustrations in the books by Lettow-Vorbeck and Ross added essential complements to their stories, graphics dominated text in the children's bi-weekly *Der heitere Fridolin* (Merry Fridolin). Published by Ullstein from 1921 to 1928, it was the first German children's magazine to make extensive use of color artwork and to base its humor largely on cartoons. Frequent references to Africa in articles, illustrations, and caricatures added a complexity that diverged from the unified narratives by Lettow-Vorbeck and Ross. The graphics in *Der heitere Fridolin* appear haphazardly associated and lack a coordinated editorial point of view. Consequently, the magazine's representations of Africa underscore the diversity of coexisting attitudes, by turn racist and enlightened, imperious and self-mocking. The works of two prominent illustrators, Ferdinand Barlog and Moritz Pathé, reveal conflicting perspectives on Africa and Africans.

Drearily predictable racist stereotypes of Africans pervaded German popular culture during the Weimar period. Cartoon caricatures of uncultivated "nature-folk" with exaggerated physical and behavioral characteristics were as much at home in Germany as in many other Western nations. Grotesque physical distortions in caricature often express aggressive derision toward its subject, and when generalized to a stereotype of Africans, the contempt is racist. In comics appearing in *Der heitere Fridolin*, however, artists muted this kind of disdain by casting the Africans more as exotic playmates.

For example, Ferdinand Barlog, a house illustrator for *Der heitere Fridolin*, employed unambiguous racist ciphers for Africans. Barlog's drawings had nothing to do with real Africans. He employed African caricatures as a comical foil for a white cartoon hero, who needed to overcome a threatening situation through ingenuity. In one instance, a German boy tames wild cannibals by charming them with the song "Oh du lieber Augustin." The tone of the comic is clearly one of delight and amusement, contradicting the ominous situation expressed in the caption's words "wild cannibals."[36] While comics of this type were crass expressions of superiority, they were neither malicious nor brutal.

Moritz Pathé, also a house illustrator at Ullstein, created all of the artwork for serious feature articles about Africa in *Der heitere Fridolin*. In 1925 Pathé actually traveled to Africa. The journey provided ample material for his series of reports, nature articles, and incidental illustrations during the subsequent years of the magazine's publication. Little evidence exists in Pathé's art of a colonialist or racist attitude toward Africans. His respectful impressions of Massai hunters, for example, highlighted their cunning, courage, and sophistication.[37] Pathé's genuine esteem for Africans suggests that the racist cartoons by Barlog and others were based more on convention than conviction, and that the magazine was more inclined to respect the integrity of African culture, rather than demean it as uncivilized.

However, admiration for Africans did not preclude the idea of European technological superiority. *Der heitere Fridolin* reported on modern technology in nearly every issue, highlighting travel, communication, and industry. Its news of larger aircraft, faster trains, and advanced communications networks implied that they could be used in developing less industrialized regions; numerous contributors to the magazine demonstrated how aircraft, ships, and land vehicles could penetrate previously inaccessible regions of the world. Modern advancements also played a role in the magazine's humor. Comics in *Der heitere Fridolin* showed silly images of "primitives" mimicking modern Europeans or expressing confusion and fear at things German children would take for granted. For example, when Moritz Pathé illustrated an article about Walter Mittelholzer's record 1927 flight from Switzerland to Capetown, he chose to show the Massai crouched beneath their shields as the airplane flew over them.[38] This drawing is one of many images in *Der heitere Fridolin*, comic and documentary, that depict "primitives" as frightened or awestruck by aircraft. Despite his admiration for Africans, Pathé's cowering Massai emblematically convey the superiority of European civilization.

Yet these comics were not always derogatory. Comic images of Africa in *Der heitere Fridolin* sometimes introduced moments of self-irony and even identification with caricatured Africans. While the magazine's basic message remained that European technological supremacy held sway over less developed parts of the world, the ambiguities of children's humor lent a subversive twist to the idea of European superiority. Pathé's own 1925 travelogue includes one of his few comic portrayals, satirizing his own ineptitude as an exotic traveler. Here he levels his ridicule not at Africans, but at himself.[39] For his only self-portrait in *Der heitere Fridolin*, Pathé breaks completely from his approach to illustrating. He employs a far cruder style than in his other artwork and caricatures, further accentuating his mocking self-irony. By casting himself as silly, he reduces his own authority in the narrative and "plays" with his readers by upsetting expectations. In the white safari hunter, Pathé ridicules the exotic adventurer, providing a corrective to assumptions of white privilege.

A different kind of identification takes place when Pathé reflects his audience of readers—German children—in the caricatures of Africans. In the six-panel comic "Ein Elefant für alles" ("An Elephant for all Occasions"), for instance, Pathé shows *African* children being inventive by using their elephant as a multipurpose appliance for work and recreation—tasks which comically imitated modern Western everyday life.[40] In such comics, Africa has little to do with the point of the humor. Rather, they encourage young readers to take delight in the ingenuity of the characters and to identify with them.

Charles Baudelaire described caricature as a quintessentially modern form of art that expresses a new attitude toward life. He believed that the complexities of modernity manifest themselves in caricatures through oppositions, contradictions, dualities, and self-irony.[41] Caricature art also contains a literary dimension, according to Baudelaire, because it conveys narratives that stem from mundane and uncultivated social contexts. While none of the illustrations and caricatures in *Der heitere Fridolin* provide the intricate commentaries on modern life that Honoré Daumier had done in Baudelaire's time or that George Grosz was doing in Weimar Germany, many of them did incorporate elements of reflexive humor, inviting the readers to identify themselves with the comic characters.

Baudelaire also distinguished between two kinds of humor, the *comique absolu* and the *comique significatif.* The former elicits joy, the latter scorn: "[W]hile superiority is a factor in both, the *absolu* connotes freedom, license, pleasure, and spontaneity, as opposed to the more rigid and limited *significatif.*" [42] The *comique absolu* expressed in Moritz Pathé's comics reinforces a common virtue that *Der heitere Fridolin* championed throughout its pages—the art and joy of being clever. Stories, historical anecdotes, articles, and comics all consistently underscore ingenuity as a primary virtue. Being intelligent and resourceful grants the cartoon characters command over their situations, enabling them to improvise spontaneous solutions and fulfill their needs. Pathé demonstrates in his comics a sympathetic and ironic "doubling," through which German children should recognize themselves in the caricatures of Africans. Moreover, the amusement in Pathé's comics lies not only in the pleasure of a witty take on an everyday situation. Silliness also adds an essential element to the humor. Together, creative nonsense and ingenuity could be used to effect an interactive, playful connection between the young reader and the images.

German children's periodicals attained massive circulation in the 1920s. *Der heitere Fridolin* alone claimed three to 400,000 readers between 1922 and 1929. Therefore, one may discuss comics and caricatures as a commonplace in Weimar youth culture. Comics, even in their childish simplicity, can contain different levels of irony. A comic artist might employ absurd, derogatory distortions of Africans to elicit in the young German reader a feeling of superiority. Yet many cartoons could also express a reflexive irony. In some cartoons depicting African natives, inventive play could reflect attributes German children would value—in this case, cleverness. Readers of *Der heitere Fridolin* would have been able to find joy in the affirmation of their own playful ingenuity.

Conclusion

Haia Safari!, *Mit Kamera, Kind und Kegel durch Afrika*, and *Der heitere Fridolin* exemplify three of the many expressions of colonialist ideas in Weimar children's literature. Lettow-Vorbeck overtly exhorts his readers to settle as German colonists in Africa; but to locate Ross's underlying imperialist agenda, one must read his children's book in light of the reactionary politics he propagates in his book for adults, *Der erwachende Sphinx*. Illustrators and authors of *Der heitere Fridolin* never allude to German colonies, but repeated images of technological superiority over "primitives" suggest latent associations with imperial power.

Attitudes toward race and Africans varied among these texts as well. Despite his military experiences in ruthlessly crushing native rebellions, Lettow-Vorbeck insists that German ingenuity, determination, gallantry, and culture inspired Africans to emulate Germans. He envisions a renewal of empire, in which Africans of noble character would serve as loyal subjects. Colin Ross, on the other hand, finds little to redeem in the nature of Africans. His characterization of the Kavirondos as degenerate savages corresponds to his conviction that future colonizers of Africa would have to enslave the natives as the only way to integrate them into a modern industrial economy. In Weimar children's literature, a more benign sense of cultural superiority, exemplified by Lettow-Vorbeck's book, was more prevalent than the naked racism of Ross. *Der heitere Fridolin* often portrayed Africans as noble hunters, highly sophisticated in adapting to their own environment. Yet the magazine also depicted the intrusion of modern Western civilization, implying eventual white hegemony over Africans.

Juvenile literature echoed many of the popular ideas about Africa during the Weimar era. Africa was a distant exotic realm, as alluring for its potential riches as it was forbidding in its wild and primitive state. Children's literature tended to idealize life in the former colonies or to present Africa optimistically as a refuge, where the next generation might find a new homeland.

Notes

1. Wolfgang J. Mommsen, *Imperial Germany 1867–1918* (London, 1995), 75–100. See also Mathew Fitzpatrick, *Liberal Imperialism in Germany: Expansionism and Nationalism, 1848–1884* (New York, 2008); Russell Berman, *Enlightenment or Empire: Colonial Discourse in German Culture* (Lincoln, 1998).
2. Marcia Klotz, "The Weimar Republic: A Postcolonial State in a Still-Colonial World" in *Germany's Colonial Pasts*, ed. Eric Ames, et al. (Lincoln, 2005), 135–47. See also Lora Wildenthal, *German Women for Empire, 1884–1945* (Durham, 2001); Michael Schubert, *Der schwarze Fremde: Das Bild des Schwarzafrikaners in der parlamentarischen und publizistischen Kolonialdiskussion in Deutschland von den 1870er bis in die 1930er Jahre* (Stuttgart, 2003).
3. Germany carried out genocide in Southwest Africa in 1904, killing between 75 and 80 percent of the Herero people. From 1905 to 1907, German forces suppressed the Maji-Maji rebellion in German East Africa, with deaths of Africans estimated between 200,000 and 300,000. Isabel V. Hull, "Military Culture and 'Final Solutions'" in *The Specter of Genocide*, ed. Robert Gellately and Ben Kiernan (Cambridge, 2003), 144–46, 161.
4. Ernst Wächter, "Die Deutsche Kolonialausstellung in Stuttgart," *Der gute Kamerad* (1929): 727–30.
5. Medardus Brehl, "'The Drama was Played Out on the Dark Stage of the Sandveldt': The Extermination of the Herero and Nama in German (Popular) Literature" in *Genocide in German South-West Africa: The Colonial War (1904–1908) in Namibia and its Aftermath*, ed. Jürgen Zimmerer and Joachim Zeller (Monmouth, 2008), 100–12.
6. In this regard, I am indebted to the seminal ideas found in Edward Said, *Orientalism* (New York, 1978) and *Culture and Imperialism* (New York, 1993) and in Homi Bhabha, *The Location of Culture* (New York, 1994).
7. Paul von Lettow-Vorbeck, *Heia Safari! Deutschlands Kampf in Ostafrika* (Leipzig, 1920), 282.
8. The author of one account claims that Lettow-Vorbeck was the "most successful guerilla leader in world history." Edwin Hoyt, *Guerilla: Colonel von Lettow-Vorbeck and Germany's East African Empire* (New York, 1981), 206.
9. Lettow-Vorbeck, *Safari*, 125.
10. Ibid., 55.
11. Arthur Dix summarized the arguments for Germany's neocolonial expansion in *Weltkrise und Kolonialpolitik: Die Zukunft zweier Erdteile* (Berlin, 1932).
12. Lettow-Vorbeck, *Safari*, 114.

13. L.H. Gann and Peter Duignan, *The Rulers of German Africa, 1884–1914* (Stanford, 1977), 239–46.
14. Lettow-Vorbeck, *Safari*, 249.
15. Ibid., 31.
16. Ibid., 99.
17. Ibid., 158–59.
18. Ibid., 251.
19. Ibid., 193. An emphasis on the alleged amicability between Germans and East Africans echoed throughout Weimar colonial politics. Germany had lost its colonies in the Treaty of Versailles due in part to accusations that the Germans had been cruel and irresponsible imperial authorities. In response, a broad spectrum of political parties, including the SPD, emphatically insisted on Germany's record of generosity and honor in its colonial administration and called for renewed initiatives to regain former colonies. Weimar politicians attempted without success to become involved in the administration of colonial mandates through the League of Nations. See Wildenthal, *Women*, 179; Dirk van Laak, " 'Ist je ein Reich, das es nicht gab, so gut verwaltet worden?' Der imaginäre Ausbau der imperialen Infrastruktur in Deutschland nach 1918" in *Phantasiereiche: Zur Kulturgeschichte des deutschen Kolonialismus*, ed. Birthe Kundrus (Frankfurt am Main, 2003), 81; Mihran Dabag, "National-koloniale Konstruktionen in politischen Entwürfen des Deutschen Reichs um 1900" in *Kolonialismus: Kolonialdiskurs und Genozid*, ed. Mihran Dabag, et al. (Munich, 2004), 44; Martin Eberhardt, *Zwischen Nationalsozialismus und Apartheid: Die deutsche Bevölkerungsgruppe Südwestafrikas, 1915–1965*, ed. Andreas Eckert and Christoph Marx (Berlin, 2007), 129–38. Lettow-Vorbeck served as a Reichstag deputy representing the German Nationalist Party (DNVP) from 1928 to 1930.
20. Lettow-Vorbeck, *Safari*, 116–17, 227.
21. Karl May was a true fraud, whereas Lettow-Vorbeck only stylized his real experiences. May posed for publicity photographs in the costumes of his heroes and even claimed that his tales were drawn from his own experiences, when in fact he traveled abroad only briefly in later life. See Reiner Wild, ed., *Geschichte der deutschen Kinder- und Jugendliteratur* (Stuttgart, 1990), 197–99.
22. Susanne Zantop, "Close Encounters: Deutsche und Indianer" in *Germans and Indians: Fantasies, Encounters, Projections*, ed. Susanne Zantop, et al. (Lincoln, 2003), 4–5.
23. Bodo-Michael Baumunk, "Ein Pfadfinder der Geopolitik: Colin Ross und seine Reisefilme" in *Triviale Tropen: Exotische Reise- und Abenteuerfilme aus Deutschland 1919–1939*, ed. Jörg Schöning (Munich, 1997), 86.
24. "Beurteilungen der Vereinigten deutschen Prüfungsausschüsse," *Jugendschriften-Warte* (1929): 64. Ufa released Ross's documentary film *Die*

erwachende Sphinx in 1927 alongside a children's version, *Als Dreijähriger durch Afrika*. Ross's films earned him as much acclaim as Germany's great globetrotting journalist as did his books. Baumunk, "Pfadfinder," 92–93.

25. Colin Ross, *Der erwachende Sphinx: Durch Afrika vom Kap nach Kairo* (Leipzig, 1927), 246.

26. Ibid., 241.

27. Ibid., 243–44.

28. Ibid., 237–39.

29. Ross, *Kamera*, 88–89.

30. Ibid., 70–71.

31. Ibid., 143–45.

32. Ibid., 112.

33. Ibid., 128–33.

34. Stephen Greenblatt, *Marvelous Possessions: The Wonder of the New World* (Chicago, 1991), 53–55 describes how explorers anticipated the nature of encounters with alien cultures, which conditioned the responses of Europeans to New World cultures.

35. As a point of comparison, Greenblatt characterizes the attitude of early European explorers and colonizers toward natives as "marvelous understanding," which presumed knowledge of other peoples and thereby disarmed fears of the unknown. Ibid., 81–82. Edward Said emphasizes the power of making the foreign familiar as a response to a perceived threat in *Orientalism*, 58–59.

36. Ferdinand Barlog, "The wild cannibals all stood around the piano with eyes and mouths agape when I played 'O du lieber Augustin' for them," *Der heitere Fridolin* 3:23 (1925): 8.

37. Editor's note: This and the other images discussed in this section can be viewed on the Internet. See http://www.archive.org/stream/heiterefridolinh06na#page/n243/mode/2up.

38. See http://www.archive.org/stream/heiterefridolinh06na#page/n197/mode/2up.

39. Indeed, one can read this account as a parody of exotic travelogues, such as those by Colin Ross. See http://www.archive.org/stream/heiterefridolinh06na#page/n27/mode/2up.

40. See http://www.archive.org/stream/heiterefridolinh03na#page/n227/mode/2up.

41. Michele Hannoosch, *Baudelaire and Caricature* (University Park, 1992), 9–74.

42. Ibid., 28.

VI

How Can a War Be Holy?
Weimar Attitudes Toward
Eastern Spirituality

Tom Neuhaus

By the beginning of the twentieth century, most areas of the globe had been explored by travelers from Europe. There was, however, one region in the heart of Asia that Europeans had attended to only very sporadically: Tibet. Yet there was an ever-growing drive to explore the culture and environment of this alien country from the first half of the nineteenth century onward. A German geography textbook explained in 1931:

> The rule of the priests over the land explains its isolation; for they feed the fanatical dislike of the "foreign devils" amongst the people. But it seems that even the state of the lamas cannot close its borders for all eternity. For centuries Tibet has belonged to China in name, but it has been situated as a buffer state between the Russian and English Empires. At the moment the English have a certain influence in this elevated country, and in 1922 a telegraph line was even installed between India and Lhasa.[1]

One of the most alien facets of Tibet for European travelers was its religion. Yet precisely because of its alien character, Tibet and its religion could serve as a blank screen onto which Germans could project fantasies, fears, and desires. This chapter examines how and why interest in both Tibetan Buddhism and a wider Eastern spirituality grew in certain sections of Weimar society. This growth reflected a desire to look for different ways of coping with the violent recent past, as well as cultural developments that were more generally perceived as pernicious, such as urbanization. The "blank screen" character of Eastern spirituality meant that these developments and possible (spiritual and Eastern) solutions could be discussed relatively freely through references to the supposedly beneficial aspects of Eastern cultures. In this sense, growing interest in the East was part and parcel of figuring out how the new Germany of the post-World War I era should and could advance.

Much of the research on religion in Weimar Germany has focused on the political and social contexts of Christian and Jewish communities.[2] However, historians have not paid much attention to religion as part of a larger, global framework that allowed people to make sense of cultural and ideological change.[3] Yet religion and spirituality were much discussed and often invoked by those members of the cultural elites who debated the nature of culture, modernity, and civilization in Germany during the interwar period. As this chapter shows, this discussion often took place within the context of comparing Germany to other areas of the globe. Therefore, we are unable to appreciate fully Weimar debates about culture, religion, and spirituality without an understanding of Weimar approaches to other religions, above all Eastern ones.

Moreover, such an understanding will also shed light on the transnational nature of debates in Weimar Germany. Germans in that era perceived themselves as very much part of a wider world, in which both problems and ideas for their solution transcended national boundaries, even entire continents. Even though there may exist at the moment a tendency to overuse the term "transnational," it can be helpful for exploring these issues. For it allows us to appreciate that ideas and people crossed the borders of nations, both conceptually and physically, yet never completely ignored or negated them.[4]

This chapter begins by outlining how the German fascination with this kind of spirituality evolved from the second half of the nineteenth century onward. The second section examines those elements that made Eastern spirituality so attractive for some Germans during the Weimar period, paying particular attention to Tibetan Buddhism as one of its most alien and unexplored forms. This section analyzes how commentators engaged, through their focus on Eastern spirituality, with the legacy of their immediate past, and how they searched for new answers to life's most pressing questions.

From Bodh Gaya to Berlin: Growing Interest in Spirituality

East and South Asia had fascinated Germans for a long time. In the seventeenth century, for instance, German Jesuit scholar Athanasius Kircher had produced one of the largest descriptions of Asia in his *China Illustrata*, and both scientists and missionaries had traveled to China and India from the early modern period onwards.[5] Inner Asia—that is, the countries north of India and west and southwest of China (mainly Tibet, Nepal, Bhutan, Ladakh, and Sikkim)—was particularly suited as a blank canvas onto which European travelers and writers could paint their fears, desires, and anxieties about the state of their home countries.

The area was extremely inaccessible, due both to its geographical isolation and to the fact that it was officially closed to all foreign visitors from Europe and North America. To the north and east, it was surrounded by deserts and comparatively empty grasslands. To the south lay the Himalayas, which together with their subsidiary mountain ranges are home to the fourteen tallest mountains in the world, including Mount Everest. Consequently, very little was known about the region, even into the twentieth century. According to one estimate, only approximately 1,250 Westerners had visited Tibet by 1975, half of whom had entered as soldiers during a short-lived British military mission in 1903/04 designed to counteract suspected Russian influence in the area.[6]

Tibetan religion was of particular interest to German travelers, who, unlike the British, had no political or economic influence in the region. Tibetans subscribed to their own brand of Buddhism, which they supplemented with older beliefs in the spiritual power of nature. These were largely derived from the so-called Bön religion that predated Tibetan Buddhism, which appeared with very little impact in the second century C.E. during the reign of King Lha Thothori Nyantsen, and then received a boost during the reign of King Songtsen Gampo in the seventh century. Over the course of several centuries, a number of Tibetan Buddhist sects developed, the most well-known of which are the so-called "yellow hats" (*gelugpa*) and the "red hats" (*nyingmapa*). Monasticism was a very important feature of Tibetan Buddhism, with large monasteries comprised of several thousand monks in Lhasa, Shigatse, Gyantse, Samye, and Sakya, to name but a few. Spiritual practice relied heavily on meditation and the devotion to gurus, and worship was aided by certain mechanical implements, such as prayer wheels and prayer flags. Leadership was provided by lamas, the most important of whom were the Dalai Lama and the Panchen Lama.[7] All this was very alien to Germans during the early twentieth century and did not resemble any of the religious practices carried out in Europe.

Already during the second half of the nineteenth century, interest in Eastern religions had grown significantly alongside the expanding study of Asian cultures and ethnography.[8] Emil Schlagintweit, who wrote one of the first German works on Tibetan Buddhism, was motivated by the awareness that the number of Buddhists worldwide was, at 340 million, possibly larger than that of Christians.[9] Wagner, Schopenhauer, and Nietzsche all integrated Buddhist ideas into their work.[10] And in 1903 a small group of people around the Leipzig Indologist Karl Seidenstücker formed the Buddhist Missionary Society in Germany (*Buddhistischer Missionsverein in Deutschland*).[11] From 1911 onward, Polgasduwa, located on the island of Sri Lanka in the Indian Ocean, was home to a hermitage of Buddhists drawn from all over the world and particularly from Germany. This had been set up by Anton Walter Florus Gueth, subsequently known as Nyanatiloka, the son of a bourgeois Catholic family and the first German to be ordained as a Buddhist monk.[12]

The most thorough exploration of Tibetan religion, culture, and history, however, was carried out by the Moravian missionaries, who settled in Ladakh in Northern India beginning in the 1850s. These missionaries were part of a community that had settled in and around Herrnhut in eastern Germany in the early eighteenth century and maintained mission stations all around the world. The Moravian missionaries in Ladakh were among the first Europeans to have any long-term interactions with Tibetans, although they were virtually never allowed to enter Tibet itself; and they produced some of the earliest grammars and dictionaries of the Tibetan language, as well as analyses of ancient Tibetan texts. They also collected religious artifacts and objects of everyday life, which they sent back to the Ethnographic Museum in Herrnhut. The missionaries had a somewhat patronizing, yet benevolent, attitude toward Tibetan religiosity. For them, Tibetans were superstitious and ignorant yet fully capable of salvation if converted to the right brand of the Christian faith. The fact that the number of converts among the Tibetans and Ladakhis remained extremely low throughout the entire sixty-year period of the Moravians' stay in the area did nothing to dispel this fascination with Tibetan religion and the ways in which it might be affected by encounters with Christianity.[13]

Interest in Asian religion and philosophy, whether expressed by missionaries, scholars, or travelers, continued with renewed vigor after the First World War. This led to a diversification of the small Buddhist groupings that had been founded before the First World War in Leipzig, Munich, and Berlin. This diversification mainly took the shape of a larger split between so-called Old Buddhists and New Buddhists. One of the first Buddhist centers of Weimar Germany was the Old Buddhist Community (*Altbuddhistische Gemeinde*) in Utting near the Bavarian Ammersee, founded in July 1920 by Georg Grimm and Karl Seidenstücker.[14] In 1924 the first Buddhist house of worship in Germany was built under the direction of Paul Dahlke, a medical doctor, in the leafy Berlin suburb of Frohnau. This consisted of a villa in the style of the other bourgeois houses in the neighborhood, an Asian front gate, and a Buddhist "temple" that was added in 1926.[15]

Many of those involved in these Buddhist groups came from the educated bourgeoisie of Berlin, Munich, and Leipzig. Paul Dahlke had been trained and continued to practice as a medical doctor; Georg Grimm had studied law and worked as a judge until 1919. Much of their discussion of Buddhism was thus rather academic in nature. This is demonstrated by the emergence of Buddhist periodicals, such as the rival publications *Zeitschrift für Buddhismus* (*Journal for Buddhism*), edited by Wolfgang Bohn and Ludwig Ankenbrand, and the *Buddhistischer Weltspiegel* (*Buddhist World Mirror*), edited by Karl Seidenstücker and Georg Grimm. The former had originally been published in 1913 and then reappeared from 1920 onward, while the latter was first published in 1919 or, as the cover of the first edition put it, in 2463 after Nirvana.[16] These journals published scholarly articles, translations of Buddhist texts, personal contributions, poems, and announcements of events and developments in the different Buddhist groupings in Germany. Events ranged from lectures for a general audience to a Buddhist opera, based on a text by the Jewish author Jakob Wasserstein and set to music by Vienna musicologist Egon Wellesz, which was performed at the Frankfurt opera house in May 1921.[17] At times, the journal editors also drew the attention of their readers to the activities of other movements, which they apparently considered somehow related to Buddhism and hence of interest to their audience.[18]

But Asian approaches to spirituality, as well as culture and politics, held a wider appeal. This can be seen perhaps most clearly in the frenzied reception one of India's most famous writers writer encountered when visiting Germany. Rabindranath Tagore, the first Asian Nobel Laureate, wrote on various themes relevant to early twentieth-century Indian politics, society, and culture. His appeal in Germany was so great that police had to be called to restrain the crowds when Tagore came to lecture on "the message of the forests" in Berlin in June 1921.[19] According to the foreign reporter of the *Daily News*, there were "scenes of frenzied hero worship" and, as the *Vossische Zeitung* reported, the crowds could only be appeased when it was announced that Tagore would repeat his lecture the following day.[20] Other high points of Tagore's visit to Germany that year were Munich and the School of Wisdom run by Count Hermann Keyserling in Darmstadt.[21]

This demonstrated the immense attraction that alternative messages about a seemingly more spiritual Asian approach to nature, culture, civilization, and modernity had on many Germans during the Weimar years. Tagore's complete works were translated and edited by Heinrich Meyer-Benfey and Helene Meyer-Franck in 1921. The publishing house taking on this enterprise was Kurt Wolff's in Munich. This was well known for producing a wide range of works on and by artists and famous literary figures, such as Georg Heym, Georg Trakl, Paul Klee, Paula Modersohn-Becker, Guy de Maupassant, Franz Werfel, Heinrich Mann and Walt Whitman. Tagore's works, in this sense, were by no means on the margins of literary life in Weimar Germany. Within just over a year of his lectures, approximately 800,000 copies of his books had been sold in Germany.[22]

Some of the major contemporary authors of the German-speaking world, too, were caught up in this excitement over Eastern religions. German-Swiss writer Hermann Hesse was fascinated by South Asia; and after a trip to Sri Lanka and Indonesia in 1911, his works began to incorporate Buddhist themes. In 1922 Hesse published *Siddhartha*, a novel tracing the life of the son of an Indian Brahmin and his spiritual development, paralleling that of Prince Siddharta, who according to Buddhist doctrine had become the Buddha Gautama.[23] Hesse's fascination with the East, however, was not tied to any specific organized religion. During the 1920s he engaged with Asian spirituality on a large scale. In 1921 he wrote that "The Speeches of Buddha" would give the West "a deepened self-knowledge, such as was the first and most holy requirement of the pupils of the wise men of Greece."[24] Two years later, he commented that he, and Europe as a whole, was "beginning to have an intimation of the greatness and wonder of this true religion of the people, Hinduism, incomparable in its plasticity."[25] In 1925, when working his way through the Chinese *I Ching*, he declaimed, "Everything is written there that can be thought or lived."[26] Ten years after the publication of *Siddhartha*, he released *A Journey to the East*. At the same time he began with the preparations for one of his major books, *The Glass Bead Game*, which tells the story of Dasa, an Indian prince, and also deals more generally with ideas about wisdom and scholarship.[27]

Asia was clearly a place that promised to let German-speaking Europeans gain deeper insights into the most basic questions of life. The social base for this interest in Eastern spirituality was to be found particularly among the educated middle and upper strata of Weimar society. This held true both in terms of who was actively interested in promoting it and of who was merely taking a curious interest in it. Students and academics were certainly the most prevalent section of society within Buddhist movements, among contributors to publications about spirituality, and in the audiences for Tagore's talks.

But Inner Asia also found its way into the publications of less mainstream authors. In Germany and in other countries, novels and short stories dealt with Tibetan mysticism. In 1919 Count Hermann von Keyserling published one of the most popular German travel narratives of all time. His *Travel Diary of a Philosopher* described his travels around the world, focusing particularly on India, where he had visited Bodh Gaya, the location where Buddha supposedly gained enlightenment, and the Himalayas. The culture and nature of the region, which he found "unearthly, cosmically-grand," led Keyserling to muse about the nature of mankind and life. "In the Himalayas," he wrote, "the human being is wonderfully close to the deity; this nature, more than any other on Earth, expands the limits of consciousness."[28] Other authors were no less mystical in their treatment of Tibetan spirituality. Otfried von Hanstein, for instance, published an intriguing novel about a young Tibetan novice searching for spiritual enlightenment, and author Gustav Meyrink wrote about a mystical Tibetan magician conjuring up images of war.[29] (Both will be discussed further below.) It is difficult to determine exactly how Weimar reading audiences received these works. Nevertheless, the fact that their authors were prolific and continuously successful at finding publishers for their books indicates that they were not just a "flash in the pan."[30] Moreover, works on Tibet by foreign authors such as the French traveler Alexandra David-Néel were translated into German and found a captivated audience.[31] It would be unwise to exclude these representations from the present analysis just by virtue of their having been produced by non-Germans. If we are serious about analyzing attitudes and perceptions we need to bear in mind that many non-German representations, such as those generated by David-Néel, were read and discussed in Germany, too, and thus influenced German attitudes.

Not all Germans were sympathetic to the ideals of Buddhism and other Eastern religions and philosophies, however. When the first postwar issue of the *Journal of Buddhism* appeared in 1920, editors Wolfgang Bohn and Ludwig Ankenbrand lamented the reaction of many of their contemporaries.

The press, dependant as it is on the demands of the day, will oppose [the publication of this journal], from the beginning hostile toward teachings that aim for finiteness and extinction. The wider public will regard it with indifference, as the flood of magazines appearing and disappearing has been rushing past it for years. The thinking reader will be skeptical of the attempt to introduce new and alien elements into a circle of chaos. Even those who have not given up on seeking salvation elsewhere will see it without confidence. However, some people, who still have the will within them, will reproach us: it is a crime to advertise teachings of "pessimism" and of "passivity," such as Buddhism, in a time of collapse when people are calling upon all available forces for the renewed construction of "positive values."[32]

Nevertheless, this suggests that Buddhism was at least talked about and appeared on the agenda of Weimar debates. Thus, Buddhism and Eastern spirituality in their various forms—and particularly in the form of Tibetan Lamaism—entered German consciousness to an extent that it had not done previously.

"Germany's Hope for the Future": Spirituality and the Problems of Weimar Germany

Given this wave of interest in Eastern spirituality during the 1920s, one has to ask which of its supposed characteristics made it so attractive, particularly to the educated circles of Weimar Germany. To begin with, Eastern spirituality appeared peaceful. This was crucial, for it provided a way in which many commentators could criticize Western culture for the development of modern warfare and, in particular, for the First World War. Germany had been defeated in 1918 and went through major political, social, and economic upheavals during the early years of the Weimar Republic. On the one hand, militarism was rife in Weimar, particularly on the right of the political spectrum; and many former soldiers organized themselves in so-called Free Corps, which engaged in street fights and assassinated demonstrators and left-wing politicians like Rosa Luxemburg and Karl Liebknecht. Ernst Jünger, whose books *Storm of Steel* (1920) and *Battle as Inner Experience* (1922) inaugurated his career as one of Weimar Germany's most prolific and militaristic authors on battle, demanded a hard, authoritarian state in Germany that would be fit for war, just like the battle community he idealized in his books. On the other hand, strong pacifist currents emerged as well, for instance within the Catholic Church and among socialist and liberal intellectuals. Erich Maria Remarque's *All Quiet on the Western Front* (1929) depicted war as a demeaning force that utterly destroyed youthful energy, enthusiasm, and lives. The uneasy coexistence of militarism and pacifism became one of the defining characteristics of the Weimar Republic.[33]

Religion and spirituality were an important theme in attitudes toward war and peace in the Weimar Republic. Not all religions had connotations of peacefulness. In Otfried von Hanstein's novel *The Novice of Tashi-lunpo* (1923), the young Tibetan novice Lobsen encounters both Christians and Muslims during his travels away from Tibet and is shocked when confronted with their warlike character. When he hears the Muslims proclaiming "holy war," he rhetorically asks, "How can a war be holy? You lunatics, how can a god incite you to murder?"[34] Later on, Lobsen expresses his horror at a vision of Christians fighting each other in the First World War; and during the German revolution of 1918. Lobsen sees a European country where "war has been raging for years and has swept away every village and every town, soaking the soil in the blood of its inhabitants. And everywhere on the borders of this horrible country stand armies under arms, and priests are praying and blessing weapons."[35] This conveys very well how von Hanstein's novel was written as a critical commentary on European warfare. It portrays warfare as a pernicious feature of modern societies across Europe and the Middle East. The answer to mankind's warlike and hypocritical aberrations, according to von Hanstein, lies in individual spirituality. This distinction between organized religion and individual spirituality is quite important, as it means that Eastern religions, too, are not necessarily portrayed as a positive force. Lobsen, in fact, leaves Tibet in the first place because he is disillusioned with the morality of both ordinary people and the monks in the monasteries. In sum, neither the Buddhism of Lobsen's home country, Tibet, nor the warlike character of the inhabitants of the Middle East or of Europe are suited to lead Lobsen to be at peace with himself. Instead, Lobsen muses at the end of the novel, "The love that...Buddha and Christ have preached is not in this world and cannot prosper...Lead me home, into solitude, so that I may become a human being."[36] The attitude that Lobsen displays in Hanstein's novel is almost nihilistic, suggesting the author's serious disillusionment with European society and with any kind of organized religion at all.

Similarly, occultist writer Gustav Meyrink used Tibet as the setting for a short story dealing with science, modern civilization, and above all, warfare. His "Grillenspiel" ("Cricket's Play") tells of a German scientist called Skoper, who encounters a Tibetan *dugpa*—a quasisorcerer who can "solve and bind," that is, who has recognized that time and place do not exist. Skoper is unconvinced of the *dugpa's* powers at first, approaching the matter with European scientific skepticism. When asked whether he wants to witness the "crickets' spell," he initially scorns this piece of magic as "a well-known trick" frequently used by Chinese tricksters.[37] The *dugpa* then conjures up a large number of crickets, which congregate on a large map of Europe. They form distinct groups and begin a terrible war against each other.[38] Witnessing this incident soon leads Skoper to recognize that science cannot explain this trick, and reality and magic gradually merge into one:

> I could not get rid of the words: "He solves and he binds"; gradually they turned into something terrible in my brain;—in my imagination the twitching heap of crickets transformed into millions of dying soldiers. The nightmare of a miraculous, immense sense of responsibility strangled me, which was even more tortuous for me as I sought in vain for its root.[39]

Skoper dies in Asia, but he is able to send one last letter, together with one of the crickets, to his scientific colleagues back in Europe. Upon reading Skoper's letters, they are able to discern the face of the *dugpa* in a cloud, causing them to have a similar sense of foreboding that science cannot explain certain things in an age marked by such major upheavals as the First World War. The custodian of the Academy ends the story by muttering, "What strange shapes the clouds are taking in these horrible times of war!... Verily, one could become superstitious in one's old age."[40]

As in von Hanstein's novel, the entire plot of Meyrink's "Grillenspiel" is really an exploration of the emotions engendered through the First World War. The crickets' forming of different warring factions is clearly meant to represent different European nations at war with each other. Not only do they physically congregate on a map of Europe, but the Tibetan name for this species of crickets is alleged to be the same word as that used to describe European "foreigners." The story begins by situating the events taking place within a few weeks of the outbreak of the Second World War. While the precise logical links between Europe and Tibet are not made explicit—in fact, part of the point of the story is that differences of space and time are merely an illusion—"Grillenspiel" is a clear invocation of the violent, frightening, and sinister character of modern war.

The link between disillusionment with what the First World War symbolized for many and their fascination for the East was also obvious in the works of other, better-known authors. In Hesse's *Journey to the East*, the narrator remembers that during the time in which he embarked on his journey to the Orient,

> [O]ur country was full of saviors, prophets, and disciples, of presentiments of the end of the world or of hopes for the beginning of a Third Reich.

Shaken by war, desperate due to want and hunger, deeply disappointed by the apparent uselessness of all the sacrifices made..., our people back then was open to many fantasies...; an inclination toward Indian, Old Persian and other Eastern secrets and cults was widespread then.[41]

Similarly, Austrian author Robert Musil commented that, "Germany is awash with sects. People look to Russia, to East Asia, to India."[42] Contemporaries like Hesse and Musil made the connection between Eastern spirituality and its appeal as an alternative to war-torn European modernity. Rabindranath Tagore, after his successful lecture tour of Germany in 1921, wrote the following to Charles Freer Andrews, an English priest with strong sympathies for Gandhi and the Indian Independence Movement:

Germany today has received a violent check in her political ambition, which has produced almost a universal longing in this country to seek for spiritual resources in man in place of external success. Germany seems to have set out on a spiritual voyage to the East, to the land of sunrise—and, in spite of her dire poverty, is not merely thinking of the spinning wheel [part of the iconography of Buddhism] and some new move in the political game of gambling but of the achievement of spiritual freedom which gives us power to soar above vicissitudes of circumstances.[43]

Tagore here explained the attraction of Eastern spirituality for his German audience in terms of its potential to present an alternative to the violent political and diplomatic failures of the past—that is, the First World War above all—as well as to the poverty and economic dislocation of the present. Tagore's publisher Kurt Wolff, by no means an easily impressionable man, noticed this trend as well. In an essay explaining why he believed Tagore was so popular in Germany, Wolff mused:

The military defeat and its consequences, perceived by many Germans as a breakdown of the ideas and ideals of Western civilization, contributed immensely to the spread of this mood. I can still see the university students of those days in parks and cafés and shop clerks on the tramway immersed in their copies of Buddha's sermons... Half a dozen translations of Lao-tsu were available, and they were all read. "*Ex oriente lux*" ["Light comes from the East"] was Germany's hope for the future.[44]

Those who were personally or academically interested in the practices of Buddhism also believed that the growing interest in Buddhism in Germany was a legacy of the First World War. Wolfgang Bohn, in an article about "Buddhism and the spiritual culture of the present age," wrote:

> It is as if the World War and its legacies are being perceived as a breakdown of our entire culture; so without exception, so complete that the searching intelligence of our times seems to be losing touch with the dead gods of the pre-war era, in order to dive far back, into that culture from which our peoples once detached themselves, into the culture of Asia.[45]

In sum, those who were fascinated by Eastern spirituality during the Weimar era frequently linked their fascination to their disillusionment with the past. This could have been a criticism of the past, as opposed to a more promising future; or it could have been a criticism of Europe, as opposed to the more peaceful alternative offered by parts of Asia. Most likely, in fact, it was a combination of both, leading parts of the educated elites of Weimar Germany to think about whether ideas acquired from the East might serve to provide Europe, and particularly Germany, with a better future.

Another element that made discussing Eastern spirituality attractive was the fact that it allowed authors of fiction, cultural criticism, and travel accounts to criticize, both implicitly and explicitly, what they perceived as the main shortcomings of Germany. In the Weimar Republic, there was a plethora of movements critical of the supposed excesses of modern civilization. Many Germans feared not only a decline in moral values in all aspects of modern life, but also a decline of quality of life more generally, due to economic dislocation and political unrest and, above all, urbanization. It is certainly true that there was genuine excitement about the potential that the Weimar Republic offered in many areas, including the buzz of life in large cities.[46] Nevertheless, across the social and political spectrum, there were voices critical of the more pernicious aspects of urbanization. Shopping streets, for instance, were described by authors like Hans Fallada as materialistic spaces in which managers exploited salesmen and saleswomen for the sake of quick profit.[47]

Criticism of Weimar urban modernity also found its way to the more abstract level of morality and religion. Hermann Hesse criticized the alleged decline of religiosity and morality in Germany in an article published in the illustrated magazine *Uhu* in 1926. "The new image of the earth's surface," he wrote, "completely transformed and recast in just a few decades, and the enormous changes manifest in every city and every landscape of the world since industrialization, correspond to an upheaval in the human mind and soul." Deploring the rapid changes that had taken place in the preceding years, Hesse believed that "irreplaceable things have been lost and destroyed forever" and told his readers that, "destroyed and lost for the greater part of the civilized world are, beyond all else, the two universal foundations of life, culture, and morality: religion and customary morals."[48]

The natural environment was one of the major areas in which many commentators suggested Europe would encounter problems. Urbanization and industrialization were frequently regarded as having eradicated the primeval landscapes of Germany and were consequently perceived, just like warfare and militarism, as one of the evils of modernity. We can find this attitude toward environmental degradation and the loss of nonurban spaces reflected in much of German writing about the Himalayas, Tibet, and Eastern spirituality. Inner Asia remained one of the most inaccessible regions of the globe even during the years of the Weimar Republic. Yet compared to the urban busyness of Weimar Germany, the desolate and barren environment of Inner Asia could appear almost calming and soothing for the traveler. In the report of his own trip to Tibet, German traveler Albert Tafel told his readership that,

> I constantly had the feeling that I had been transported back into the grey pre-history of our homeland, as if I were suddenly living in the days of the migration of peoples or of Attila the Hun. To those who love to look back to past times, this primeval character exerts a magical fascination. I lived in past times and, at the same time, could see all the hustle and discoveries of our modern Europe like a faraway dream, as if it were the future.[49]

As a consequence of the preoccupation with the meaning of civilization and its effects on the environment, the Inner Asian environment itself became endowed with positive powers as it offered an alternative to those who were searching for a break from this civilization. Walter Bosshard ended his 1930 account of his travels through Tibet and Turkestan by regretting that, when arriving back in Germany, "gone were all the glories of the free and foot-loose life on the road. Central Asia lay far, far behind. Only the yearning remains and the memory of all the fine experiences."[50] In other words, the urban, industrialized, and regulated life of Weimar Germany constituted a constraining force that had been absent in Inner Asia.

For some, the environment they encountered in Tibet and the Himalayas even acquired spiritual powers. Paul Bauer, one of the many German and Austrian mountaineers who attempted to climb Kangchenjunga and Nanga Parbat during the 1920s and 1930s, elevated and personified the mountains above everything else. About Kangchenjunga, he wrote in 1933, "Like a metaphor of the greatest, inviolable by the weather, by all earthly things, he sat on his throne, in majestic calm, on top of endless spaces—so big that nothing human can persist in front of him other than longing adulation and jubilant devotion."[51] Again, Germans were looking for a higher spirituality that would allow them to make sense of contemporary developments, and they thought they would be able to find this in individual encounters with Asian nature and cultures, particularly in Tibet and the Himalayas.

Not all commentators agreed on the exact manner in which rural natural environments were linked to the potential for benefiting the human spirit. While Bauer was inspired by the sheer grandeur of Himalayan nature, university professor Konrad Guenther developed a more complex argument in an essay exploring why Buddhism, even though nihilistic in character, arose first in the lush nature of tropical India. He compared the diverse and rich nature of the tropics with that of temperate Europe, concluding that the former would eventually tire the observer precisely because of its grandeur, whereas the latter was comparable to a watercolor and much easier on the eye. Having tired of tropical nature, Guenther argued, Buddha came to recognize the vanity of human emotions and desires.[52]

Nor would all Germans have liked to exchange the "civilization" of their home for the seemingly fancy-free life of a traveler in Inner Asia. Many of the criticisms of life in Weimar Germany were voiced in the knowledge that their authors would never have to forsake all the comforts of their home country for good. Hettie Dyhrenfurth, for instance, the wife of a German mountaineer, was quite happy to be back in polite company after returning from the mountain. Having been invited to a ball at the Everest Hotel in Darjeeling, she was excited that she "could finally dress as a lady again." During her final night on the Indian subcontinent, she "was hardly able to sleep," because she was "far too excited and full of gratitude that [she] had survived everything and was allowed to return home."[53]

The intuitive nature of Eastern spirituality was another component that made it attractive to the Weimar public. In previous decades, missionaries and amateur scholars alike had criticized Tibetan Buddhism and older native belief systems for encouraging superstition and ignorance among the poorer strata of Tibetan society. Tibetan spirituality had been regarded as backward compared to European progress and rationalism. After the First World War, however, criticisms of supposed Eastern superstitiousness became both much rarer and much less acerbic and patronizing. Instead, more and more commentators defended the importance of intuition and inner visions over that of positivism. An excellent example of the debate on the importance of intuition is an exchange between the Polish occultist Ferdinand Ossendowski and the Swedish scientist Sven Hedin, which took place through the medium of German publishing houses and newspapers. This debate erupted in 1925 around Ossendowski's depiction of Inner Asia (both Mongolia and Tibet) and grew to question the very nature of truth and knowledge itself. Ossendowski had published an account of an alleged journey through Mongolia and Inner Asia in the wake of the Russian Civil War. His account, which was accessible to a readership in Germany through translations, detailed a series of prophecies uttered by the "King of the World," who, as a lama had allegedly told Ossendowski, lived in an underground kingdom north of Tibet. According to Ossendowski, the king had prophesied in 1890 that,

> All the earth will be emptied. God will turn away from it and over it there will be only night and death. Then I shall send a people, now unknown, which shall tear out the weeds of madness and vice with a strong hand and will lead those who still remain faithful to the spirit of man in the fight against Evil. They will found a new life on the earth purified by the death of nations. In the fiftieth year only three great kingdoms will appear, which will exist happily for seventy-one years. Afterwards there will be eighteen years of war and destruction. Then the peoples of Agarthi will come up from their subterranean caverns to the surface of the earth.[54]

The question that Ossendowski and Sven Hedin hotly debated was whether Ossendowski had really been to northern Tibet during his escape from the Bolsheviks. Hedin, who had attained great fame in his native Sweden and in Germany by publishing one of the most authoritative studies of Inner Asian geography, believed that Ossendowski's narrative was fabricated, since his camels could never have survived such a trip and since the few dates and locations that Ossendowski provided just did not add up. Ossendowski himself admitted that his aim had not been to provide a geographical work. For him, science could not explain the real meaning of human existence. Instead, he proposed, it was necessary to explore spiritual developments and dig beneath the supposedly superficial fact gathering of scientists such as Hedin. His book, therefore, was "supposed to become a book that had been written not with the dry, indifferent pen of the scholar but with my blood...The terrible ghost of the awakened Asia appeared to me worthier of the attention of the civilized world than the question at what point in Tibet the Hwangho River has its source."[55] In other words, the spirituality he associated with Inner Asia was far more important to Ossendowski than scientific research. Thus this debate attests to a growing skepticism with regard to the validity of Western positivism and confidence in "progress" and "civilization."

Critical attitudes toward science, however, also surfaced elsewhere, couched in a more conciliatory and less obscurantist language. Not all criticism of science needed to include dire predictions about the fate of the world, but much of it was conceived with the desire to help mankind to greater happiness. In the inaugural issue of the *Buddhistischer Weltspiegel*, published in 1919, Georg Grimm told his readers:

> Due to their very methodology, the natural sciences can never get to the true foundation of the forces active in nature; instead they always take these forces as a given. Thus they are particularly inept at shedding light on the essence of human beings. They can only show the force or forces at work in human appearance, while that true essence of a human being is the object of religious awareness, and therefore the theme of religion. Only concentrated inner vision [*Innenschau*], as practiced by the so-called religious genius, will lead into its depths,... not by the point of view of scientists, who look outwards. Precisely because of this, thoroughgoing help for our time and our people can only be expected to come from a new religious genius.[56]

The following year, Grimm took up this topic again, arguing that gathering human knowledge was futile. Buddha, he argued, sought to teach happiness, and "what does a truly happy person still need to know?"[57] Given Grimm's background as an academic and judge, this statement might seem somewhat surprising. But Grimm did not mean his statements as an exhortation to cease all scientific activity. In fact, he merely argued against the opposite extreme, an attitude in which the pursuit of science precluded the search for all deeper truths. He claimed that science had "revolutionized the heads of the masses, so that all belief is regarded as old-fashioned."[58] This, he feared, would foreclose the path to faith and real meaning forever. Grimm therefore provides yet another example of how parts of the educated elite in Weimar Germany attempted to find new and different approaches to life, as well as answers to life's most important questions, by focusing on Eastern spirituality.

Again, these sentiments did not go unchallenged. As Douglas McGetchin has argued, many in the older generation of Buddhological and Indological scholars were rather uneasy with the enthusiasm with which some of their disciples approached Eastern religion.[59] Nevertheless, the idea of acting according to intuition and seeking deeper truths hidden from science became relatively more popular during the Weimar years.[60]

Conclusion

Eastern spirituality, and Buddhism in particular, exerted a great fascination over Germans during the Weimar era, and it was especially popular among the educated elites.[61] It is difficult to determine the extent to which these ideas impacted the wider culture and politics of Germany in this period. Nevertheless, events such as the frenzy surrounding Tagore's talks in 1921, as well as the popular success of the published works discussed above, suggest that their appeal was anything but marginal. What made Buddhism, and to a lesser extent other Asian religions, so appealing in the Weimar years?

At the most basic level, Eastern religions allowed people to seek alternatives—alternatives to the mistakes of the past (such as those that had led to the outbreak of the First World War), to the rapidly increasing urbanization of Weimar society, and to the supposed overreliance on science to explain the human condition. In many ways, focusing on the East as a source for these alternatives involved a good deal of escapism and idealizing of foreign cultures. However, it involved more than that. Commentators used the East as a point of reference, as many believed that Eastern spirituality could point the way out of the problems of the past and the present, leading into a brighter future. In this sense, interest in spirituality was one of the many ways in which Weimar Germans tried to make sense of their time and find the inspiration that would allow them to answer the most basic questions of human existence. Thus, their fascination with Eastern spirituality—even if it stemmed from a critique of modern life itself—was an integral part of Weimar modernity.

Notes

1. *Teubners Erdkundliches Unterrichtswerk. 3: Die Ostfeste* (Leipzig, 1931), 89.
2. See for instance Heinz Hürten, *Deutsche Katholiken 1918 bis 1945* (Paderborn, 1992); Gerhard Besier, *The Holy See and Hitler's Germany* (Basingstoke, 2007, transl. W.R. Ward); Kurt Nowak, *Evangelische Kirche und Weimarer Republik* (Weimar, 1988); Michael Brenner and Derek Penslar, eds., *In Search of Jewish Community: Jewish Identities in Germany and Austria 1918–1933* (Bloomington, 1998); Cornelia Hecht, *Juden und Antisemitismus in der Weimarer Republik* (Bonn, 2003); Wolfgang Benz, Arnold Paucker, and Peter Pulzer, eds., *Jüdisches*

Leben in der Weimarer Republik (Tübingen, 1998); Walter Grab and Julius Schoeps, eds., *Juden in der Weimarer Republik* (Stuttgart, 1986).

3. An exception, at least in part, is Volker Zotz's excellent study of Buddhism in Germany, *Auf den glückseligen Inseln: Buddhismus in der deutschen Kultur* (Berlin, 2000).

4. For methodological discussion, see for instance Jürgen Osterhammel, "Transnationale Gesellschaftsgeschichte: Erweiterung oder Alternative?," *Geschichte und Gesellschaft* (2001), 464–79; Michael Werner and Bénédicte Zimmermann, "Vergleich, Transfer, Verflechtung: Der Ansatz der Histoire Croisée und die Herausforderung des Transnationalen," *Geschichte und Gesellschaft* (2002), 607–36. This interest in Eastern religions was also transnational in scope, not just in content. Germans and other Europeans, as well as North Americans, all became more interested in Eastern spirituality during this period, for interrelated reasons.

5. Athanasius Kircher, *China monumentis: quà sacris quà profanis, nec non variis naturæ and artis spectaculis, aliarumque rerum memorabilium argumentis illustrata* (Amstelodami, 1667); Jürgen Offermanns, *Der lange Weg des Zen-Buddhismus nach Deutschland* (Stockholm, 2002), 115–32.

6. Peter Bishop, *The Myth of Shangri-La: Tibet, Travel Writing and the Western Creation of Sacred Landscape* (London, 1989), 245. For details of the military expedition, see Patrick French, *Younghusband: The Last Great Imperial Adventurer* (London, 1995).

7. Elisabeth Booz, *A Guide to Tibet* (London, 1986), 138–9; Donald Lopez, *The Story of Buddhism* (San Francisco, 2001).

8. Indra Sengupta, *From Salon to Discipline: State, University, and Indology in Germany, 1821–1914* (Heidelberg, 2005).

9. Emil Schlagintweit, *Buddhism in Tibet: Illustrated by Literary Documents and Objects of Religious Worship, With an Account of the Buddhist Systems Preceding It in India* (Leipzig, 1863), 12.

10. Douglas McGetchin, "Wayward Disciples: Indology and Buddhism in *fin-de-siècle* Germany" in *Sanskrit and "Orientalism": Indology and Comparative Linguistics in Germany, 1750–1958*, ed. Douglas McGetchin et al. (New Delhi, 2004), 309; Heinrich Dumoulin, "Buddhism and Nineteenth-Century German Philosophy," *Journal of the History of Ideas* (1981): 457–70; Offermanns, *Weg*, 205–8.

11. Walter Schmidt, "Die 'Fremdreligionen' in Deutschland: Hinduismus—Buddhismus—Islam," *Evangelische Zentrale für Weltanschauungsfragen, Information Nr. 46* (Stuttgart, 1971): 8.

12. Zotz, *Inseln*, 171–81.

13. The majority of the inhabitants of Ladakh were ethnically Tibetan, and almost all Western Tibetan trade with South Asia (mainly in wool and salt) took place through Ladakh. This had made the area an ideal place for studying Tibetan culture for those Europeans who did not have the permission

to enter Tibet proper. For some accounts by and about the Moravians, see August H. Francke, *A History of Western Tibet: One of the Unknown Empires* (London, n.d.); Heinrich A. Jäschke, *Handwörterbuch der tibetischen Sprache* (Gnadau, 1871); Frank Seeliger, *"Einer prügelt uns und der andere bringt uns Religion…": Fremdheitserfahrungen im West-Himalaya-Gebiet aus Sicht der Herrnhuter Missionare* (Herrnhut, 2003); Hartmut Walravens, "The Moravian Mission and Its Research on the Language and Culture of Western Tibet," *Oriens Extremus* (1992), 159–69.

14. Klaus-Josef Notz, *Der Buddhismus in Deutschland in seinen Selbstdarstellungen* (Frankfurt, 1984), 46; Schmidt, "Fremdreligionen," 9.

15. See the website of the Buddhistisches Haus at www.buddhistisches-haus. de/history.php?lang=de; B. and R. Hildebrandt and Christiane Knop, eds., *Gartenstadt Frohnau* (Berlin, 1985), 31. Dahlke opposed some of Georg Grimm's interpretations of Buddhism and distanced himself from the practice of using Western philosophy to explain central tenets of Buddhism. Notz, *Buddhismus*, 65.

16. *Buddhistischer Weltspiegel* (1919–1920), cover.

17. *Zeitschrift für Buddhismus* (1921), 181.

18. Each edition of the *Zeitschrift für Buddhismus* contained an overview of related events and occurrences across the world, as well as book reviews. The *Buddhistischer Weltspiegel* devoted even more space to announcements of events, albeit more limited to Buddhist ones.

19. *DAAD Letter* (2007), 14.

20. Krishna Dutta and Andrew Robinson, eds., *Selected Letters of Rabindranath Tagore* (Cambridge, 1997), 273; "Rabindranath Tagore in Berlin," *Vossische Zeitung* (June 2, 1921).

21. Dutta and Robinson, *Selected Letters*, 270.

22. Ibid., 271, note 2.

23. Hermann Hesse, *Siddhartha: Eine indische Dichtung* (Berlin, 1922).

24. Hermann Hesse, *My Belief: Essays on Life and Art*, ed. Theodore Ziolkowski, transl. Denver Lindley (London, 1976), 382.

25. Ibid., 379.

26. Ibid., 391.

27. Hermann Hesse, *Die Morgenlandfahrt* (Zürich, 1932), and *Das Glasperlenspiel* (Zürich, 1943).

28. Graf Hermann Keyserling, *Das Reisetagebuch eines Philosophen* (Darmstadt, 1920, two vols., 4th ed.), 375.

29. Otfried von Hanstein, *Der Klosterschüler von Taschi-lunpo* (Hamburg, 1923); Gustav Meyrink, *Fledermäuse: Erzählungen, Fragmente, Aufsätze*, ed. Eduard Frank (Munich, 1981), 53–67.

30. Von Hanstein wrote several dozen entertainment novels, many of which had Asian themes. Meyrink was one of the most famous occultist writers of Weimar Germany, producing a wealth of novels and short stories that were often set

in the Orient. His novel *The Golem* sold almost 150,000 copies between 1915 and 1917, making Meyrink known beyond a narrow audience of occultists. *Deutsche Biographische Enzyklopädie* (Munich, 1995–2000), vol. 4, 378 and vol. 7, 118.

31. Alexandra David-Néel, *Heilige und Hexer: Glaube und Aberglaube im Land des Lamaismus* (Leipzig, 1931).

32. "Geleitwort des Verlegers und Herausgebers," *Zeitschrift für Buddhismus* (1920): 1.

33. Nikolaus Wachsmann, "Marching under the Swastika: Ernst Jünger and National Socialism, 1918–33," *Journal of Cotemporary History* (1998): 578; Rolf von Bockel, *Kurt Hiller und die Gruppe Revolutionärer Pazifisten, 1926–1933* (Hamburg, 1990); Dieter Riesenberger, *Die katholische Friedensbewegung in der Weimarer Republik* (Düsseldorf, 1976); Modris Eksteins, "*All Quiet on the Western Front* and the Fate of a War," *Journal of Contemporary History* (1980): 350.

34. Hanstein, *Klosterschüler von Taschi-lunpo*, 149.

35. Ibid., 185.

36. Ibid., 193.

37. Ibid., 63.

38. Meyrink, *Fledermäuse*, 53–67.

39. Ibid., 65.

40. Ibid., 67.

41. Hesse, *Morgenlandfahrt*, 14.

42. Christoph Gellner, *Weisheit, Kunst und Lebenskunst: Fernöstliche Religion und Philosophie bei Hermann Hesse und Bertolt Brecht* (Mainz, 1994), 103.

43. Dutta and Robinson, eds., *Selected Letters*, 274.

44. Michael Ermarth, ed., *Kurt Wolff* (Chicago, 1991), 127.

45. Wolfgang Bohn, "Buddhismus und Geistes-Kultur der Gegenwart," *Zeitschrift für Buddhismus* (1921): 3.

46. See, for instance, Janet Ward, *Weimar Surfaces: Urban Visual Culture in 1920s Germany* (Berkeley, 2001).

47. Quoted in Deborah Small, "Sadly materialistic…: Perceptions of Shops and Shopping Streets in Weimar Berlin," *Journal of Popular Culture* (2000): 150.

48. Quoted in ibid., 365.

49. Albert Tafel, *Meine Tibetreise* (Stuttgart, 1923, second ed.), 212.

50. Walter Bosshard, *Durch Tibet und Turkistan: Reisen im unberührten Asien* (Stuttgart, 1930), 239.

51. Paul Bauer, *Um den Kantsch: Der zweite deutsche Angriff auf den Kangchendzönga 1931* (Munich, 1933), 7. Bauer later became one of the most prominent Himalayan mountaineers of the Third Reich, participating in several expeditions to Nanga Parbat, the so-called "German mountain" or "mountain of loyalty".

52. Konrad Guenther, "Die Tropennatur als Führerin zur Abkehr vom Leben," *Zeitschrift für Buddhismus* (1920): 24.

53. Hettie Dyhrenfurth, *Memsahb im Himalaja* (Leipzig, 1931), 71.

54. Ferdinand Ossendowski, *Tiere, Menschen und Götter* (Frankfurt, 1924), 358–60; Ferdinand Ossendowski, *Beasts, Men and Gods* (London, 1922), 314.

55. Sven Hedin, *Ossendowski und die Wahrheit* (Leipzig, 1925), 31.

56. Georg Grimm, "Zur Einführung," *Buddhistischer Weltspiegel* (1919): 3.

57. Georg Grimm, "Ist die Lehre des Buddha Wissenschaft?," *Buddhistischer Weltspiegel* (1920): 100.

58. Ibid.

59. McGetchin, "Disciples," 313–26.

60. Interestingly, historians have noted similar trends in other realms of Weimar culture, such as the geopolitics of Karl Haushofer and Ewald Banse—although it must be clear that we are talking here about similarities in method, not in aims or content. David Thomas Murphy, *The Heroic Earth: Geopolitical Thought in Weimar Germany, 1918–1933* (Kent, OH, 1997), 56.

61. This interest continued throughout the 1930s and early 1940s. Mountaineers and scientists continued to write about Eastern religions, and occultist literature expanded on some of the themes developed in the 1920s. See Thomas Neuhaus, "British and German Representations of Tibet and the Himalayas, c. 1890–1959" (Dissertation, University of Cambridge, 2008).

VII

Visualizing the Republic: State Representation and Public Ritual in Weimar Germany

Nadine Rossol

Visual impressions shape our perception of historical time periods and remind us of the importance of photographs, pictures, or films for the reconstruction of the past.[1] The term "Weimar culture" generally evokes a set of mental images, despite the fact that very few of us will have personal experiences of 1920s Germany. Some of these snapshots are of the stunning Marlene Dietrich, the modern architecture of the Bauhaus, or Charleston-dancing girls in short dresses. Breathtaking cultural prosperity stands in sharp contrast to political turmoil and economic depression. In these images, Weimar Germany was crisis-ridden and exciting at the same time, although we need to keep in mind that the admiration of Weimar culture is in part a post-1945 phenomenon.[2]

After the collapse of the Nazi regime, the limelight of Weimar culture shone even more brightly. The division into spectacular culture on the one hand and disastrous politics on the other has long impeded scholars from concentrating on an area in which the fusion of culture and politics was practiced—republican state representation. Attempts of the young republic to promote its democratic state to the German population with the help of symbols, monuments, and festivities have long been neglected in historical research. Instead, republican representation has been negatively contrasted to the allegedly more successful Nazi propaganda.[3]

Recently, historians have started to challenge this negative evaluation of Weimar Germany's self-representation.[4] In what follows, I will argue that republican officials not only were well aware of the need to create a positive impression of their young democratic state, but that they also applied highly innovative means to achieve this end. State representation in 1920s Germany echoed modern cultural developments with a stress on three areas: the visual, the inclusive, and the spectacular. Both mass entertainment and elite culture in the Weimar Republic were largely "a culture of the visual"[5]; and the same holds true for the republic's state representation, which was also characterized by a particular "inclusiveness"—that is, the encouragement to participate actively in public festivities, great state occasions, and even the designing of the republic's symbols and monuments. In addition, there was an emphasis on the overall impression of representative events, as can be seen in the ways in which they were planned and staged. This is what I mean by the "spectacular" aspect of representative culture in Weimar Germany.

This chapter will examine the ways in which the Weimar Republic represented itself, but it will also show that Weimar state representation was a matter of some controversy. Not everyone wanted to be part of the new republic, no matter how inclusively and openly the young democratic state presented itself. Popular participation entailed scathing criticism of the republic by some, while others felt that the republic needed to elaborate a more distinctive message to win the support of the German public.[6] Of course, these contested and unresolved issues of republican representation reflected the pluralism of Weimar democracy. Even within the republic's framework no unified blueprint existed, but rather different and sometimes contradictory opinions on how democracy should be presented.

Shaping the Face of the Republic: State Symbols and Republican Representation

The totality with which the Weimar Republic approached cultural state representation still amazes nowadays, mainly because we would not expect the young republic to have taken representational issues so seriously. After the end of the First World War and the collapse of the monarchy, a democratic state was introduced to the German population for the first time. To deal appropriately with the challenges of republican state representation, a new official position, the *Reichskunstwart,* was created on a full-time basis in 1920. The art historian Dr. Edwin Redslob, director of the state arts collection in Stuttgart, was appointed the first *Reichskunstwart* and was charged with the task of giving artistic shape to republican representation. The *Reichskunstwart* or, as one newspaper later called him, "the advertising chief of the republic,"[7] was to be involved in all areas of cultural state representation. This included the creation of new state symbols, the staging of state celebrations, and the erection of monuments as well as the redesign of stamps, seals, coins, and bank notes. Redslob contacted artists, designers, and craftsmen who would help to shape the public image of the republic. In practice, the work of the *Reichskunstwart* was made difficult by limited financial means, a small staff, and the unwillingness of several ministries to collaborate. The *Reichskunstwart*'s office had a consultative function for all areas of cultural state representation, but its power was limited when, for example, the post ministry did not want to cooperate in the redesign of its stamps. Politicians of the nationalist right repeatedly demanded the complete abolition of the office. More often than not, the *Reichskunstwart* had to defend his office, with its very limited funds, from further cuts.[8] In hindsight it seems difficult to understand why an office with the goal of advertising and promoting the republic lacked a sufficient budget and the wider competencies that were necessary for it to perform effectively. But we have to keep in mind that the republic was testing the water with Redslob's office and had no experience to build upon.

Although the removal of former imperial insignia by the republican state was a measure that followed clear-cut official regulations, it was less clear what a new representative style should look like. Historians of state representation have argued that purely democratic representative forms do not exist, because democratic states always adopt, change, and reinterpret symbols of previous periods.[9] This observation should not surprise us, because in fact most kinds of state partially rely on older ways of representation, and the Weimar Republic was no exception. The young democracy kept the German eagle, the traditional German state symbol, and modernized its design. In October 1922, *Reichskunstwart* Edwin Redslob informed the Reich Ministry of the Interior that he wanted to encourage industry, craftspeople, and artists to use the German eagle more frequently in order to popularize the symbolic representation of the new state.[10] Consequently, the eagle was woven onto pillows and curtains and printed on decorative pictures, wallpaper, official forms, and envelopes.[11] For these activities the *Reichskunstwart* relied strongly on commercial artists. Redslob was convinced that commercial art fitted the new republic well, because it represented simplicity, efficiency, and artistic quality without superfluous decoration; and he argued that the spread of well-designed products held an enormous potential for introducing good artistic quality to a mass audience.[12] The *Reichskunstwart* believed sincerely that German citizens could be educated to appreciate modern art at a time when the young republic wanted to present itself as a modernizing and progressive state. The German populace did not always share this priority.

When the *Reichskunstwart* supervised the redesign of the new German eagle, the artistic taste of Weimar society was put to the test. The republic's state symbol needed to be stripped of its imperial signs and redesigned. To do so, Redslob invited several famous modernist artists to suggest drafts of their ideas for a modification of the traditional state symbol. Among them were the expressionists Karl Schmidt-Rottluff and Ludwig Gies, Siegmund von Weech and Peter Behrens as representatives of the modern reform movement, and Rudolf Koch standing for a modernist direction inspired by craftsmanship. The *Reichskunstwart* favored the Expressionist design of Schmidt-Rottluff's eagle and suggested this draft in April 1920 to the Reich Ministry of the Interior, which passed it on to the cabinet for approval. But the cabinet rejected Karl Schmidt-Rottluff's eagle in the summer of 1920, and the press tore it to shreds, comparing the eagle's appearance to "a frightened parrot."[13] A new solution needed to be found, and in the end, the republican state used a number of different versions of the German eagle.[14] For Redslob, a clear and modern design of the German eagle stood for more than a successfully reshaped state symbol; he found that it fit the new republican state well.

Nevertheless, the republic's "advertising chief" admitted that hasty public reactions in newspapers and letters had prevented a calm and concentrated working process. The *Reichskunstwart* lamented that, "The speed and impatience of our time impedes and complicates anything that does not immediately lead to successful results...[O]ur society seems to prefer artificial flowers to seeds that need time and patience to grow."[15] While the importance of the visual dimension of state representation was obvious for an art historian and experienced museum curator like Edwin Redslob, including the population in the process of its development was a more difficult task.

Naturally, republican officials, with the *Reichskunstwart* at the forefront, knew well that successfully popularizing the reshaped symbols was as crucial as designing them. Redslob published relentlessly on aspects of republican state representation, attempting to enhance a wider understanding of the goals and responsibilities of the republic.[16] In 1926 the *Reichskunstwart* staged an exhibition offering the first overview of the development of republican symbols. Not limited to the presentation of coins, stamps, or coats of arms, the display included designs for honorary presents and decorative objects for offices, as well as photographs of republican festivities.[17] Redslob convinced the Reich Ministry of the Interior to support his project by drawing attention to the public interest in how the new German democracy presented itself, an interest that did not always make his job an easy one, as we have seen. According to Redslob, "[A]n exhibition of the republic's new symbols would be of great help to spread the republican idea to a wider public."[18] Indeed, Redslob's aim was twofold— to improve popular acceptance of the new symbols, and to strengthen the position of his office at the same time. For three weeks, the exhibition on republican state representation was shown within the parliament buildings in Berlin. Although it was open to everyone, it was aimed more specifically at ministerial officials than the general public. While the liberal press praised the results, it criticized the somewhat hidden location and the limited opening hours.[19]

This criticism might have been justified for the Berlin exhibition. However, unlike other small exhibitions, this one traveled throughout Germany. From 1927 to 1928, it was shown in Munich, Nuremberg, Düsseldorf, Kassel, Frankfurt, and Hamburg, to name but a few of the venues.[20] Redslob's exhibition was frequently part of others in museums or local city halls. In Darmstadt, for example, it was incorporated into a display dedicated to the works of Rudolf Koch.[21] While municipal authorities were clearly interested in having the *Reichskunstwart*'s exhibition in their city halls or museums, financial difficulties created problems. The costs of transportation from one location to another had to be paid by the cities or museums.[22] Redslob tried to persuade the Reich Ministry of the Interior to cover some of the costs, but to little avail. Eventually, the Ministry granted 3,600 RM to Redslob for making changes to the original exhibition that would allow it to be transported more easily.[23]

In 1928 parts of Redslob's exhibition were also included at the international publishing fair *Pressa* in Cologne. While the public presentation of state symbols at the 1926 exhibition had concentrated on the recent efforts of the young republic, at the *Pressa* the new republican symbols were part of a presentation stressing the historical and political roots of the German nation. Reshaped state symbols were framed by political and historical documents covering German history from 1815 to the Weimar years. With this inclusion of the Weimar Republic in the development of German history, the state communicated an important message: republican democracy was not atypical for Germany, as nationalists liked to suggest, but linked to the historical development of the country.[24] The *Reichskunstwart* was in charge of decorating the room in Cologne in which the republic presented its symbols. Here we find a visually striking and almost playful arrangement of different republican signs. The walls were painted red with 3,000 small golden eagles printed on them. Furthermore, the introduction of the Weimar Constitution and the German eagle were produced as stain glass windows and put on display in the room.[25] This decor underlined the presence of the republican state and stressed the political context of the exhibition. Redslob remained faithful to his idea of educating the public. When part of the exhibition was held again in 1929—this time as part of an advertising convention in Berlin—the journal *Gebrauchsgraphik* praised the originality of a display of different versions of the German eagle. The writer captured Redslob's leitmotiv when he stated that "the usual way of simply adding one artist's design after another has been abandoned here. Attempts have been made to illustrate how different artists solved the same task, showing us the right path for the creation of artistic solutions."[26]

One issue that was closely related to the idea of enhancing the appeal of the republic through visual signs remained unresolved in Weimar Germany. This was the highly controversial question of whether the republican state should bestow decorations and medals. Such insignia had been an obsession of the governing and military elites of Imperial Germany; and in order to assert the principle of democratic equality, the Weimar Constitution did not allow medals and titles to be bestowed or accepted.[27] However, some republicans disagreed with this policy, claiming that decorations and medals could provide a good opportunity to honor deserving citizens of the democratic state. Publicly, the *Reichskunstwart* never criticized the status quo. In his diary, however, Redslob described the republic's decision not to use these signs of community as "plain stupid."[28] Some republican newspapers expressed a similar point of view. In 1922 the *Vossische Zeitung* was the first democratic newspaper to state that honorary republican decorations could reach the hearts of the citizens better than other representative forms.[29]

Not all republican newspapers agreed. Some accused the supporters of republican decorations of playing into the hands of the republic's enemies.[30] The Social Democratic newspaper *Vorwärts* called titles, decorations, and medals "fuss of Imperial Germany"; and the left-wing journal *Die Weltbühne* asserted that it was one of the republic's moral principles for citizens to fulfill their tasks and serve the state without receiving awards for it.[31] These diverse views persisted throughout the existence of the Weimar Republic. Not surprisingly, nationalist and antirepublican newspapers observed with amusement the uneasiness of the republican side when discussing this matter.[32] Eventually, republican organizations and democratic parties filled this vacuum with their own badges and signs.[33]

From the foregoing we can see how the republic was trying to find a new way of representing itself that would break with imperial traditions. While some republicans believed that any similarities to Imperial precedents were a discredit to the republic, others sought to endow traditional representative forms with new republican connotations. Yet their attempts to achieve popular participation often generated reactions that were different from those that republican officials had hoped for.

"Death is black, blood is red, and golden shines the flame": State Funerals in Weimar Germany

The Weimar Republic outlived several of its leading politicians. Foreign Minister Walther Rathenau was assassinated in 1922, Reich President Friedrich Ebert died unexpectedly in 1925; and Foreign Minister Gustav Stresemann passed away in 1929. Republican politicians and officials hoped that state funerals for these important figures would help stabilize the republic's political culture.[34] Republican officials and liberal newspapers told the German public that the tragic deaths should be turned into defining moments of national unity and expressions of republican dedication that would honor the work of the deceased politicians. Although republicans liked to claim otherwise, the success of this strategy was debatable. The deaths of Rathenau, Ebert, and Stresemann did not unite German society behind a republican cause. Political divisions, which extended to questioning the legitimacy of a republican democracy as the right political system, were not overcome by collective mourning. However, the staging of memorial ceremonies undoubtedly served as practice for other and more original ceremonial concepts tried out by republican governments.

State funerals and memorial ceremonies were characterized by representative methods that were typical of Weimar Germany's performance culture. Their staging became increasingly spectacular with growing emphasis on their visual effect and the involvement of onlookers, both of which were intended to create a long-lasting impression. State funerals and memorial ceremonies fell under the jurisdiction of Edwin Redslob, who believed that there was more at stake than just a respectful farewell. For the *Reichskunstwart*, the republican state defined itself by the way it honored its dead.[35] Historian Volker Ackermann argues rightly that the new style of memorial ceremonies owed much to Redslob's involvement.[36]

In the summer of 1922, the assassination of Foreign Minister Walther Rathenau by nationalist forces shocked the republic. Following on from the murder of the politician Matthias Erzberger in the previous year as well as several other assassination attempts, Rathenau's demise was considered a serious threat to the survival of the republican state.[37] Rathenau's memorial ceremony on June 27, 1922 was the first state-staged ceremonial event to take place in the German parliament in the Weimar years.[38] Similar to the shaping of state symbols, Walther Rathenau's funeral had to embody a republican style. This style, however, had to be created from scratch, because there was no republican tradition to build on. The memorial ceremony in the Reichstag started with Beethoven's "Coriolanus Overture." Reich President Ebert then bowed to the coffin of his dead friend and delivered a speech; this was followed by a speech by the parliament's vice-president. To the sound of Wagner's "Götterdämmerung" lamenting the killing of the heroic Siegfried, the doors of the Reichstag opened and the coffin was carried outside where crowds of people and the military had gathered to honor Rathenau.[39] Afterwards, the coffin was taken to the cemetery.

Edwin Redslob had chosen the pieces of music played at the ceremony. In particular, the mourning piece for Siegfried captured brilliantly the nature of the event. The cowardly assassination of the foreign minister was equated with the killing of the young Siegfried, the hero of the medieval Nibelungen saga. As historian Manuela Achilles writes, "it seems fair to assume that the audience knew the story behind the music: Siegfried slain by Hagen is lifted on the shield by King Gunther's men. While the corpse is carried out of sight, the mourning tune transforms into a triumphal praise of Siegfried's heroism."[40] With this obvious reference, the republic connected its late foreign minister to a legendary figure of German national culture and showed that the national narratives of the country did not necessarily have to be dominated by the Right.[41] But these were not just efforts to create national heroism—the republican state needed to be made visible at the ceremony as well. The *Reichskunstwart* focused on the republican colors present at the ceremony when he summarized his impressions. Redslob remarked: "When I put the flag with the German eagle over the coffin, I felt that from now onwards this flag was again part of our history. The shining colors black-red-gold were repeated in the dark of the coffin and in the red and yellow flowers of the wreaths. The colors recalled Hoffmann von Fallersleben's words: death is black, blood is red, and golden shines the flame."[42]

In his diary of the Weimar years, Harry Graf Kessler commented on the effects of Rathenau's memorial ceremony. He described the moment at which the performance of Wagner's funeral music for the dead hero provided the emotionally overwhelming climax to the event as the coffin was carried outside the parliament building. According to Kessler, everyone in the parliament felt the extraordinary character of this moment.[43] The predominant atmosphere in the days and weeks after Rathenau's assassination was a sense of shock combined with the feeling that republican democracy needed to be defended against the nationalist right.[44] Eight years afterwards, the left-wing journalist Carl von Ossietzky reminded his readers that this event had been one of the few occasions when the German people had been willing to fight for the republic.[45] Effectively, the killing turned Walther Rathenau into a republic martyr, a role his life and his works had never predestined him for.[46]

With its decoration, the choice of music, moving gestures, and speeches of praise, the mourning ceremony for Rathenau had conveyed an atmosphere of mythical heroism with the republican state at its core. The parliament as the location, the republican flag on the coffin, the Reich President bowing respectfully to his dead foreign minister—all these elements visually illustrated republican state authority. It was a sad but spectacular beginning for republican ceremonies, with an obvious stress on the overall emotional and historical impression. Three years later, in 1925, Redslob remembered that the greatest difficulty had been to "fill the ceremony with actions" and connect it emotionally to the people. The *Reichskunstwart* found that the opening of the parliament's doors and the carrying of the coffin outside had achieved this popular involvement.[47] Indeed, the opening of the Reichstag doors, linking indoor ceremonies for selected audiences to the crowds gathered outside, found its way into the standard ritual repertoire of Constitution Day festivities in Weimar Germany (as we will see in the last section).

Attempts to increase popular participation became more important in the arrangements of Friedrich Ebert's funeral. Here we see the shift from an indoor to an outdoor event, a development typical of public performance culture in the 1920s. The death of President Ebert happened unexpectedly on February 28, 1925, shortly after the press had reported that he was on the way to recovery from his illness. The Social Democratic Party and its leading politicians insisted on a ceremony in the parliament and a long cortège through Berlin, so that republican organizations and the general public alike could see the coffin. The office of the Reich President feared that this might turn the memorial ceremony into a party-based political event.[48] After all, although Friedrich Ebert had tried to be a president for all Germans, he had also been a leading figure of Social Democracy. Eventually a compromise was reached. The main ceremony was held in the house of the president, while the cortège went from the Brandenburg Gate to the Reichstag building, where it stopped outside for a short mourning ceremony before continuing on to the Potsdam railway station, where the coffin remained for a while so that people could say their farewells. Afterwards it was taken to Ebert's hometown of Heidelberg for the funeral.[49] Ebert's coffin was covered with the flag of the Reich President in which the black-red-gold colors of the republic were present. The black eagle, designed by Rudolf Koch and Siegmund von Weech, was displayed on a yellow background with a red frame around it. Redslob had been involved in the creation of this flag,[50] and it had been present whenever the Reich President or his office engaged on official business. At Friederich Ebert's funeral, crowds of people saw the coffin covered with it.

The *Reichskunstwart* prepared the house of the president for the memorial service. Redslob covered the mirrors and windows to create a dignified and solemn atmosphere.[51] Republican newspapers described the decoration as "tasteful," "simple and dignified," and they found that it "was giving form to republican mourning." The atmosphere was almost unreal with the dark rooms, candlelight, and overpowering smell of flowers.[52] The memorial ceremony started with the funeral march from Beethoven's *"Eroica"* Symphony, played by the orchestra of the state opera, followed by a choir and a speech by Chancellor Luther. A choir then sang again, and the ceremony ended with music by Mozart. A select audience attended, among them representatives of different ministries as well as of Germany's cultural elite.[53]

In the procession, members of the police force and the military preceded the coffin on its way through Berlin, followed by family members and relatives, officials from the office of the Reich President, and the organizers of the state funeral. Then came representatives of the government, the parliament, and the German states, who were followed by highly placed civil servants, state secretaries, representatives of German cities, and other participants from the memorial ceremony. Bringing up the rear of the procession were organizations, associations, and anyone else who wanted to join in.[54] The cortège passed between street lights covered with black cloth, pillars crowned with bowls of incense, and republican flags.

The SPD newspaper *Vorwärts* praised Ebert's funeral as an event that had brought together people from different classes of society. The liberal *Vossische Zeitung* stated that the republic had now found its representative form.[55] Nationalist newspapers saw this differently, of course. The *Deutsche Tageblatt* claimed that the republic had always despised the great traditions of the country but had buried Friedrich Ebert like a hero to offer something spectacular to the people. According to this nationalist newspaper, "a people robbed of its soul and tradition needed more than staged republican festivities."[56] Despite this criticism of style and form, the impact of the event must have been very impressive when even antire-publican newspapers felt bound to comment on its staging. A short silent film of Ebert's state funeral, showing scenes from Berlin and Heidelberg, communicated the solemn atmosphere with crowds of people, military and police parades, flowers, and flags. It appeared in the cinemas as part of the newsreels before the main film began.[57]

By increasing the possibility of popular participation, Friedrich Ebert's funeral continued a development that was still in its infancy at the memorial ceremony for Walther Rathenau. Although Rathenau's coffin had been deliberately shown to the crowds outside, the funeral arrangements for Ebert enabled people to participate actively in the event by paying their respects to the coffin. For the state funeral of Gustav Stresemann, efforts to involve the population increased even more. Like Ebert, Foreign Minister Stresemann died suddenly after a brief illness. He passed away in the autumn of 1929. Stresemann's funeral, like Ebert's, was filmed and scenes from it were featured in cinema newsreels. They offer remarkable impressions of the atmosphere and the staging of the event. The sound of drums and church bells enhanced the atmosphere of mourning as crowds of people waited for the coffin to pass. The coffin was covered with the republican flag.[58]

When the arrangements for Stresemann's memorial ceremony were discussed, Edwin Redslob suggested to Chancellor Müller to bow to the coffin before the chancellor began his commemorative speech. The late Reich President Ebert had done the same at Rathenau's coffin and, in so doing, had created a very impressive image. According to Redslob, this gesture would provide a moment of contemplation and express a last farewell.[59] The memorial ceremony for Stresemann was again held in the Reichstag. Afterwards the cortège moved to the Foreign Ministry, where it paused for several minutes before continuing to the cemetery.[60] The *Reichskunstwart* considered this silent pause as the emotional climax of the event.[61] People could not only watch the cortège and pay their respects when the coffin passed, but they could also actively participate by following the coffin. Harry Graf Kessler emphasized that Stresemann's funeral was not just a state funeral, but also the people's own farewell to their late foreign minister.[62]

In April 1925 the *Reichskunstwart* asserted that the importance of these state ceremonies reached far beyond paying tribute to dedicated politicians of the young republic. He stated, "[I]t is sad that the great festivities of the republic which united the country and its people have been memorial ceremonies. The representation of the state has to be based on the spirit of these events."[63] Again we find the hope that a foundation had been created for future republican festivities that would represent the whole nation.

Republican Aesthetics and Mass Choreography: Constitution Day Festivities in the Republic

National holidays and state festivities are essential for states, particularly for new ones, because they offer a sense of belonging and community.[64] To achieve this unifying effect in Weimar Germany, the events celebrated needed to be important enough for people from different classes, affiliations, and parties to appreciate them. Many supporters of the republic believed that the signing of the Weimar Constitution on August 11, 1919 provided the appropriate date for a republican holiday.[65] However, Constitution Day did not become an official holiday for the whole country, because the German parliament never voted with a majority for it. There were alternative suggestions that represented different political reference points in the sharply divided Reichstag. The extreme left suggested November 9; sections within the SPD were in favor of May 1; and the nationalist parties proposed to commemorate the foundation of the German *Kaiserreich* on January 18.[66] A consensus on this issue never emerged, and the young democratic state missed the opportunity to write a national holiday into its constitution.

Nevertheless, the fact that Constitution Day never became a public holiday did not mean that it was not celebrated. Its first celebration, initiated by the Wirth government, took place in August 1921 with a ceremony in Berlin's opera house. In August 1922 the official celebration moved to the Reichstag building, a location that had been "consecrated through the memorial ceremony for Walther Rathenau" staged there a few weeks before.[67] The set-up for annual Constitution Day festivities organized by the government remained rather traditional, with classical music, choral pieces, and poetry framing the main speech in front of a selected audience. During the celebration, military and police bands played to entertain the people gathered outside the building. After the official festive act, the parliament doors opened, and politicians stepped outside and beheld, together with the crowds, the Reich President receiving the military honors. Two elements clearly derived from the ceremony for Rathenau: the parliament as location for important celebrations and the opening of its doors. Indeed, Redslob stated with satisfaction in 1925 that the style of Constitution Day celebrations "is sober and serious, but at the same time the celebration is connected to music and military spectacle for the people

gathered in front of the parliament who have shown their wish to participate in the event."[68] This element of public involvement was important for
the *Reichskunstwart*, who believed that state celebrations should include a
combination of political, cultural, popular, and sporting aspects to create
genuine popular festivities.[69]

Republican officials in charge of organizing activities for Constitution
Day realized quickly that annual ceremonies in the Reichstag had to be
complemented by more popular and inclusive festivities to create true celebrations for the people. Parades, sport competitions, children's festivals,
and other forms of popular entertainment were slowly added to the day's
festivities. Redslob demanded in April 1923 that, "[T]he youth should
celebrate Constitution Day with dances, singing, and competitions,
because this will help to root the commemoration of the republican constitution in their minds." He suggested that celebrations take place in all
stadiums and sports fields. Government representatives should attend, and
local officials—school principals or mayors—should give out awards for
sporting achievements signed by the president of the republic.[70] Schools
and sports clubs put most of these ideas into practice from the mid-1920s
onwards.[71]

Organizers of Constitution Day celebrations in Berlin and elsewhere
considered the inclusion of sporting and popular entertainment necessary
to enhance the general appeal of such events. Many republicans, among
them *Reichskunstwart* Redslob, saw the incorporation of such attractions as
the right way to stage inclusive festivities. In 1925 the journal of the republican organization *Reichsbanner Schwarz-Rot-Gold* published two juxtaposed
photographs on its cover, which ironically compared the styles of Weimar
and Imperial Germany. The caption was "Once and Nowadays." This jux-
taposition suggests that a military parade devoid of ordinary citizens was
once considered to be a popular celebration in Berlin in 1913. The 1925
Constitution Day celebration in Berlin, on the other hand, had citizens celebrating together. According to this representation, republican celebrations
were not just inclusive but also were a festive community of equals, thereby
representing in microcosm the main principle of the young German democracy. However, other republicans believed that this strategy had no benefits.
On the contrary, it seemed to them that the republican and democratic
aspect of these events—their political character—was being watered down
and the celebrations turned into an apolitical festive circus. We have seen
that this was the basic conflict on many representative issues within the
republican camp. It was to remain unresolved. *Die Weltbühne* objected that
parades staged by the republic simply imitated traditions of the nationalist

right without creating genuine republican forms. The journal cautioned that the republic wrongly equated big parades with deep-rooted republican beliefs.[72] The warning was not unjustified, in that the appeal of popular festive elements, parades, and sports activities did not necessarily turn the people enjoying them into convinced republicans. Republican newspapers and organizations reported that sports competitions held at schools were a distraction from the real purpose of these events, which was to celebrate Constitution Day. Antirepublican schoolteachers preferred to focus on sports instead of finding words of praise for the Weimar Constitution.[73] In 1929 the SPD politician Carlo Mierendorff commented on this problem when outlining his ideas for increasing the popularity of Constitution Day in a report to the *Reichskunstwart*. Mierendorff pointed out that sports competitions in honor of Constitution Day had to be closely related to the reason for their staging in order to prevent them from turning into apolitical entertainment events.[74]

In August 1929, the republic celebrated its tenth anniversary on an unprecedented scale in Berlin and elsewhere. Sports competitions, parades and marches, public concerts, car races, air shows, and celebrations of political parties characterized the day. For the first time, the republican state expanded its official festival schedule and included an afternoon celebration in Berlin's sports stadium. This event consisted of a mass spectacle with a cast of thousands choreographed by the *Reichskunstwart*; 11,000 pupils from the schools of Berlin-Brandenburg participated. The choir groups consisted of 7,500 schoolchildren and mass movement groups of 3,000 performers. A male choir, a police band, and other dance and gymnastic groups complemented the cast.

Witnessed by 45,000 spectators, the spectacle began when 500 working men entered the stadium and attempted to connect ten golden poles to construct a symbolic representation of a bridge. The men failed to do so and called upon the German youth for help. Dressed in black, red, or gold, the young people entered, successfully connected the poles, and positioned themselves in the stadium to provide a visual representation of the republican flag. Sports exercises, games, songs, and dances were performed, and the workmen reminded the young people of the importance of the day. The youth swore an oath to the fatherland. At the end, the republican flag was raised, and the national anthem played.[75]

Some historians have argued that the 1929 spectacle offered a counterproductive founding myth in which, after ten years of republican democracy, the national community could still only be achieved with the help of its youth.[76] This criticism neglects the fact that the young people in the celebration, in helping to create unity, represented a positive symbol for the future. The event conveyed a very clear message of a unified society under the republican flag. Workers and young people, the foundation and future of the republic, were the main participants; and the display of the republican colors made up of youths suggested that the republic consisted of individuals who together formed the state. The Reich Minister of the Interior congratulated Edwin Redslob on "the new way of celebrating in the stadium."[77] Due to the popularity of this event, another great stadium celebration was planned for Constitution Day in the following year. Redslob coordinated it again with much success. However, financial cuts in the state budget jeopardized plans for a similar event in 1931.[78]

In these spectacles, and in other forms of republican representation, the influence of theater, gymnastics, and modern dance is obvious. Experiments with mass amateur choirs and movement groups were an important aspect of performance culture in the 1920s. Many dance choreographers and theatre directors believed that their venues had become too small for their performances and moved to sports grounds. Communist groups used mass choirs to mobilize their audiences for the political struggle, and the Social Democrats extolled the communities they represented through mass plays and sports performances. Attempts to involve large groups of people as participants and viewers alike, often outdoors, could be found in enormous variety in the Weimar Republic.[79]

Redslob was well aware of this tendency but stressed an aspect that he saw as even more important—the active participation of the republican citizen in state representation. In a radio lecture given shortly before the staging of the 1929 spectacle, he pointed out that, "One demands of the state the power to express its sovereignty visually, not because one wants to be entertained as a spectator, but rather out of the citizen's desire to be an active part of the state." Redslob stressed the importance of community and togetherness, concluding that, "[T]he Constitution Day is a popular celebration that aims to overcome the sharp division between participants and spectators. It has developed a form that represents the people's state."[80] The journal *Deutsche Republik* agreed and praised the spectacle for showing how the young people brought their brightness and joyfulness to the republican state.[81] Once again, we see how modern festive forms were explicitly connected to a political message, which simultaneously claimed that they represented the true characteristics of the Weimar Republic and voiced the hope that they would influence the wider German population.

Conclusion

Weimar German society was fascinated with visual culture, ranging from films and theatrical productions to republican state representation and political demonstrations. Republican officials made use of this fascination. In addition to the importance of the visual, the republican state also focused on increased participation and spectacular staging in many of its representative efforts. These tendencies shaped republican representation in varying degrees, and they sometimes created problems. In fact, the *Reichskunstwart* would have preferred fewer participatory attempts in the reshaping of state symbols than actually occurred. For instance, Redslob felt that too much participation, public discussion, and hasty criticism had hindered rather than helped the artistic development of the new eagle design.

Republican representation was in a period of transition, deliberately breaking away from Imperial Germany, and facing the hurdles and welcoming the opportunities to start anew. The creation of an appropriate symbolic language for the republic was the goal. Less clear was how to achieve it. Innovative representative methods were combined with optimistic hopes that the young democracy could educate its citizens in better artistic taste, a deeper communal spirit, and more republican dedication. The *Reichskunstwart* believed that the emancipated and educated citizen reflected upon his role in the republican state when witnessing a spectacle or paying respect to the late republican President. In November 1931, the *Reichskunstwart* wrote a letter to his wife Charlotte describing his ideas for the republic's festivities for the coming year. He stated that, "[C]elebrations as an end in themselves are Hitlerism. We need other motifs."[82] This conviction that the German population could be educated was the basis for Edwin Redslob's work on modern state representation. Redslob realized he had to communicate his ideas in representative forms with contemporary popular resonance. In so doing, he became a modernizer of German state representation without losing sight of the educational message he wanted to convey. It was due to Edwin Redslob that the public face of the Weimar state was shaped by modern artists, inclusive celebrations, and spectacular performances.

Notes

1. See Harald Welzer, "Die Bilder der Macht und die Ohnmacht der Bilder" in *Das Gedächtnis der Bilder: Ästhetik und Nationalsozialismus*, ed. Harald Welzer (Berlin, 1995), 165–93. I would like to thank the Irish Research Council for the Humanities and Social Sciences.

2. See Paul Betts, "Die Bauhaus-Legende: Amerikanisch-Deutsches Joint venture des Kalten Krieges" in *Amerikanisierung: Traum und Alptraum im Deutschland des 20. Jahrhunderts*, ed. Alf Lüdtke, et al (Stuttgart, 1996), 270–90.

3. Lothar Kettenacker, "Sozialpsychologische Aspekte der Führerherrschaft" in Karl-Dietrich Bracher, ed., *Nationalsozialistische Diktatur 1933–1945* (Berlin 1986), 114; Gerhard Paul, *Aufstand der Bilder: Die NS-Propaganda vor 1933* (Bonn 1992), 54; Hagen Schulze, *Weimar 1917–1933* (Berlin 1994), 123.

4. Nadine Rossol, "Visualising the Republic—Unifying the Nation: The Reichskunstwart and the Creation of Republican Representation and Identity in Weimar Germany" (Dissertation, University of Limerick, 2006); Christian Welzbacher, *Die Staatsarchitektur der Weimarer Republik* (Berlin 2006); Manuela Achilles, "Re-Forming the Reich: Symbolics of the Republican Nation in Weimar Germany" (Dissertation, University of Michigan, 2005); Bernd Buchner, *Um nationale und republikanische Identität: Die Sozialdemokratie und der Kampf um die politischen Symbole in der Weimarer Republik* (Bonn, 2001). For a short overview on new, mainly cultural history approaches to the republic, see Andreas Wirsching, *Die Weimarer Republik: Politik und Gesellschaft* (Munich, 2008), 118–41.

5. Eve Rosenhaft, "Lesewut, Kinosucht, Radiotismus: Zur geschlechter-politischen Relevanz neuer Massenmedien in den 1920er Jahren" in Lüdtke et al, *Amerikanisierung*, 119–43. For an examination on the lack of politicians in Weimar's visual culture, see Thomas Mergel, "Propaganda in der Kultur des Schauens: Visuelle Politik in der Weimarer Republik" in *Ordnungen in der Krise: Zur politischen Kulturgeschichte Deutschlands 1900–1933*, ed. Wolfgang Hardtwig (Munich, 2007), 531–59.

6. A re-evaluation of Weimar Germany's representative style also influences our understanding of the Third Reich. If we acknowledge that some aesthetic elements thought to be typically National Socialist had their roots in the Weimar Republic, we need to rethink the field of state representation and propaganda in the Nazi period. See Nadine Rossol, *Performing the Nation in Interwar Germany. Sport, Spectacle and Political Symbolism 1926–36* (New York, 2010).

7. "Zu Besuch beim Reichsreklamechef," *Berliner Tageblatt* (February 13, 1931).

8. On Edwin Redslob and his office, see Annegret Heffen, *Der Reichskunstwart: Kunstpolitik in den Jahren 1920–1933* (Essen, 1986); Gisbert Laube, *Der Reichskunstwart: Geschichte einer Kulturbehörde 1919–1933* (Frankfurt, 1997); Christian Welzbacher, *Edwin Redslob: Biographie eines unverbesserlichen Idealisten* (Berlin, 2009). For works connecting the *Reichskunstwart* to republican identity, see Winfried Speitkamp, "Erziehung zur Nation: Reichskunstwart, Kulturpolitik und Identitätsstiftung im Staat von Weimar" in *Nationales Bewusstsein und kollektive Identität*, vol. 2, ed. Helmut Berding (Frankfurt, 1994), 541–80; Rossol, "Visualising."

9. Hans Vorländer, "Demokratie und Ästhetik: Zu Rehabilitierung eines problematischen Zusammenhangs" in *Zur Ästhetik der Demokratie: Formen der*

politischen Selbstdarstellung, ed. Hans Vorländer (Stuttgart, 2003), 18; Jürgen Hartman, *Staatszeremoniell* (Cologne, 2000), 11.

10. Bundesarchiv Berlin (hereafter BArch), R1501/224, p. 28.

11. BArch, R32/224, p.144, p.147; BArch, R32/298a, p.1, p. 97.

12. Germanisches National Museum, Deutsches Kunstarchiv (hereafter GNM, DKA), NL E. Redslob: "Die Bedeutung der Gebrauchsgraphik für unsere Gegenwart," *Mitteilungen der VGV Wirtschaftlichen Rundschau* (September 18, 1922).

13. Cited in Speitkamp, "Erziehung zur Nation," 566.

14. For a more detailed account of the design's development, see Heffen, *Der Reichskunstwart*, 92–98, 110–13.

15. GNM, DKA, NL E. Redslob I;B-2: E. Redslob, "Amtliche Graphik des Reichs," *Die Woche* (no date).

16. See *Mitteilungen des Reichskunstwart* (1920, 1921, and 1922).

17. BArch, R32/254, pp. 122–32; Edwin Redslob, *Die künstlerische Formgebung des Reichs* (Berlin, 1926).

18. BArch, R1501/116489, p. 7.

19. "Offizielle Kunst, eine Reichskunstwart Ausstellung," *Vossische Zeitung* (October 29, 1926); "Die künstlerische Formgebung des Reichs," *Vorwärts* (October 29, 1926); "Die Bilanz des Reichskunstwarts," *Lokal Anzeiger Berlin*, (October 29, 1926); GNM, DKA, NL E. Redslob, I,B-2: "Die künstlerische Formgebung des Reichs," *Querschnitt* (no date).

20. BArch, R32/245, p. 122.

21. BArch, R32/256, p. 62.

22. BArch, R32/256, p. 9.

23. BArch, R32/256, p. 41.

24. BArch, R1501/125268, pp. 202-3; BArch, R1501/125269, p. 13; *Pressa Cologne: Amtlicher Katalog* (Cologne, 1928).

25. BArch, R1501/125270, pp. 49–51. For photographs see BArch, R32/533 and R32/421b.

26. "Die künstlerische Form als werbende Kraft," *Gebrauchsgraphik* (September, 1929): 74.

27. See Hans Hattenhauer, *Geschichte der deutschen Nationalsymbole* (Munich, 1990), 240–47.

28. GNM, DKA, NL E. Redslob, 345: diary (September, 1927).

29. "Ein Orden für die Republik?," *Vossische Zeitung* (January 7, 1922).

30. "Titel und Orden in der Republik," *Berliner Tageblatt* (March 8, 1927).

31. "Ordens- und Titelfragen," *Vorwärts* (January 6, 1927); "Bemerkungen: Titel und Orden," *Die Weltbühne* (May 4, 1926): 712–13.

32. "Die Leere des Knopfloches," *Deutsche Zeitung* (January 9, 1926); "Republikanisches Zeremoniell," *Deutsche Zeitung* (January 2, 1926); "Die republikanischen Ordenssorgen," *Kreuz Zeitung* (January 6, 1927); "Die bunte Republik," *Kreuz Zeitung* (August 23, 1927).

33. On different ways of expressing republican support, see Nadine Rossol, "Flaggenkrieg am Badestrand: Lokale Möglichkeiten repräsentativer Mitgestaltung in der Weimarer Republik," *Zeitschrift für Geschichtswissenschaft* (2008): 617–37.

34. For an overview on state funerals, see Volker Ackermann, *Nationale Totenfeiern in Deutschland* (Stuttgart,1990).

35. Edwin Redslob, "Die staatlichen Feiern der Reichsregierung," *Gebrauchsgraphik* (1925): 56–7.

36. Ackermann, *Nationale Totenfeiern*, 283–84.

37. For the reaction of several newspapers to Rathenau's assassination, see Burkhard Asmuss, *Republik ohne Chance? Akzeptanz und Legitimation der Weimarer Republik in der deutschen Tagespresse 1918–1923* (Berlin, 1994), 384–450.

38. BArch, R32/168, pp. 79–80.

39. For a detailed examination of the ceremony and of the speeches delivered, see Achilles, "Re-forming," 209–20.

40. Ibid., 216.

41. For the antirepublican use of the Nibelungen story, see Buchner, *Identität*, 194–6.

42. BArch, R32/168, p. 81. August Heinrich Hoffman von Fallersleben was a German patriotic poet writing in the nineteenth century. As a supporter of the national-liberal movement and the revolutionary uprising in 1848, his poems expressed the longing of many Germans for a unified state. Von Fallersleben also wrote the lyrics for the German national anthem.

43. Harry Graf Kessler, *Tagebücher 1918–1927* (Frankfurt, 1961), 327.

44. See Martin Sabrow, *Der Rathenaumord* (Munich, 1994), 157–69.

45. Carl v. Ossietzky, "Von Kapp bis…?," *Die Weltbühne* (March 11, 1930): 376.

46. Shulamit Volkov, "Überlegungen zur Ermordung Rathenaus als symbolischer Akt" in *Ein Mann vieler Eigenschaften: Walther Rathenau und die Kultur der Moderne*, ed. T.P. Hughes (Berlin, 1990), 100–1.

47. Redslob, "Die staatlichen Feiern der Reichsregierung," 52–53.

48. BArch, R601/35, no page numbers: "Niederschrift über die Vorbereitung und den Verlauf beim Ableben des Reichspräsidenten Ebert veranstalteten Trauerfeierlichkeiten."

49. BArch, R601/35.

50. BArch, R32/302, pp. 20–21.

51. GNM, ABK, NL E. Redslob, I, A-2: diary. See also BArch, R601/35: "Bericht über die Ausführung der Trauerdekoration für den verstorbenen Herrn Reichspräsidenten."

52. "Der Tag des Abschieds," *Berliner Volkszeitung* (March 4, 1925); "Vor Eberts letzter Fahrt," *Berliner Tageblatt* (March 4,1925); "Der Tag der Trauerfeier," *Berliner Tageblatt* (March 4, 1925); "Im Totenhaus nach der Feier," *8 Uhr Abendblatt* (March 5, 1925).

53. BArch, R601/38.

54. GNM, DKA, NL E. Redslob, I,B-3c: Ordnung des Trauerzuges.

55. "Millionen neigen das Haupt: Die Republik ehrt ihren toten Führer," *Vorwärts* (March 5, 1925); "Trauerfeier der Republik," *Vorwärts* (March 4, 1925); "Der Trauertag der Republik," *Vossische Zeitung* (March 4, 1925).

56. "Maskerade," *Deutsche Tageblatt* (March 6, 1925); "Keine byzantinische Legendenbildung," *Reichsbote* (March 3, 1925); "Sinnlosigkeit von Überführungstagen," *Deutsche Tages Zeitung* (March 5, 1925); "Die Presse zum Tod Eberts," *Deutsche Zeitung* (March 1, 1925).

57. BArch, Filmarchiv, no. 1285.

58. BArch, Filmarchiv, no. 298, no. 249, no. 28.

59. BArch, R43I/3511, p. 114.

60. BArch, R43I/1936, p. 32.

61. GNM, DKA, NL E. Redslob, 3154: diary; Edwin Redslob, *Von Weimar nach Europa: Erlebtes und Durchdachtes* (Berlin, 1972), 198–9.

62. Kessler, *Tagebücher*, p. 597.

63. GNM, DKA, NL E. Redslob, I,B-2: "Die Inszenierung der Republik," *Vossische Zeitung* (April 12, 1925).

64. Buchner, *Identität*, 24. On Imperial Germany, see Alon Confino, *The Nation as a Local Metaphor* (Chapel Hill, 1997).

65. See Fritz Schellack, *Nationalfeiertage in Deutschland 1871–1945* (Frankfurt, 1990); Rossol, "Visualising," 131–61; Achilles, "Re-forming," 233–304.

66. Detlef Lehnert and Klaus Megerle, eds., *Politische Identität und nationale Gedenktage: Zur politischen Kultur in der Weimarer Republik* (Opladen, 1989); *Verhandlungen des Reichstags: Stenographischer Bericht*, vol. 423 (June 13, 1928–February 4, 1929), 124–45.

67. Arnold Brecht, "Die erste Verfassungsfeier," *Der Heimatdienst* (1929): 275.

68. BArch, R32/273, p. 115; E. Redslob, "Die staatlichen Feiern der Reichsregierung," *Gebrauchsgraphik* (1925), 54.

69. BArch, R32/426, p. 81, p. 96.

70. BArch, R1501/116871, pp. 9–12.

71. Brandenburgisches Landeshauptarchiv Potsdam (hereafter BLHA), Rep.34/994: "Verfassungsfeier im Gaue," *Das Reichsbanner* (September 1, 1926).

72. "Zum Geburtstag der Verfassung," *Die Weltbühne* (1929): 189–90.

73. See Friederike Schubart, "Zehn Jahre Weimar: Eine Republik blickt zurück" in Heinrich A. Winkler, ed., *Griff nach der Deutungsmacht* (Göttingen, 2004), 142; BLHA, Rep.34, 994, pp. 174–80; Geheimes Staatsarchiv Preussischer Kulturbesitz Berlin, NL Becker.

74. BArch, R32/427, p. 18.

75. Historisches Archiv der Stadt Köln, Best. 6, 702: official programme of the celebration. For a photograph of the formation of the republican flag see GNM, DKA, NL E. Redslob, I, B-240, *Das 12-Uhr Blatt*, 187, 12.8.1929, "Verfassungsfeier im Grunewald-Stadion."

76. Pamela Swett, "Celebrating the Republic Without Republicans: The Reichsverfassungstag in Berlin, 1929–32" in *Festive Culture in Germany and Europe from the Sixteenth to the Twentieth Century*, ed. Karen Friedrich (Lewiston, 2000), 288–89.

77. BArch, R32/426, p. 98.

78. BArch, R43/573, p. 173; BArch, R32/438a, p. 4.

79. See Matthias Warstat, *Theatrale Gemeinschaften: Zur Festkultur der Arbeiterbewegung 1918–33* (Tübingen, 2005), 307-61; Inge Baxmann, *Mythos Gemeinschaft: Körper und Tanzkulturen in der Moderne* (Munich, 2000); Yvonne Hardt, *Politische Körper: Ausdruckstanz, Choreographien des Protests und die Arbeiterbewegung in der Weimarer Republik* (Münster, 2004).

80. BArch, R32/426, p. 79, p. 96.

81. "Das Volk feiert seine Verfassung," *Deutsche Republik* (August 17, 1929), 1434.

82. GNM, DKA, NL E. Redslob, II C 1: Redslob to Charlotte (November 26, 1931).

VIII

THE PARTY DOES INDEED FIGHT LIKE A MAN: THE CONSTRUCTION OF A MASCULINE IDEAL IN THE WEIMAR COMMUNIST PARTY

Sara Ann Sewell

The sketch below (Figure 8.1), from *Sozialistische Republik*, the local organ of the German Communist Party (KPD) in Cologne, depicts the front line of communist struggle. Men and women clasp hands in defense of the working classes. Toward the center are two women standing strong and resolute alongside their male comrades. In this rendering and others like it, women were depicted as integral to the defense of the working classes, as emphasized in the accompanying caption: "Women and men of the proletariat must stand firmly together in the fight against hunger and immiseration."

Figure 8.1   Drawing in *Sozialistische Republik* (July 20, 1923).
Source: Archiv der sozialen Demokratie and Bibliothek der Friedrich-Ebert-Stiftung in Bonn.

This image was created during an era of acute economic and political crisis. 1923 was the year of Germany's hyperinflation, which led to immense economic, social, and political upheaval, including a number of attempted coups d'états, such as the Nazi Beer Hall Putsch. For communists, too, it appeared that the moment was ripe for revolution. In fact, the KPD initiated several failed coup attempts that year.[1] In such an urgent context, it is not surprising that the dominant motif in the communist visual arsenal was revolutionary struggle. Guided by the belief that a communist state was on the immediate horizon, communists asserted that women would occupy pivotal roles in the new society, and their representations thus prominently featured strong female warriors.

The fact that these female representations display distinctly masculine features, including builds that suggest masculine physical prowess and facial structures that depict strong bone lines and pronounced jaws, underscores the ambivalent nature of communist femininity.[2] Communists' views of women were steeped in paradox. On the one hand, the KPD consistently advocated women's rights; on the other hand, the cadre as well as party leaders never fully committed themselves to gender equality.[3] That Rosa Luxemburg, Ruth Fischer, and Clara Zetkin occupied the highest echelons of the KPD should not obscure the fact that women's presence at all ranks in the party was marginal. The KPD was, as described by the contemporary statistician Dr. Hartwig, an "out-and-out men's party."[4] Silvia Kontos advanced this argument in 1979, concluding "that the party fights like a man"[5]; and there is ample evidence to corroborate Kontos's assertion that the KPD was not fully committed to gender equality, either in the party or in society more generally. This helps to explain why communists depicted female warriors with masculine characteristics, for they believed, sometimes latently and sometimes overtly, that masculine prowess was essential on the frontlines of revolutionary struggle.

But what did it mean to "fight like a man"? While Kontos stressed the word "man" to highlight the KPD's exclusion of women from the institutional realm of party politics, the word "fight" offers even greater insight into how the KPD constructed its public profile. As a revolutionary party, the KPD shaped itself into an organization that was committed to armed struggle. Its emphasis on aggressive politics and violent tactics contributed decisively to the fashioning of a political culture that prioritized not only men's issues but also the male fighter. Despite significant efforts to recruit women and promote women's issues, particularly during the late 1920s, communists, especially at the grassroots, cultivated a distinctly masculine culture that was dedicated to militancy. This fierce masculine ethos became even more pronounced during the final years of the Weimar Republic, as communists all over Germany devoted increasing energy to fighting Nazis in an epic battle whose gendered composition effectively excluded women.

Although groundbreaking, Kontos's study of women in the KPD was limited by its narrow institutional focus. Since the publication of her monograph, a handful of historians have furthered the understanding of some aspects of women and gender in the KPD. However, no scholar has completed a thorough analysis of gender within the party or the communist movement more broadly.[6] Particularly neglected is the study of communist masculinity. Eric Weitz has argued that the KPD underwent a process of masculinization that was "defined by male productive labor and male physical prowess."[7] Yet further research is necessary to understand how this process of masculinization developed and flourished. This chapter investigates the emergence of a militant hypermasculinity that came to dominate communist political culture in the final years of the Weimar Republic.

Reconstructing Gender after the Great War

One of the most prominent developments to emerge out of the ashes of the Great War was a significant shift in gender roles in Germany as well as throughout much of Europe. Profound apprehension about the new femininities and masculinities accompanied these changing gender norms. The deepest anxieties responded to the emergence of the "New Woman," recognized in popular culture by her bobbed hair, raised hemline, masculine attire, make-up, cigarettes, sexual liberation, and independence.[8] This rejuvenated female stood in stark contrast to the physically and psychologically mutilated male, whose masculinity was continuously called into question with every reminder of the lost war and the lost generation. Indeed, Weimar Germany suffered from a crisis of masculinity, to which a wide array of men responded by constructing an ultramasculine ideal.[9]

Communists' efforts to assert a masculine ideal were tied to the ways in which they viewed revolutionary femininity. At its inception, the KPD resolutely advocated gender equality. As a wave of female emancipation swept through Europe in the wake of World War I, communists were among the staunchest proponents of gender equality. The Communist International's Third Congress in 1921 affirmed that "women must be included in all the militant class organizations...with equal rights and equal responsibilities."[10] In Germany, which enfranchised women in 1919, communist women echoed this stance, as expressed by the KPD's Red Women and Girl's League (*Roter Frauen- und Mädchen Bund*, R.F.M.B.): "The basis of complete and true equality of woman is this: that one has granted her equal rights in every domain, whether it is in economic or political or cultural matters."[11] Communists created a wide array of visual propaganda that placed women on the frontlines of revolutionary struggle in the early 1920s, even though many of these female representations assumed masculine features.

Communists forged their notion of masculinity within the context of war and revolution. Indeed, the experience of trench warfare, mounting casualties, male camaraderie, and isolation from the home front were decisive in shaping the ways in which communists reconceptualized masculinity in the postwar years. Compounding a culture that tolerated, even promoted, violence were the ideological battles that devolved into fierce street fighting, especially during the first months of the new regime. From the outset, the Weimar Republic was characterized by an acceptance, indeed a fascination, with violence. This helps to explain the normalization of violence at various moments during the republic's tumultuous existence, reflected in the ubiquitous uniformed organizations that boldly paraded through the streets, the tacit acceptance of paramilitary units often associated with radical politics, and most notably the numerous attempts to overthrow the state. In a historical context that was distinguished by such a culture of violence, a number of social and political groups valorized an extreme model of manliness. Tapping into a culture that had been laid in the trenches and further fostered during the immediate unstable postwar years, German males, particularly those who were ideologically driven, cultivated a masculine ethos that was characterized by militancy, belligerency, virility, and sacrifice.[12]

Despite declarations that championed a new vision of humanity, communists nurtured a notion of manliness that corresponded to a normative masculinity, rooted in moral and physical fortitude, which had come into existence in the modern age.[13] Above all, they called upon working-class men to demonstrate their ideological commitment by participating in physical and armed struggle. As the battles unfolded throughout the streets of Germany, especially in the final years of the republic, this male fighter was elevated to heroic status.

Although KPD leaders consistently stressed gender equality in their public proclamations, signs of the masculinization of communist political culture and the construction of a hypermasculine archetype were already evident in the 1920s. The years 1924 and 1925 witnessed an important step toward the masculinization of communist culture. In response to a wave of economic and political crisis in the early 1920s that had paralyzed the young republic, the German government enacted a series of reforms beginning in late 1923. This move fundamentally altered the sociopolitical context, as revolution subsided. Recognizing that Germany was entering a new phase of relative political and social stability, KPD leaders initiated a significant organizational shift known as "into the masses" (*Heran an die Massen*), which they hoped would transform the party from a cadre organization into a mass movement. At the heart of this shift was the establishment of ancillary organizations designed to integrate members and sympathizers more fully into party activity.

One of these organizations was a paramilitary group called the Red Front Fighters League (*Roter Frontkämpferbund*, RFB), founded in 1924 with great fanfare.[14] The birth and development of the RFB contributed decisively to the masculinization of communist political culture. From the outset, the RFB had a distinct martial tenor, with its ranks engaged in physical struggle against political rivals that included fascists and members of the Social Democratic paramilitary organization, the Reichsbanner.[15] Dominated by war veterans and young men who longed for military camaraderie and adventure, the RFB prided itself for its warlike solidarity rooted in male companionship and violence. Committed to creating a mass political movement, however, KPD leaders sought to rein in the RFB men and fashion them into "propaganda troops" who were to build a mass organization, not a cadre of professional soldiers.[16]

But the RFB contained a formidable rebellious faction, who asserted that the organization's main task was to combat political enemies. In fact, the RFB was a significant source of factional dissent within the communist movement, as a sizable portion of its members fiercely sought to maintain not only the RFB's nominally autonomous status, but also its militant character.[17] KPD leaders responded by either disciplining or expelling the renegade RFB men, whom they denigrated as "ultra-leftists."[18] This relatively successful disciplining of the RFB's ranks laid the groundwork for remolding the men into the KPD's honorary guard, which the party prominently showcased. Indeed, by the end of 1926, the RFB had come to represent the public face of communism, signaling the masculinization of communist political culture more generally. Although RFB men devoted less time to physical combat, they continued to appear as communist soldiers. Never without their military-style uniform and always marching in disciplined formation, RFB men displayed a regimented masculine soldiery, even though armed confrontation temporarily receded to the background of communist tactics.[19]

When KPD leaders founded the RFB, they initially welcomed women into its ranks. In fact, female members marched alongside male comrades, wore the same uniform, and even ran military drills. At the end of 1925, however, party leaders expelled the women, reasoning that the physical demands of the RFB made the organization unsuitable for women. Subsequently, they directed female members into the newly created all-female auxiliary, the Red Women and Girl's League (RFMB).[20] The establishment of the RFMB was an important step in the party's attempt to build a mass following. Hoping to expand the KPD far beyond its male-dominated revolutionary cadre, party leaders erected a host of organizations that they believed would appeal to working-class women. In addition to the RFMB, they established a Women's Commission to head efforts to recruit women. They also founded factory cells in industries dominated by female labor and neighborhood cells to connect with working-class home-makers. Furthermore, they promoted an array of issues that concerned women, such as equal pay, welfare, education, and reproductive rights.[21] Thus by the mid-1920s, the KPD had undertaken significant measures to recruit women to the communist banner and to advance women's rights. Indeed, the KPD's efforts to mobilize working-class women and advocate women's issues positioned it as the most profeminist party on the Weimar political spectrum.

At the same time that KPD leaders created the ancillary organizations, they also redirected organizational work from working-class neighbor-hoods to factories through the establishment of a factory cell system.[22] Believing that revolutionary struggle would be waged in the industrial workplace and not in the neighborhood, party leaders instructed the rank and file to focus on recruiting workers in heavy industry. They called upon members to dedicate themselves to shop floor politics; and in a work environment characterized by a prominent and pervasive gender divide, communist organization inherently privileged working-class men's issues over those of women. While the party did establish numerous factory cells in businesses with predominantly female laborers, it emphasized the organization of workers in male-dominated factories.[23] Furthermore, the party brass came to view neighborhood cells, which women dominated, as sub-ordinate to the more important task of factory organization. Repeatedly advancing the slogan "Every Factory is our Fortress," KPD leaders maintained that factory organization must be a priority.[24] Thus, even though the KPD did attempt to organize working women in factory cells and homemakers in neighborhood cells, it oriented itself toward the masculine industrial world. This too contributed decisively to the masculinization of communist political culture and the promotion of a militant working-class masculine archetype.

The fact that the KPD appeared to pursue contradictory policies regarding the organization of women underscored the uncertainty that characterized communists' views on women. Although the KPD devoted significant effort to recruiting women, it consistently prioritized appealing to men in arenas that excluded women. It was no wonder, then, that female membership leveled out at around only 15 percent throughout the Weimar years.[25] An examination of gender relations in the communist movement sheds critical light on why women were consistently underrepresented in the KPD. The former communist Helmuth Warnke explained gender relations in the communist home. When a man came home, he wanted "food on the table right away because he has to go out again to an important meeting." When "he is at home, the wife cannot talk about her everyday woes. He has to read the party paper, several brochures along with it, and, in general, he needs peace and quiet."[26] A female communist reiterated this belief in women's subordination, asserting that a working-class wife's primary function was to "stand next to her husband every day in the struggle that he fights against the exploitation of his labor in the factory."[27] Communist men's reluctance to see women as their political equals was summed up by a woman at the district party congress in May 1930: "Very many male party comrades still hold the petty-bourgeois-opportunist viewpoint that women belong at the cooking pot. They don't believe it is necessary to inform their wives or to bring them to meetings."[28] Thus, despite the KPD's profeminist stance and despite its efforts to appeal to working-class women, communists' attitudes toward women's political activism, especially at the grassroots level, were laced with a deep ambivalence, as a culture of gender inequality resonated more widely with communists than the party rhetoric of equality.

Constructing the Communist Hero

As communists energetically worked to organize working-class men, they fashioned the communist man into the embodiment of proletarian manliness. Casting off their bourgeois Sunday suits, a mainstay of prewar labor demonstrations led by the Social Democratic Party, communist males proudly donned their work clothes during party events and demonstrations to emphasize their working-class pedigree. One of the key symbols that identified communist males with their proletarian heritage was the ubiquitous Lenin-style cap popularized by Ernst Thälmann, leader of the KPD beginning in 1925. KPD leaders advocated such distinctly working-class attire as a means to link the communist agenda visually with working-class culture. By affixing various party patches to the affordable caps, men could easily tailor them to identify themselves publicly with the communist movement. In fact, the KPD, like other social and political organizations in the wake of the First World War, encouraged the wearing of uniforms to construct a cohesive public profile that highlighted martial solidarity.[29] Communists' enthusiasm to don unitary clothing underscored the fact that a broad spectrum of the German public was attracted to militarism.

The shop floor provided the stage to showcase communist working-class masculinity. Agitating in the workplace, communists fashioned a powerful masculine figure whose innate proletarian strength was capable of defeating capitalism. Images of muscular, determined men towering over factories had become stock figures in the KPD's visual arsenal by the late 1920s. The oversized brawny, tenacious representations personified the ideal warrior: he was from the working classes, employed in heavy industry, imposing, strong, politically committed, battle ready, and male.

One of the most potent symbolic practices that exhibited communist male physical prowess was the raised clenched fist. While certainly not associated with only male comrades, the clenched fist was a militant gesture that implied masculine might. The origin of the clenched fist is unknown, but its genesis among German communists was linked to the founding of the RFB, which used it originally as a salutation ritual. Departing dramatically from the prewar labor symbol of the clasped hands that stood for international fraternity, communists transformed the clenched fist from a ceremonial greeting into a bellicose gesture that had become fully integrated into communist cultural practices and iconography by the late 1920s.[30] It was, as Gottfried Korff argues, a "disintegrative symbol" that catalyzed conflict.[31] Repeatedly invoked at party gatherings as a statement of commitment to revolutionary struggle, the clenched fist was a visible tribute to the increasing militancy of the communist movement and of Weimar politics more broadly.

As the clenched fist implied, the communist hero was to be prepared at all moments to defend the cause. Battle readiness was best articulated with one of the most popular slogans in the communist rhetorical armory, *"Immer Bereit!"* ("Always Ready!"), which signaled that communists were willing to defend their political ideals at all costs. As the Weimar

Republic wore on and the political stakes increased, KPD leaders called upon communist men to be "always ready" to fight their ideological enemies. This image from the front page (Figure 8.2) of the 1931 May Day issue of *Sozialistische Republik* prominently depicts a metal worker/soldier who seizes the product of his labor, a rolled steel bar, and wields it as a weapon. As he charges an unseen enemy with his mouth open in a battle cry, his tensed and ready muscles grip his weapon. He lunges forward, wearing nothing more than his workpants, shoes, and hat. Indeed, his bare chest serves to reinforce the virile nature of his pose. The visual distortion of his work cap into a military helmet reinforces the worker's duty as a communist soldier in the battle for the factory. Meanwhile, behind him an overdimensioned red flag flutters in front of an industrial skyline, symbolically linking communist struggle to heavy industry. This representation illustrates many elements of communist masculinity in late Weimar, especially the importance of military preparation and personal volition to take up arms against political adversaries.

But battle readiness demanded much more than an eagerness to fight ideological enemies, for it also required trained, physically fit male bodies. Similar to other labor organizations, the KPD devoted considerable energy to the sporting movement, which had been an integral feature of German labor organization since the late nineteenth century.[32] Party leaders believed that sports were essential to rally workers, especially young ones, to the communist banner, and the KPD thus sought to mobilize workers via sporting activities under its umbrella organization Red Sport.[33] Athletes served a variety of functions in the communist movement and were even charged with explicit political tasks that required the summoning of steeled, healthy bodies to advance the communist agenda.[34] For example, Red Bicyclists regularly distributed KPD literature. Most significantly, the communist sporting movement played a pivotal role in molding a battle-ready body type.[35] In fact, no communist celebratory gathering was complete without performances by athletes, such as gymnasts in pyramid formations, who demonstrated "the energy of the revolutionary proletariat."[36] Displaying their protruding muscles and athletic abilities and draped in communist uniforms, athletes' bodies came to personify the male aesthetic in communist political culture.

For communists, masculine prowess hinged above all on physical victory over political enemies. Since the founding of the KPD, party leaders had worked assiduously to prepare male comrades for armed conflict. While the prominence of paramilitary maneuvers waned in the

Figure 8.2 Front page of *Sozialistische Republik* (April 30, 1931). By permission of the Archiv der sozialen Demokratie and the Bibliothek der Friedrich-Ebert-Stiftung in Bonn.

mid-1920s as revolutionary opportunities dissipated, the tactical deployment of violence once again assumed acute importance in the final years of the Weimar Republic as communists aggressively combated their ideological opponents, principally the Nazis. Facing an ominous enemy that was quickly gaining strength, communists grew considerably more militant in the final years of the republic. To confront the escalating Nazi threat, the KPD founded an array of antifascist "united front" organizations, including the Fighting League Against Fascism (*Kampfbund gegen den Faschismus*), the Red Mass Self-Defense (*Roter Massenselbstschutz*), and the Antifascist Action (*Antifaschistische Aktion*).[37] Communist leaders designed these organizations primarily to rally a broad spectrum of sympathizers to confront National Socialism through mass public protest under the KPD banner. However, these antifascist units also regularly served as quasiparamilitary forces that defended working-class streets, even though party leaders continually reminded members that the organizations were not "substitutes for the banned Red Front Fighters League."[38]

Challenging Nazis to maintain control of working-class districts became a critical task of communist men by the early 1930s. While scholars have documented the armed conflict that raged between communists and Nazis at the end of the Weimar Republic,[39] they have devoted little attention to the gender politics associated with this new era of militancy. Armed confrontations with Nazis provided communist men with forums to flex their muscles. Indeed, when the communist movement underwent a fundamental programmatic shift in the early 1930s as it aggressively confronted Nazism, so too did it transform its male archetype. Above all, communists increasingly exalted a masculine warrior who was prepared to take up arms against his political foes.

Party propaganda disseminated a vision of militant men leading the antifascist struggle. One 1932 sketch in the KPD journal *Roter Stürmer*, for example, depicted uniformed RFB members charging Nazi men who have just thrown a rock through a window of a working-class home.[40] The communist antifascist fighters are drawn in militant poses, complete with clenched fists that express their determination to fight the Nazis. This image implied that the battle against Nazism should be waged exclusively by men who were willing to deploy violence to protect working-class neighborhoods.

Communists' efforts to mold the communist man into a steeled antifascist fighter had a dramatic impact on how they conceptualized revolutionary femininity. Most notably, their commitment to armed struggle anchored a femininity that placed women in the rearguard of the revolutionary struggle. By the early 1930s, the rhetoric and images of men and women united together in revolutionary struggle vanished in KPD publications, supplanted by a linguistic and visual lexicon that emphasized a hypermasculinity that was defined foremost by the commitment to armed struggle against Nazism. The KPD leadership, for its part, welcomed women into the antifascist ranks and consistently directed members to recruit women actively:

> The fight against fascism is not only a thing for men. More than half of all working people are women, and the working woman is affected the hardest by the measures of a fascist dictator... Every local group, every squadron, is obligated to accept the organization of women and girls immediately into the attack. Whoever refuses or sabotages this work has no place in our ranks.[41]

Such declarations, however, were usually a direct response to male comrades' refusal to work with women, especially in the antifascist struggle. Indeed, party leaders repeatedly reprimanded male members for their political "backwardness" and "reactionary attitude."[42] As an internal report summarized, "From the start, we had to overcome the significant resistance among the male comrades who, because of their political backwardness, took the position that women have nothing to seek in a military organization. Even today, this view has not yet been conquered."[43] Thus at the grassroots level, communist men widely resisted working with women in the antifascist battalions.[44] While they generally accepted women as antifascist propaganda troops, the majority of male comrades believed that women should work in "women's organizations" such as the Red Aid (*Rote Hilfe*), not in the antifascist "red mass self-defense brigades." KPD leaders responded to the defiance of their male members by repeatedly reprimanding them for their political "backwardness." But as the reports on the KPD's antifascist activities reveal, communist leaders made little headway in changing deeply entrenched antifeminist views among a significant portion of the rank and file.[45]

To persuade men to fight Nazis, the KPD bombarded them with a barrage of hortatory propaganda. By 1930 the party press published daily entreaties that urged followers to combat fascism aggressively. After the murders of several working-class men by Nazis in Cologne in July 1932, for instance, the local KPD exhorted, "In all the streets and neighborhood blocks, the antifascist mass self-defense must be organized immediately."[46] Party members themselves readily became antifascist propagandists, decorating their homes' exteriors with red flags and placards that called upon residents to defend their neighborhoods. One member described the visual impact of communist propaganda in a working-class neighborhood in Cologne-Kalk in 1932 as follows: "We go through the working-class streets. From the asphalt, large letters shoot out at us: 'Arm yourself for the red army review!' The short street is swimming in red. One flag after another. Banners call everyone to the united front."[47] The message was clear—communists should prepare for battle.

As the Weimar Republic edged closer to its demise, the militancy of the communist movement intensified, as reflected above all in the nightly brawls between communist men and Nazis. When mixed with the bravado gained from a night of drinking, such confrontations were regular occurrences in Germany's working-class districts. Beer glasses, chairs, and tables flew through working-class establishments, accompanied by fistfighting and sometimes gunfire, followed by the inevitable arrival of the riot squad.[48] This daily political violence fed the militant masculinity of the communist movement. Emboldened by their battle scars and mourning their fallen comrades, communist men cultivated a fierce radical culture that glorified armed conflict. The increasing presence of combative uniformed men who took to the streets to deter Nazi activity testified to this escalating militancy. Marching in closed ranks, the young communist men conveyed political resolve as they prepared themselves for armed confrontation. From their caps to their jackboots, they projected an unmistakable aura of militant masculinity and thus embodied the militant communist hero of late Weimar. Women, by contrast, were nowhere to be found in their ranks, for they did not fit the image of a communist fighter in the late Weimar Republic. Underlining such a militant masculine profile was the belligerent public language of the male troops. Typical of this rhetoric was the *Rot Front der Jung Prolet*'s response to the murders of five communist youths in Berlin in 1930: "We will answer these murders with 'Revenge'! We will find the murderers of our young comrades and we will avenge their deaths."[49] Even though the KPD's political apparatus defined the antifascist fight as primarily a mass "united front" protest movement, male fighters conceived of it as an instrument to combat their enemies. No wonder then that the antifascist fighters advised members to keep a "revolver at [their] breast" at all times.[50]

Blood and Martyrdom

By the final months of the Weimar Republic, the ultimate test of communist masculinity was martyrdom. In death, communist men were idolized by the cadre, welcomed into the pantheon of communist heroes that included the iconic Karl Liebknecht and Rosa Luxemburg. George Mosse maintains that "heroism, death, and sacrifice on behalf of a higher purpose in life became set attitudes of manliness" beginning with the French Revolution.[51] Weimar communists readily conformed to this conception of masculinity, as communist political culture, particularly during the final years of the Weimar Republic, fashioned a cult of death that venerated the male working-class hero who had sacrificed his life in violent political struggle. The fact that Luxemburg stood alongside her male comrades in this cult of death should not obscure the fact that it was primarily men who filled the ranks of communist martyrdom.[52]

Martyrdom obviously required the shedding of one's blood. However, spilled blood was much more than a physical manifestation in communist political culture, for it also symbolized men's personal sacrifice for the communist revolution. Indeed, blood assumed critical metaphoric meaning in communist political culture that linked it explicitly to a valiant masculine ethos.

The symbolic significance of blood in the working-class cultural lexicon dated from at least June 1848, when the French provisional government killed approximately 3,000 Parisians in what came to be known as the June Days. Subsequently, European labor organizations came to identify working-class politics with the blood-soaked flags of the June Days' fighters. This idea was perhaps best articulated by Karl Marx himself when he explained that the June Days had demonstrated that the revolutionary banner was now red: "Only after baptism in the blood of the June insurgents," he wrote, "did the tricolor become the flag of the European revolution—the red flag."[53] Saturated with the blood of those who had mounted the barricades in June 1848, the bloodied tricolor flag became the new banner of the future working-class revolution. Weimar communists, following the cues of their Russian comrades, appropriated the blood red flag as one of the most meaningful emblems in their symbolic repertoire. As one rank-and-file communist declared, "[We] were proud to be led by a red flag, which we, at all times, will defend with our blood."[54] Upon its founding, the KPD immediately recognized the potent rhetorical connotation of the blood red flag by naming its central political organ *Red Flag*.

During the Weimar Republic, communists repeatedly invoked blood imagery to showcase a masculine ideological conviction. As Comrade Schreiner explained, "The Communist Party is the holiest thing for which...thousands upon thousands of fighters have suffered by [shedding] their blood."[55] May Day 1929 marked a watershed moment in the increasing importance of blood sacrifice as a test of masculinity in communist political culture. Defying a December 1928 ban on open-air demonstrations in Berlin issued by the SPD police president Karl Friedrich Zörgiebel, communists marched through the streets of the working-class districts Neukölln and Wedding. Police responded with armed force, leaving approximately 33 dead and 200 wounded.[56] Labeled "Bloody May Day" by communists, this event marked the fiercest street fighting in Berlin since 1919, and it instantaneously gained critical weight in the history of communist martyrdom. Indeed, after 1929, the party consistently called upon the cadre to avenge the deaths of the demonstrators, particularly in conjunction with their annual May Day demonstrations.[57]

Communists gave blood sacrifice a distinctly masculine subtext, as illustrated in a 1925 report about an old miner, nicknamed the "Flagwaver," which was penned by a rank-and-file communist. According to the author, the Flagwaver used a little red flag to signal to locomotive engineers when the coal was loaded onto the train. The old miner explained, "My views are like my flag. I wave this little one now, but someday, I will attach a large red flag to the tower." During a strike at the mine, the Flagwaver washed his flag so that it reportedly was "once again red—red like true blood." But in 1925, the Flagwaver was killed in an accident at the mine. The author explained that he had died "desperately holding the flag in his hand so that it was smeared through and through with blood—with the blood of the Flagwaver."[58] Although replete with hyperbole, this tale offers a rich illustration of the symbolic significance of blood in communist political culture. Through the shedding of his blood, the old miner demonstrated valor, thus becoming a communist hero. He embodied all of the traits of a communist martyr—ideological fortitude, commitment to working-class struggle, and blood sacrifice. His story contains an additional masculine dimension, for not only was the hero male, but the sociopolitical context, the mining industry, was also an exclusive masculine domain. Thus the political struggle that resulted in the act of heroism effectively excluded communist women, who would never gain full entrée into the masculine world of revolutionary struggle where heroes were forged.

Communists exalted men who shed their blood for the communist cause as martyrs, particularly when their deaths were the result of armed conflict with Nazis. By the final months of the Weimar Republic, the communist calendar was overflowing with funerals for fallen male heroes who had lost their lives in physical confrontations with Nazis. The funerals for the slain revolutionaries provided communists with the consummate public forums to propagate a militant masculine martyrdom. Replete with pageantry that extolled the virtues of sacrificial manliness, these funerals invoked the death of the fallen in a didactic narrative to remind mourners of the qualities that communist men were to exhibit.

The rich dramaturgy of the communist funeral—including a sea of red flags, uniformed RFB pallbearers, "Red Front" chants accompanied by raised clenched fists, and the obligatory collective singing of *The International*—reinforced the urgency of personal sacrifice for communist men. Indeed, communist funerary practices politicized every aspect of mourning to fashion martyrs and persuade mourners to recommit themselves to battle. The March 1931 funeral for Ernst Henning, a victim of Nazi violence, offers an excellent moment to examine how communists instrumentalized the death of one of their heroes to promote a masculine fighting ethos. According to *Rote Fahne*, the cemetery was filled with over one hundred wreaths, hundreds of red flags, delegations of communist athletes, funerary music, raised fists, and approximately 35,000 mourners, all exercising "exemplary discipline."[59] In his eulogy, Ernst Thälmann narrated Henning's life story to convince mourners to take up his revolutionary mantle.

> The working-class fight for freedom has demanded a new victim. This will not be the last victim in the fight for freedom and socialism. But our brother has fallen nonetheless. Like his struggle, so too does his death consecrate the future... Henning was a true soldier of the revolution. Today, where the March sun shines upon us, where the call to fight resounds throughout the entire world, where the workers of Hamburg march in a protest strike as a pledge to fight, we say: The retaliation will be brought upon this history. We will avenge our comrade and all of our dead brothers.[60]

Remembering Henning's life and death as a didactic tool to convey the importance of blood sacrifice in the struggle for communism, Thälmann's words revealed the KPD's masculine ethos. The deaths of the "dead brothers" were to be "consecrated" and "avenged" in an epic battle, he cried. Mourners were to fashion themselves after Henning, who "was a true soldier of the revolution." Thus this communist funeral, like the many others held in the early 1930s, offered the bereaved the opportunity to honor the fallen by rededicating themselves collectively to revolutionary struggle and publicly promising to take up arms against their ideological foes. As such, the communist funeral ritual was the quintessential cultural expression of communist militant masculinity.

Working energetically to recruit women, and advocating an agenda that included reproductive rights and equal pay, the KPD positioned itself as the most profeminist political party of the Weimar polity. Nevertheless, the communists' efforts to organize women were laced with deep ambivalence. While KPD leaders asserted that women should enjoy equal rights both within the party and society at large, communists widely viewed the organization of women and the advocacy of women's issues as subordinate to the more important task of organizing men, particularly those employed in heavy industry. A latent sexism undermined communists' efforts to appeal to women, which helps to explain why women were consistently underrepresented in the ranks of the party and within its leadership structure.

This tension between the rhetoric of equality and a culture of inequality translated into ongoing disputes about how to construct the communist male and female. These debates concluded with the overt reassertion of a traditional gender divide by the early 1930s, especially as rank-and-file communists devoted increasing energy to battling Nazis. In such a charged atmosphere, theoretical discussions about gender equality gave way to political imperatives that prioritized physical confrontation against ideological foes. In the battle against fascism, communists promoted an image of the antifascist fighter as strictly male, effectively relegating women to the status of adjunct revolutionary. While the KPD's propaganda urged women to join the party, the movement's masculine culture turned them away.

The creation of a communist male archetype who was working-class, politically resolute, physically fit, battle ready, and willing to sacrifice his life for the cause signaled a reconceptualization of masculinity that responded to the specific political and social context of late Weimar. This reconceptualization began in the trenches of World War I, and it was battle tested on the streets of Germany in the final years of the republic. The stakes were high, as the country's future teetered on a thin tightrope. Such a situation called for an epic hero. The protagonist propagated by the communist movement corresponded with many traditional cultural assumptions about heroism. Above all, this hero, like most who have been held up as ideal types before him, was male.

Notes

1. See Werner T. Angress, *Stillborn Revolution: The Communist Bid for Power in Germany, 1921–1923* (Princeton, 1963); Ben Fowkes, *Communism in Germany under the Weimar Republic* (New York, 1984), 91–109.
2. Examining early Soviet iconography, Victoria Bonnell shows that female figures were often replications of male figures with the mere alteration of dress and hairstyle to indicate gender. Victoria Bonnell, "The Representation of Women in Early Soviet Political Art," *Russian Review* (1991): 267–88.

3. Other scholars have argued that communists' views on women and their organization contained deep-seated contradictions, including Klaus-Michael Mallmann, *Kommunisten in der Weimarer Republik* (Darmstadt, 1996); Eric Weitz, *Creating German Communism, 1890–1990* (Princeton, 1997); Julia Sneeringer, *Winning Women's Votes: Propaganda and Politics in Weimar Germany* (Chapel Hill, 2002), 100–7.

4. Quoted in Helen Boak, "Women in Weimar Germany: The *'Frauenfrage'* and the Female" in *Social Change and Political Development in Weimar Germany*, ed. Richard Bessel and E. J. Feuchtwanger (Totowa, NJ, 1981), 157.

5. Silvia Kontos, *Die Partei kämpft wie ein Mann: Frauenpolitik der KPD in der Weimarer Republik* (Frankfurt, 1979).

6. For scholarship that examines women and gender among Weimar communists, see Karen Hagemann, "Men's Demonstrations and Women's Protest: Gender in Collective Action in the Urban Working-Class Milieu during the Weimar Republic," *Gender History* (1993): 101–19; Atina Grossmann, *Reforming Sex: The German Movement for Birth Control and Abortion Reform, 1920–1950* (New York, 1995), and "German Communism and the New Women: Dilemmas and Contradictions" in *Women and Socialism/Socialism and Women*, ed. Helmut Gruber and Pamela Grave (New York, 1998), 135–68; Mallmann, *Kommunisten in der Weimarer Republik*, 131–41; Weitz, *Creating*, 177–78, 216–17.

7. Weitz, *Communism*, 205. For an investigation of gender roles in the international communist movement in the early twentieth century, see Eric Weitz, "The Heroic Man and the Ever-Changing Woman: Gender and Politics in European Communism, 1917–1950" in *Gender and Class in Modern Europe*, ed. Laura Frader and Sonya Rose (Ithaca, 1996), 311–52.

8. On the New Woman in Weimar Germany, see Atina Grossman, "*Girlkultur* or a Thoroughly Rationalized Female: A New Woman in Weimar Germany?" in *Women and Culture and Politics: A Century of Change*, ed. Judith Friedlander, et al. (Bloomington, 1986), 62–80, and "The New Woman and the Rationalization of Sexuality in Weimar Germany" in *Power of Desire: The Politics of Sexuality*, ed. Ann Snitow, Christine Stansell, and Sharon Thompson (New York, 1983), 153–71.

9. For recent studies on masculinity during the Weimar Republic, see George Mosse, *The Image of Man: The Creation of Modern Masculinity* (New York, 1996); Sabine Kienitz, "Der Krieg der Invaliden: Helden-Bilder und Männlichkeitskonstruktionen nach dem Ersten Weltkrieg," *Militärgeschichtliche Zeitschrift* (2001): 367–402; David Bielanski, "Front Line Weimar: Paramilitary Mobilization and Masculine Representation in Postwar Germany" (Ph.D. Dissertation, University of Illinois, 2002); Karen Hagemann and Stefanie Schüler-Springorum, eds., *Home/Front: The Military, War, and Gender in Twentieth-Century Germany* (New York, 2002); Raymond Sun, "'Hammer Blows': Work, the Workplace, and the Culture of Masculinity among Catholic Workers in the Weimar Republic," *Central European History* (2004): 245–71.

10. "Methods and Forms of Work among Communist Party Women: Theses," passed at the Third Congress of the Communist International, June 1921, reprinted in *Theses, Resolutions, and Manifestos: The First Four Congresses of the Third International*, ed. Alan Adler, trans. Alix Holt and Barbara Holland (Atlantic Heights, NJ, 1980), 217.

11. SAPMO-BA, Zentrales Parteiarchiv, RY1 I 2/8/66: RFMB paper, n.d.

12. On the construction of militant masculinities in interwar Germany, see Bernd Hüppauf, "Langemarck, Verdun, and the Myth of a New Man in Germany after the First World War," *War & Society* (1988): 70–103; Klaus Theleweit, *Male Fantasies*, trans. Erica Carter and Chris Turner (Minneapolis, 1988, two vols.); Stefanie Schüler-Springorum, "Flying and Killing: Military Masculinity in German Pilot Literature, 1914–1939" in Hagemann and Schüler-Springorum, *Home/Front*, 205–32; Bernd Weisbrod, "Military Violence and Male Fundamentalism: Ernst Jünger's Contribution to the Conservative Revolution," *History Workshop Journal* (2000), 68–94.

13. See Mosse, *Image of Man*, 126–32.

14. On the RFB see Kurt Schuster, *Der Rote Frontkämpferbund 1924–1929* (Düsseldorf, 1975); James Diehl, *Paramilitary Politics in Weimar Germany* (Bloomington, 1977); Günter Bers, ed., *"Rote Tage" im Rheinland: Demonstrationen des Roten Frontkämpfer-Bundes im Gau MR 1925–1928* (Hamburg, 1980); Kurt Finker, *Geschichte des Roten Frontkämpferbundes* (Berlin, 1982).

15. On RFB violence against Reichsbanner men see, for example, "Die rote Front an Mittelrhein: Gaukonferenz des Roten Frontkämpfer-Bundes, Gau Mittelrhein," *Sozialistische Republik* (July 7, 1925); "Gaukonferenz des roten Frontkämpferbundes Mittelrhein," *Sozialistische Republik* (November 24, 1925).

16. For example, "Die Osterfahrt der roten Front-Kämpfer," *SR* (May 15, 1925); "Gaukonferenz des roten Frontkämpferbundes Mittelrhein," *SR* (November 24, 1925).

17. "Gaukonferenz."

18. For example, see a report from the January 1927 RFB Middle Rhine regional conference, quoted in Bers ed., *Rote Tage*, 19–20. On the factional fighting in the RFB, see Schuster, *Frontkämpferbund*, 157–91.

19. On the militant character of the RFB, see SAPMO-BA, RY1 I 4/2/7: *Beschlüsse der IV. Reichskonferenz des RFB Aufbau und Aufgaben des RFB u. Rote Jungfront* (1927).

20. SAPMO-BA, RY1 I 4/3/1: "Die Tagung des 1. Reichskongresses der Roten Frauen- und Mädchen-Bundes," Material III (November 20-22, 1926); Hans-Jürgen Arendt and Werner Freigang, "Der Rote Frauen- und Mädchenbund," *Beiträge zur Geschichte der deutschen Arbeiterbewegung* (hereafter *BzG*) (1979): 249–58.

21. Hans-Jürgen Arendt, "Eine demokratische Massenbewegung unter Führung der KPD im Frühjahr 1931: Die Volksaktion gegen den §218 und die päpstliche Enzyklika 'Casti commubit,'" *Zeitschrift für Geschichtswissenschaft* (1971): 212-23; Johanna Piper, *Die Frauenpolitik der KPD in Hamburg 1928 bis 1933* (Cologne, 1988), 25–29.

22. Freya Eisner, *Das Verhältnis der KPD zu den Gewerkschaften in der Weimarer Republik* (Frankfurt, 1977), 97-113; Erika Kücklich and Stefan Weber, "Die Rolle der Betriebszellen der KPD in den Jahren der Weimarer Republik," *BzG* (1980): 116-30; Weitz, *Creating*, 148–49, 155–56.

23. A review of existing factory cell papers, such as those found in the Bundesarchiv, demonstrates that the overwhelming majority of them came from cells in heavy industry, dominated by male workers.

24. For example, see "Jede Fabrik sei unsere Burg!" *SR* (July 4, 1923).

25. Hans-Jürgen Arendt, "Weibliche Mitglieder der KPD in der Weimarer Republik," *Beiträge zur Geschichte der deutschen Arbeiterbewegung* (1977): 654. However, as Atina Grossmann points out, the KPD sent the largest percentage of female delegates to the Reichstag out of all the political parties. In 1930, 17.1 percent of KPD delegates were female, compared to only 11.1 percent for the SPD. Grossmann, "Communism," 141.

26. Helmuth Warnke, *". . . nicht nur die schöne Marianne": Das andere Eimsbüttel* (Hamburg, 1984), quoted in Mallmann, *Kommunisten*, 136. In his study on working-class attitudes during the Weimar Republic, Eric Fromm confirmed that patriarchal roles were pronounced in most working-class families. Eric Fromm, *The Working Class in Weimar Germany*, ed. Wolfgang Bonss, trans. Barbara Weinberger (Leamington Spa, 1984), 163.

27. "Die soziale Lage der Stollwerckarbeiterinnen," *SR* (August 29, 1925).

28. Genossin Th., quoted in "Im Zeichen der revolutionären Selbstkritik," *SR* (May 14, 1930).

29. This attempt to appropriate everyday clothing for the communist movement highlighted the fact that rank-and-file communists were responsible for purchasing their own uniforms. As the economic status of most workers deteriorated considerably after the onset of the Depression in 1930, the party became more inventive in its uniform choices, encouraging members to adapt clothing they already owned to the new uniforms. See "Bericht und Resolutionen. 1. Reichsführer-Tagung 14. –15.4., Berlin," *Alarm* (April, 1931).

30. Gottfried Korff, "From Brotherly Handshake to Militant Clenched Fist: On Political Metaphors for the Worker's Hand," *International Labor and Working-Class History* (1992): 70–81.

31. Gottfried Korff, "Rote Fahnen und geballte Faust: Zur Symbolik der Arbeiterbewegung in der Weimarer Republik" in *Transformation der Arbeiterkultur*, ed. Peter Assion (Marburg, 1986), 93.

32. Vernon Lidtke, *The Alternative Culture: Socialist Labor in Imperial Germany* (New York, 1985); Hans Joachim Teichler, ed., *Arbeiterkultur und Arbeitersport* (Clausthal-Zellerfeld, 1985).

33. W. L. Guttsmann, *Workers' Culture in Weimar Germany* (New York, 1990); Peter Friedemann, "Die Krise der Arbeitersportbewegung am Ende der Weimarer Republik" in *Arbeiterkultur zwischen Alltag und Politik*, ed. Friedhelm Boll (Vienna, 1986); Hartmann Wunderer, *Arbeitervereine und*

Arbeiterparteien: Kultur- und Massenorganisationen in der Arbeiterbewegung (1890–1933) (Frankfurt, 1980).

34. For example, see *Technische Winke: Für die Agitation* (March, 1932).

35. George Mosse in his *Image of Man* argues that the physical appearance of the male body as a measure of masculinity distinguished modern masculinity from its predecessor, which emphasized aristocratic chivalry. In this modern notion of masculinity, strong and healthy bodies were a key feature.

36. "Proletarische Feierstunde RFB Abt. Mülheim," *SR* (October 14, 1925).

37. On the KPD's antifascist movement, see Fowkes, *Communism*, 166–71; Erika Kucklich and Elfriede Liening, "Die antifaschistische Aktion: Ihre Rolle im Kampf um die Abwehr der faschistische Gefahr im Jahre 1932 und ihr Platz in der Strategie und Taktik der KPD," *BzG* (April 4, 1962): 872–97; Mallmann, *Kommunisten*, 365–80.

38. SAPMO-BA, RY1 I 4/9/5: "Bericht und Resolutionen, 1. Reichsführer-Tagung, 4.15, Berlin," *Alarm* (April, 1931). While some branch organizations adhered to the KPD leadership's instruction to keep the Fighting League Against Fascism as a mass united front organization, other branches (e.g. the Ruhr district) fashioned their local Fighting League into a paramilitary organization. For example, see SAPMO-BA, RY1 I 4/9/3: Fritz Lange, "Bericht über den Kampfbund gegen den Faschismus" (January 28, 1931).

39. For instance, Eve Rosenhaft, *Beating the Fascists? The German Communists and Political Violence, 1929–1933* (New York, 1983); Anthony McElligott, *Contested City: Municipal Politics and the Rise of Nazism in Altona, 1917–1933* (Ann Arbor, 1998).

40. SAPMO-BA, RY1 I 4/9/3: *Roter Stürmer, Mittel- u Norddeutsches Kampforgan für die soziale und nationale Bereitung* (c. 1932).

41. *Alarm: Mitteilungsblatt für die Funktionäre des Kampfbundes gegen den Faschismus* (February, 1931).

42. SAPMO-BA, RY1 I 4/9/1: "Kampfbund gegen Faschismus. II. Bezirksverbandkonferenz am 14. u. 15. Feb. 1931 in Hamburg" (1931); SAPMO-BA, RY1 I 4/9/4: "Richtlinien für die Arbeit der Frauen und Mädchenstaffeln des Kampfbundes gegen den Faschismus" (c. 1931/32).

43. SAPMO-BA, RY1 I 4/9/3: "Bericht der Reichsfrauenleitung des Kampfbundes gegen den Faschismus" (c. 1931).

44. Women made up 10 to 15 percent of the Fighting League's membership. SAPMO-BA, RY1 I 4/9/3: "Bericht der Reichsfrauenleitung des Kampfbundes gegen den Faschismus" (c. 1931).

45. For example, SAPMO-BA, RY1 I 4/9/3: "Bericht"; SAPMO-BA, RY1 I 4/9/1: "Kampfbund"; SAPMO-BA, RY1 I 4/9/5: "Bericht," and "Gewinn die Betriebsarbeiterinnen für die antifaschistische Front!," *Alarm* (January, 1932).

46. "Die braune Mordbestie in Nippes!," *SR* (July 12, 1932).

47. Worker Correspondent 371, "Kampfstimmung überall," *SR* (September 24, 1932). Worker correspondents were rank-and-file communists and

sympathizers who wrote articles for the KPD press. In KPD organs, worker correspondents were generally given numbers to protect their identity. For more on the KPD's Worker Correspondent Movement, see Christa Hempel-Küter, "Die kommunistische Presse und die Arbeiterkorrespondentenbewegung in der Weimarer Republik: Das Beispiel der *Hamburger Volkszeitung*" (Frankfurt, 1989); Sara Ann Sewell, "From the Lives of Workers: Worker Correspondents in Cologne, 1924–1933" (Ph.D. Dissertation, University of Wisconsin, 2000).

48. For example, "Besoffene Nazis überfallen einen Arbeiter," *SR* (June 18–19, 1932); "Naziprovokation am Holzmarkt," *SR* (June 21, 1932).

49. SAPMO-BA, RY1 I 2/8/65: *Rot Front der Jung Prolet* (May, 1930).

50. Ibid.

51. Mosse, *Image of Man*, 51.

52. For example, see a list of workers who were killed by National Socialists throughout Germany in 1930, which does not list a single woman. SAPMO-BA, RY1 I 4/9/3: "69 Tote in einer Reih," (c. 1931).

53. Karl Marx, *Class Struggles in France, 1848–1850* (New York, 1976), 59.

54. Worker Correspondent 420, "Rheinische Zeitung schwindelt und verleumdet," *SR* (May 22, 1931).

55. A. Schreiner, "Jeder Rote Frontkämpfer werde Mitglied der KPD," *SR* (September 17, 1927).

56. See Chris Bowlby, "*Blutmai* 1929: Police, Parties and Proletarians in a Berlin Confrontation," *The Historical Journal* (1986): 137–58; Thomas Kurz, *Blutmai: Sozialdemokraten und Kommunisten im Brennpunkt der Berliner Ereignisse von 1929* (Bonn, 1988).

57. For example, "Rote Fahnen heraus!," *Rote Fahne* (April 30, 1930).

58. "Der Fahnenschwenker," *SR* (April 28, 1925).

59. See "Im Geiste des ermordeten Genossen Henning: 35,000 im Kampfgeleit des roten Hamburg," *Rote Fahne* (March 22, 1931).

60. "Genosse Thälmanns revolutionäre Anklage," *Rote Fahne* (March 22, 1931).

IX

Sweat Equity: Sports and the Self-Made German

Erik Jensen

In June 1930, the French sculptor Aristide Maillol sat poolside in Frankfurt and marveled at how much more fit and athletic German youth appeared than those back home in France. His friend and host, the German states-man Harry Kessler, explained to Maillol that "a new sense of life" had taken hold in Germany since the end of the war. "One wants to really *live*," Kessler continued, "to enjoy the light, sun, happiness, one's own body."[1] Two years later, when Kessler visited France, he was similarly struck by the contrast between the cultures of physical development in the two countries. Germans exuded a sense of physical liberation that, in Kessler's estimation, their neighbors to the west noticeably lacked: "One hardly sees a sign of bourgeois stiffness [in Germany] anymore, but instead beautiful, strong bodies, naked or half-clothed. Here, by contrast, the petite bourgeois style in clothing and Sunday leisure still completely dominates."[2]

While the French took their Sunday strolls, the Germans were develop-ing the "beautiful, strong bodies" that Maillol had so admired in Frankfurt, a self-fashioning that went beyond just fitness. It pointed, instead, to a fun-damental shift in the horizon of individual possibility, in which Weimar society invited Germans to remake themselves—economically, socially, and psychologically, as well as physically. In the aftermath of the First World War's carnage, people all across Europe turned their attention to their own bodies, but nowhere more so than in Weimar Germany, where this tendency manifested itself in such diverse movements as rhythmic gymnastics, eastern meditation, vegetarian diets, and nudism. More than any of these other currents in Weimar society, however, it was competitive sports that promoted a program of re-making oneself in closer accord with modern society. The athlete embodied not only streamlined efficiency, but also such characteristics as aggression and ambition, qualities that seemed critical to getting ahead in the new era.

Stefan Zweig may have criticized sports in 1925 for contributing to "the extinction of the individual in favor of the type," but competitive sports actually developed and promoted the individual to a greater extent than any other social movement in the Weimar Republic.[3] These sports offered men and women a vehicle for self-discovery and emancipation, as the author Vicki Baum herself realized when she learned to box at a Berlin gym in the 1920s. "I became conscious of my strength," she boasted, after decades of having family members, teachers, and colleagues shelter her from any sort of physical exertion.[4] Zweig's observation neatly captured the tendency of athletic training to develop remarkably similar stream-lined forms in men and women, but he erred in equating this physical convergence with the erasure of individuality. Competitive sports pushed the individual more decisively into the foreground than ever before.

It was the individual athlete who won the match, who set the record, and who received the adoration of fans. It was his or her personal triumphs and failures that provided the fodder for conversations and debates across the country in the postwar decade. The athlete exemplified personal ambition and self-advancement. Moreover, because sports measured success in terms of winning alone, athletes felt pressure to stay ahead of the pack, to boost the performance of their hearts, lungs, and quadriceps, to make themselves faster, stronger, and more efficient. This striving, this quality of continual self-making, defined male and female athletes and suggested the potential that lay within everyone—the slim, muscular physique just waiting to be developed.

The self-made quality of the champion athlete extended beyond the cultivation of biceps and stamina alone. Elite athletes had star power in the 1920s, which they converted into financial and social opportunities. Athletes appeared on the covers of leading magazines, mixed freely with the country's literary elite, and enjoyed access to business leaders and public officials. Because competitive sports rewarded merit alone and made a claim to democratic openness, they seemed perfectly suited to Germany's new postwar republic. This aspect of sports appealed particularly to those who had existed on the margins of Wilhelmine society, like single women, Jews, and working-class men. To these groups, athletic success now offered an *entrée* into the social elite. The most famous athletes attracted lucrative endorsements and parlayed their celebrity into film roles and entrepreneurial ventures. Others capitalized on their expertise by forging careers in sports journalism, coaching, and club management. Sports like boxing, meanwhile, offered top contenders immediate opportunities to compete for money, and this same prospect lured a few pioneering tennis players into the world of professionalism over the course of the decade as well.

In this chapter, I argue that male and female athletes modeled the quality of "self-madeness" in Weimar Germany. I focus on men's boxing and women's tennis, both of which highlighted individual achievement, fostered a competitive environment of accelerating expectations, and afforded opportunities for a professional income. Elite boxers and tennis players drew the attention of sports reporters, commentators, and fans. By examining the media coverage of these two sets of figures, I will chart the contours of a new and important discourse of self-improvement, upward mobility, and reinvention in the new republic. The nation's flourishing print culture—everything from sports weeklies to daily newspapers to highbrow literary journals—shaped a narrative of "self-madeness" around these athletes that did not limit itself to just physical fitness. This discourse reinforced a general and wide-ranging postwar sense of new opportunities and challenges, even for the great majority of readers and fans who never once stepped into the ring or onto the tennis court. The life stories of male boxers and female tennis players represented the promise of success and self-determination.

In the most visible and immediate sense, these athletes remade themselves physically. This, in itself, was not new in German history. The *Turnen* movement, which propagated a communal form of gymnastics, had been actively encouraging Germans to remake their bodies since the early nineteenth century, after its founder had interpreted Prussia's loss to Napoleon as a sign of physical weakness in the male population. That movement to remake bodies, however, emphasized the collective rather than the individual, and it explicitly promoted national ambitions instead of personal ones. Indeed, although the *Turnen* movement gradually introduced athletic competitions at its regular gatherings, it purposely downplayed celebrations of personal achievement and remained distinctly uneasy with any elements that glorified the individual. The guiding philosophy of *Turnen* pursued exercise in the service of the national community and continually oriented its members' attentions toward this larger cause and identity. Because of its relatively hierarchical structure and political conservatism, moreover, commentators such as Walter Schönbrunn dismissed the *Turnen* movement as a practice best suited for "the subjects of a monarchical government," not for the "republican men" of the postwar era.[5]

Individual competitive sports like boxing and tennis, on the other hand, promoted physical training for the sake of the individual alone. The process of remaking the body through athletic training had a liberating quality and instilled a sense of confidence and personal ambition that the athlete often found exhilarating. This was particularly true for women in the postwar period. The commentator Annemarie Kopp insisted in a 1927 article, boldly entitled "Emancipation through Sports," that athletic training created high-performance female bodies designed to thrive in a postwar society that now demanded strength, speed, and stamina.[6] Kopp went even further, though: sports "shall release [the woman] from a mindless machine-like existence, as well, and make her human, make her into a [fully formed] personality." Sports, according to Kopp, developed an autonomous individual, the antithesis of Zweig's generically interchangeable athlete. This fully individuated sportswoman also served as a counterpoint to the young women of the popular kick-line troupes, whose indistinguishable uniformity the cultural observer Siegfried Kracauer famously criticized in 1927 as an indistinguishable and interchangeable "mass ornament."[7] After "centuries of deforming and neglecting" the woman's body, Kopp insisted, only athletic training would enable the woman finally to emerge as a complete person, and it therefore represented the necessary first step in a woman's more far-reaching emancipation.

Female athletes overcame those centuries of neglect by incorporating the cutting-edge principles of industrial engineering into their athletic regimens, which resulted in the sleek, disciplined, and performance-oriented bodies that helped to define the New Woman ideal. Whereas women in prewar Germany had managed to feign an hourglass shape with the external aid of a corset, women in Weimar society disciplined their bodies from within, via a strict regimen of exercise. The corseted woman may have appeared lean, but her body lacked the speed, agility, and stamina that its form suggested. The postwar body, on the other hand, performed at a level commensurate with its self-presentation.

Men remade their bodies through sports, too, and in no sport did they do so with the attention to corporeal detail that they did in boxing. Here, as in so many aspects of sports, the German media tended to present the boxer's quest for physical self-development as a decidedly American one. According to one 1927 article in the sports monthly *Sport und Sonne*, "The American does not take it easy...This training is strenuous [and] exhausting, but it forges complete men."[8] Just as Annemarie Kopp's article, also from 1927, had encouraged women to pursue sports in order to make themselves whole, this article argued that boxing forged the "complete" man. It, too, saw athletic training as emancipatory, since only a "strenuous, exhausting" investment in the self would liberate man's full potential. An article two years later on Hein Müller, Germany's light-heavyweight champion at the time, depicted his life in just such a narrative of self-completion. When Müller first started to box, he was an incomplete man, "a tiny, pale boy of 90 pounds, so tiny, so pale, and so light." Boxing initiated a metamorphosis. Looking at the strapping boxer today, the article concluded, "Müller provides the living example of what courage, tenacity, and hard work can achieve."[9] Through boxing, Müller had made himself into a strong, successful, and completed man.

Boxing reportage in the 1920s helped fans to get a handle on the exact contours of the complete man by diagramming the prizefighter's physique with an engineer's precision. This corporeal mapping not only allowed for an ostensibly objective comparison of two or more fighters, but it also provided a blueprint of the ideal body, a standard against which German men could chart their own efforts at physical remaking. One German sports encyclopedia began its entry for heavyweight fighter Max Schmeling with a catalog of statistics: "Height 186 cm, weight 175 pounds, reach 189 cm, chest 104 cm (with a full breath 115 cm), waist 82 cm, upper arm 37 cm, neck 43.5 cm, thigh 59 cm, forearm 34 cm, calf 40 cm."[10] Portrayals such as this one purposely blurred the distinction between a person and a high-performance engine, lending the impression of a human body that one could simply calibrate, as long as one knew the proper technique. References to the pugilist as a "fighting machine" emerged as the most repeated cliché in boxing journalism. Commentators had a tendency to treat the comparison more literally than figuratively, as when the literary journal *Querschnitt* described the body of the heavyweight boxer Hans Breitensträter as "built entirely according to machine-like principles."[11] The Taylorized prizefighter had arrived.

In addition to promoting somatic efficiency, competitive sports promoted individual compensation, that second key principle of the American industrial engineer F.W. Taylor, whose influential theories were taking the German business world by storm in the 1920s. Just as Taylorism advocated basing a worker's pay on his rate of output, boxing and tennis began to reward their top athletes for producing victories. These sports offered cash prizes and the alluring prospect of remaking oneself financially, as well as physically. At a time when strictly enforced amateurism remained the ideal in almost all sports, boxing and—gradually—tennis presented the option of turning professional. According to the popular narrative in Weimar Germany, boxers and tennis players could rise from modest backgrounds through hard work and astute self-marketing. The famous examples of those who had done so seemed to prove that postwar Germany had scrapped the rigid social structures of the Wilhelmine period in favor of a more American-style upward mobility.

For the public in Weimar Germany, boxing seemed to exist only its professional form, and the prizefighter's iconic status owed just as much to his financial achievements as to his skills in the ring.[12] During this era of extreme economic uncertainty, the possibility of remaking one's circumstances appealed to just about everyone, and the sports pages fueled this fantasy by lavishing attention on a champion boxer's newfound wealth and status. As early as 1921, when professional boxing was still new in Germany, the trope of the suddenly-rich prizefighter had already established itself, and articles like that by cultural commentator Hans von Wedderkop could refer to heavyweight Hans Breitensträter's success as a "boxing fairy tale."[13] During the entire Weimar period, no more than perhaps 700 men actually boxed professionally, and only a fraction of those managed to earn a decent living at it. But the image of the self-made champion circulated widely in the media and suggested a society of upward mobility for those with the skills and dedication to achieve it.[14]

Rags-to-riches stories set in the world of boxing formed a staple of Weimar popular culture. In Hannes Bork's 1925 tale "Der deutsche Teufel" (The German Devil), a former sailor, who had boxed in the navy and now worked in a blue-collar job, quickly succumbs to a boxing promoter's enticing offer to make him "a famous and rich man!"[15] Naturally, this promise comes true. The protagonist in a 1926 short story similarly decides to make his career in the ring, because "that was the only way to make money."[16] As the daily *Frankfurter Zeitung* commented in 1928 about the ubiquity of such success stories, "Everyone who is a good boxer moves into the professional boxing class in the hopes of there earning the famous mountain of gold, which one reads so much about in the papers."[17] This lure of riches through such a physically punishing sport as boxing particularly attracted men from humbler origins, and Germany's most visible champions throughout the 1920s came from a proletarian background. Max Schmeling recalled in 1928 that the money especially drew him to boxing. After learning as a 19-year-old just how rich the sport had made the American champion Jack Dempsey, Schmeling redoubled his training efforts: "When I then heard what he [Dempsey] earned, my courage, my drive, my determination grew."[18] Schmeling longed for that mountain of gold.

Once Schmeling had made that mountain, his own life story provided further grist for the myth-making mill, according to which a young man with a certain amount of talent and lots of hard work could remake himself, Horatio-Alger-style, through the sport of pugilism. The coverage of Schmeling's 1929 U.S. tour in the journal *Sport und Gesundheit* immediately steered readers' attention to his financial windfall: "Not only did he earn…$72,000 [in the main fight], but [he] also did a good business with the exhibition fights at 26 locations."[19] The analysis of Schmeling's actual performance in the ring took a clear back seat. The boxing journal *Boxwoche*, meanwhile, ran a cover illustration of Schmeling in which he wore a business suit and balanced atop a rolling dollar coin, looking more like a high-rolling entrepreneur than a hard-training athlete.[20]

The satirical journal *Ulk* also commented on Schmeling's dazzling income in 1929, pointing out that it far surpassed even that of the nation's leading author, Thomas Mann. Under the headline "Two Powerhouses," a caricature showed a muscled, colossally imposing Schmeling standing next to a thin, effete-looking Mann, who—despite the fact that he stood atop a pile of six of his famously thick novels—still did not reach the level of Schmeling's shoulders. The caption, meanwhile, juxtaposed two quotations from news organization, the first of which announced that Mann had received 200,000 Marks for his Nobel Prize, which was based upon a lifetime of literary work. The second reported that Schmeling's next fight—less than an hour's worth of work—had already guaranteed him $250,000, the equivalent of more than four times the Nobel award. Schmeling, Breitensträter, and a handful of other top professional boxers in the 1920s had clearly made themselves through the sport. During a period of entirely unpredictable economic vacillations in Germany, the boxer offered seeming proof that Weimar society would make good on its meritocratic promise, and that training and hard work would eventually pay off.

The financial promise of a boxer derived from more than his ability to win fights. As one of the pioneering figures at the intersection of sports and commerce, the professional fighter also represented a level of innovative self-marketing worthy of P. T. Barnum. Here, too, the fact that he managed successfully to exploit his own iconic status reflected an "American" sensibility in the eyes of many Germans. Precisely this aspect of the professional boxer fascinated Bertolt Brecht, who outlined the story of a fighter making his fortune in the mid-1920s in the unfinished novel *Das Renommee—Ein Boxerroman* (The Renown—A Boxer Novel). In this text Brecht expressed his belief that, rather than the action in the ring, "It is much more interesting to see how a man earns fame and fortune through boxing and how he begins to translate that fame into even more money—in short, how a man

'makes himself.' "[21] Brecht based this particular story on his close association with the prizefighter Paul Samson-Körner, but he could have chosen
any number of boxers who had crafted larger-than-life personas with an
eye to fostering their own commercial appeal.

For one thing, the celebrity status of boxers in Weimar Germany made
them obvious candidates for product endorsements. Max Schmeling, for
instance, struck a deal to model suits for a ready-to-wear clothing manufacturer almost immediately after beating Franz Diener for the German
heavyweight title in April 1928. Diener himself, meanwhile, supplemented
his prize money by promoting Kressin-Mohar cigarettes as well as a brand
of salt.[22] Boxers were also positively entrepreneurial in the commodifica-
tion of their own well-trained bodies, which they willingly and compli-
antly offered up to visual scrutiny, both professional and prurient. Postwar
boxers picked up where prewar bodybuilders had left off in cultivating
the German public's appreciation of male physical beauty.[23] Prizefighters
aggressively hawked their likenesses on everything from photographs to
collectible knick-knacks. Almost every issue of the journal *Boxsport* during
the 1920s contained at least one advertised collection of snapshots for the
avid fan, and the luxury porcelain manufacturer Rosenthal even designed
a statuette of Hans Breitensträter that, according to one account, "sold like
hotcakes."[24]

Furthermore, the male boxer consciously invited heartthrob status by
showcasing himself as an object of sexual desire. Prizefighters like Max
Schmeling, Horst Schade, and Erich Brandl posed nude for photographs
and helped to establish the genre of the male pin-up. Such photographs
also appeared in mainstream journals, such as *Sport und Sonne* and *Der
Querschnitt*, the latter of which became famous for regularly featuring nude
photos of fighters who had been carefully positioned to accentuate their
muscular figures. These photos mirrored the long-established portrayal of
the female form in that they consciously eroticized the boxer's body, pre-
senting it much less as a fighting machine than as a desirable object.

Boxers readily acknowledged the erotic nature of their appeal. As Jack
Dempsey acknowledged in one interview, "[I]t's no longer enough to
have speed and a good right arm to be the favorite. You have to be good-
looking, too, now that ladies go to the fights."[25] Hans Breitensträter certainly learned the importance of appealing to women as soon as he rose
to prominence in the early 1920s, and the profiles of him in the German
press invariably commented on his legions of female fans. The feuilletonist
Rumpelstilzchen joked that when it came to open displays of passion,
the Germans had caught up with southern Europe, "especially when the

blonde Hans, the gold-crowned Breitensträter, is there." Lest there be any doubt as to the sexual nature of this passion, Rumpelstilzchen added that Berlin's women awaited each upcoming match "with flared nostrils."[26] In a 1932 article in *Der Querschnitt*, Breitensträter himself acknowledged the number of "male and female admirers" who lavished attention on him at social gatherings, and he showed no hesitation in capitalizing on his good looks to boost his own celebrity status and marketability.[27]

The importance of looking good was also a central theme in the story "Der deutsche Teufel," in which the manager tells his charge, "Man, if I looked and punched like you, I'd be a famous and rich man in a couple of weeks!" In order to underline the importance of surface appearance, the manager exclaims just a few moments later, "How good you look, man!"[28] In *Das Renommee*, Brecht nicknamed his protagonist "Beautiful George," a good-looking fighter who modeled on the side and caused women to pursue him "like a pack of bloodthirsty hounds."[29] This fictional character did not differ all that much from the real-life French boxer Georges Carpentier, of whom *Sport im Bild* wrote in 1921 that he "captivates every heart, especially the female ones, with his handsomeness and strength."[30]

Prizefighters cultivated their physical appearance not only in order to appeal to new fans of the sport, but also because they often had one eye focused on a post-boxing career in the movies. The aforementioned 1921 article on Carpentier commented on his star turn in the film *The Wonder Man*, about which the author noted simply that Carpentier was "so strong, so noble, and so-o-o good-looking!"[31] Many of the biggest names in German boxing similarly pursued careers on the silver screen, in an ongoing pursuit of social and financial success that transcended the confines of the boxing ring. Hans Breitensträter appeared in movies as early as 1921, and the middleweight boxer Kurt Prenzel got a role in 1925. Max Schmeling probably came closest to achieving a synthesis of the prize fighter and the matinee idol by starring in two films that nevertheless still relied far more on his well-trained physique than on his abilities as a thespian: *Liebe im Ring* in 1930 and *Knockout* in 1934.[32]

If the male boxer had a counterpart anywhere else in the world of sports, it was in women's tennis, whose elite players followed the career trajectory of prizefighters to a remarkable degree. The media in Weimar Germany fawned over the formidably trained bodies of female players, just as they did over those of male boxers. Commentators, furthermore, described the control that female champions demonstrated on the court in the same mechanical metaphors to which readers had grown accustomed in boxing reportage. The tennis-player-turned-sports-reporter Ilse

Friedleben, for example, described her fellow tennis ace Cilly Aussem as having "achieved an astounding, machine-like accuracy in her shots and wonderful footwork through systematic, excellent training." Friedleben went on to praise Aussem's "goal-oriented will and undaunted competitiveness...which conducts things soberly and cold-bloodedly to her own advantage."[33] Aussem's "systematic training" revealed an embrace of Taylorism that any striving male boxer in the 1920s would have immediately recognized. Friedleben's gushing admiration for the "goal-oriented will and undaunted competitiveness" that she perceived in Aussem's on-court performances, moreover, idealized precisely those qualities in the female player that commentators had long celebrated in the male boxer. Women, Friedleben suggested, should also continually strive, improve themselves, and shoot for the top.

Female tennis players shared with boxers a similar relationship to the media, too. Both sets of athletes garnered just as much attention for their physical appearances, social doings, and enviable lifestyles as they did for their athletic skills. The champion female player was remaking her physical self in an even more dramatic fashion than the male boxer, given the prewar ideal of female delicacy from which she was departing. At the same time, her capacity to remake herself in a financial and social sense remained far more circumscribed than that of the prizefighter. Tennis was at a much earlier stage of professionalization than boxing in the 1920s, for one thing, and female athletes did not enjoy nearly the status and fan base that male athletes did. Because female players tended to come from middle- and upper-class backgrounds, their rise in social status lacked the unmistakable drama of the prizefighters, who had climbed their way out of the working-class milieu. Nevertheless, the mere fact that female champions had emerged as highly visible public figures in postwar society signaled a sea change in itself. Women, especially single women, occupied the public attention, a fact that opened up unprecedented opportunities to lead more independent lives.

Female tennis players pioneered the introduction of professionalism to women's sports in the postwar decade, as a few of them began to translate their athletic skills directly into personal income. This transition drew on the example of men's boxing, but it required an even greater degree of courage on the part of the first women to turn professional. Unlike boxing, which the public had long associated with gambling and cash prizes, tennis enjoyed a reputation into the 1920s as a purely amateur undertaking, free from commercial taint. When the French player Suzanne Lenglen made her trail-blazing decision to turn professional in 1926, she defiantly bucked tennis tradition and faced an outcry from sports purists. Lenglen, however, saw her decision as an act of self-empowerment. As she told a German sports magazine in 1928, "Why shouldn't I think about my future now that everyone for whom I've played has made their fortune?"[34] Her statement pointed to precisely that emancipatory element in sports that Annemarie Kopp had recognized in the previous year. Moreover, because the promoters and managers whose fortunes Lenglen helped to earn were men, readers could interpret her decision to turn professional as an act of specifically female emancipation, and not merely a generic liberation of the individual. Tennis, in Lenglen's view, had already evolved into a cutthroat business, and the female player faced only one decision: exploit the situation or be exploited by it. Lenglen chose the former.

Like the typical boxer in the 1920s, Suzanne Lenglen's life story opened itself up to an appealing—and strategically self-crafted—narrative of social mobility and up-by-the-bootstraps success. She had risen, by virtue of her own skill and business acumen, from a relatively modest lower-middle-class background to become one of the wealthiest and most prominent self-made women in interwar Europe. Just as in its reporting on professional boxers, the German press placed her remarkable financial success in the foreground of its stories on her career, on women's tennis, and on professional sports in general. The sports journal *Die Leibesübungen* reported in 1927 that Lenglen had taken in almost a million dollars during just one four-month tour. It went on to catalog her other business enterprises, which included public appearance fees, film roles, and royalties for articles that she regularly penned for newspapers and fashion magazines.[35] The sports commentator Willy Meisl compared Lenglen's skillful self-marketing to that of a professional boxer, noting that the hype and high ticket prices surrounding the legendary tennis match between Lenglen and the American player Helen Wills "had more in common with a prizefight."[36]

Lenglen's financial earnings easily rivaled that of professional boxers, but she represented an exceptional case of self-made wealth among female tennis players at the time. Only a very few had turned professional during this period, and none of them came close to Lenglen in terms of marketability. Even players who did not follow Lenglen into the world of professional sports, though, could still take advantage of money-making opportunities. Nominally amateur tennis players, according to one German sports magazine, easily found ways around the game's prohibition against appearance fees, and *Der Querschnitt* quipped in 1932 that tennis players readily explained away any suspect income by simply claiming "to be a representative for a tennis equipment manufacturer."[37] Celebrity status alone opened plenty of doors, of course, a fact that the tennis writer Burghard von Reznicek illustrated with the example of the American champion Helen Wills. "If Wills, the world champion, wants to go into film," he wrote in 1932, "or if she, a well-known illustrator, arranges an exhibition of her sketches, the type-setting machines of the world press will bow down [before her] with greedy joy."[38]

Paula von Reznicek, who divorced Burghard in order to chart her own path, was a good example of a tennis player who capitalized on her experiences and celebrity. In a series of moves that would have made even the most entrepreneurial prizefighters slightly envious, Reznicek used her top ranking in German tennis during the late 1920s, as well as her brief marriage to Burghard, as a platform to launch a second and far more lucrative career as a tennis commentator, author of women's handbooks, and overall social fixture. Celebrity of this kind proved comparatively easy to attain for a talented and highly motivated young player, given the general media attention to sports in the Weimar Republic and the fascination with female tennis players in particular. A 1930 article declared that just one impressive victory could mark "the moment when a tennis ace is born"; and the 1929 tennis novel *Lill* contained a passage in which the title character attracts legions of male and female fans overnight after winning a brilliant tournament victory.[39]

After capturing the 1931 singles titles at the French and Wimbledon championships, Cilly Aussem established herself as a national hero and one of the central figures on the German sports scene, male or female. Even before those triumphs, though, Aussem's youth, beauty, and powerful style of play attracted the spotlight. Her fame and success, and the financial stability that came with it, enabled her to engage in practices not widely available to German women in the 1920s, such as owning and driving her own automobile. As a 1928 article giddily reported, Aussem tooled around the French Riviera from tournament to tournament in her new Mercedes. The report cast Aussem both as a financial success, in that this nineteen-year-old daughter of a salesman had been able to afford her own car, and as a happily independent woman with a comfortable lifestyle, in that she drove herself and did so in the warm and scenic environs of the south of France.[40] Indeed, numerous profiles of female players featured the automobile as a symbol of these women's independence and self-made success. As the commentator and former player Nelly Neppach insisted, female players drove themselves to tournaments, "with the same sense of entitlement that the men have."[41] Profiles of both boxers and tennis players in the 1920s emphasized the good life that these athletes had attained through their own hard work and ambition.

More so than the automobile, though, the female tennis player's status as a single woman symbolized her independence and formed a defining component of her self-made image. The fictional Lill, whose author had conceived her as the quintessence of the tennis-playing New Woman, openly rebelled against her mother's persistent campaign to find her a husband. "We want to be free people for just a couple of years and not merely sheep on the marriage market," Lill declared in exasperation. "We want, first of all, to find ourselves physically and spiritually."[42] In an echo of Annemarie Kopp, Lill insisted on an opportunity to complete herself before deciding whether to marry, an opportunity that the world of tennis readily afforded. Then, and only then, might she enter into a relationship with a man on an equal footing.

A 1926 article presented women's tennis as notoriously resistant to family life and as a sport in which players had a tough time deciding between a "career as a mother" or "the winning of so many more tournament victories."[43] One retired female player even caricatured the "muscular" female tennis champion "who will spring around [on the court] until her old age, at which time I assume she will suitably decorate her childless home with silver trophies."[44] Rix, a supporting character in the 1929 novel *Lill*, possesses precisely the muscularity and self-sufficient spirit of this unnamed tennis champion. Her imposing and purportedly manly physique prompts hostile comments from both sexes, including her good friend Lill. Regarding her increasingly butch appearance and behavior, however, Rix responds: "I've adopted just enough from the men … that I'm man enough to defend myself against them."[45] Such calculated rejection of the prevailing standards of femininity illustrates the extent to which the figure of the tennis player had come to represent female independence in the Weimar Republic.

Although the preceding examples viewed the unmarried female player with hostility, their presentations of an alternative to matrimony would no doubt have appealed to a number of readers. The traditional priorities of *Kinder*, *Küche*, and *Kirche* (children, kitchen, and church) almost never appeared in connection with the tennis player. Instead, she pursued her financial, emotional, and sexual self-interest, living for herself and not others.[46] Even for married players, the sport nurtured independence and an opportunity to get out of the home. The establishment of all-women's tennis clubs, in particular, provided sanctuaries from the potentially constricting social roles that still prevailed in the Weimar Republic. In one of her ladies' handbooks, Paula von Reznicek celebrated these tennis clubs as places where women "make the rules, can do and have done what we want, can come and go without having to ask, 'Is it still OK to go into this bar?'...We are in control of the situation that we have created!"[47] Such clubs also gave women valuable leadership and administrative experience, thus providing yet another marketable skill with which the players could forge an independent path in the world.

As the sports advocate H. Reinking argued in 1925, the postwar woman particularly needed to cultivate the skills and temperament associated with elite athletes, because she "is more than ever in competitive life. She has to compete in public life, for her living, for her rights."[48] All Germans, Reinking agreed, though, could learn from the champion athlete about what it took to thrive in the new postwar order. In an economic and political climate that seemed to require rapid and continual adaptation, athletes like the male boxer and the female tennis player emerged as important models of successful self-transformation. These athletes dangled before the eyes of many in the Weimar Republic the tantalizing prospects of reinvention and social advancement, prospects that appealed especially to the working-class men and single women whose opportunities for advance the prizefighter and the tennis champion represented.

Notes

1. Harry Graf Kessler, diary entry for June 1930 in *Harry Graf Kessler: Tagebücher, 1918–1937*, ed. Wolfgang Pfeiffer-Belli (Frankfurt, 1996), 661.
2. Entry for August 1932 in ibid., 729.
3. Stefan Zweig, "The Monotonization of the World" (1925), reprinted in *The Weimar Republic Sourcebook*, ed. Anton Kaes, Martin Jay, and Edward Dimendberg (Berkeley, 1994), 398.
4. Vicki Baum, *Es war alles ganz anders* (Frankfurt, 1962), 377. Fan Hong has argued that sports played a similarly emancipatory role in Republican China in the 1920s. Fan Hong, *Footbinding, Feminism, and Freedom: The Liberation of Women's Bodies in Modern China* (Portland, 1997).
5. Walter Schönbrunn, "Körperliche Ertüchtigung," *Die Leibesübungen* (1930): 415. See Arnd Krüger, *Sport und Politik* (Hannover, 1975); Christiane Eisenberg, *"English Sports" und deutsche Bürger: Eine Gesellschaftsgeschichte 1800–1939* (Paderborn, 1999).
6. Annemarie Kopp, "Emanzipation durch Sport" (1927), reprinted in Gertrud Pfister, ed., *Frau und Sport* (Frankfurt, 1980), 69.
7. Siegfried Kracauer, "The Mass Ornament" (1927), reprinted in Kaes, et al., *Sourcebook*, 404–7.
8. Ted Kid Lewis, "Amerika gegen Europa," *Sport und Sonne* (1927): 551.
9. Joe Biewer, "Heinrich Müller: Wundersame Geschichte einer Entwicklung," *Das elegante Köln* (July 2, 1929): 4.
10. *Beckmanns Sport Lexikon A-Z* (Leipzig, 1933), 1951–52.

11. See Kai Marcel Sicks, "'Der Querschnitt' oder: Die Kunst des Sporttreibens" in Michael Cowan and Kai Marcel Sicks, ed., *Leibhaftige Moderne: Körper in Kunst und Massenmedien, 1918 bis 1933* (Bielefeld, 2005), 45.

12. On this iconic status, see David Bathrick, "Max Schmeling on the Canvas: Boxing as an Icon of Weimar Culture," *New German Critique* (1990): 113–36.

13. H. von Wedderkop, "Hans Breitensträter," *Die Weltbühne* (September 22, 1921): 296.

14. Christiane Eisenberg, "Massensport in der Weimarer Republik," *Archiv für Sozialgeschichte* (1993): 165.

15. Hannes Bork, "Der Deutsche Teufel," *Boxsport* (January 16, 1925): 24.

16. Karl Heinz Grétschel, "Sein letzter Kampf!," *Boxsport* (July 14, 1926): 25.

17. "Was waren uns die Olympischen Spiele?," *Frankfurter Zeitung* (August 13, 1928).

18. Max Schmeling, "Wie kamen Sie zu Ihrem Schicksal?" *Das elegante Köln* (December 1, 1929): 20.

19. "Schmelings zweite Heimkehr," *Sport und Gesundheit* (1929): 656.

20. "Da rollt der Dollar," *Boxwoche* (March 10, 1929): cover.

21. Bertolt Brecht, *Das Renommee—Ein Boxerroman* in *Werke*, vol. 17 (Frankfurt, 1989), 423.

22. For Schmeling's endorsement, see Birk Meinhardt, *Boxen in Deutschland* (Hamburg, 1996), 22. Franz Diener's ad for "Stuvkamp" salt appeared in *Boxsport* (March 29, 1927): 17 and for "Kressin-Mohar" cigarettes in *Boxsport* (December 15, 1926): 15.

23. On bodybuilding, see Bernd Wedemeyer, *Starke Männer, starke Frauen: Eine Kulturgeschichte des Bodybuildings* (Munich, 1996).

24. Regarding the photographs, see the advertisement in *Boxsport* (October 6, 1921): 17. On the porcelain figurine, see Dietrich Pawlowski, "Plaudereien über Prominente—mit Prominenten" in *Arena der Leidenschaften: Der Berliner Sportpalast und seine Veranstaltungen, 1910–1973*, ed. Alfons Arenhövel (Berlin, 1990), 102. Bernd Wedemeyer argues that bodybuilders pioneered self-marketing at the turn of the century, which included everything from endorsing training equipment to selling nude photos of themselves. See Wedemeyer, "Körperkult als Lebenskonzept: Bodybuilding und Fitnessboom" in *Schneller, höher, weiter: Eine Geschichte des Sports*, ed. Hans Sarkowicz (Frankfurt, 1996), 415.

25. Jack Dempsey interviewed by Djuna Barnes (1921) in *I Could Never Be Lonely Without a Husband: Interviews by Djuna Barnes*, ed. Alyce Barry (London, 1987), 284.

26. Rumpelstilzchen, feuilleton of October 16, 1924 in *Haste Worte?* (Berlin, 1925, vol. V), 43.

27. Hans Breitensträter, "Soll ein Sportsmann heiraten?," *Der Querschnitt* (1932): 394.

28. Hannes Bork, "Der Deutsche Teufel," *Boxsport* (January 16, 1925): 24.

29. Brecht, *Das Renommee*, 424.

30. Kurt Doerry, "Carpentier im Film," *Sport im Bild* (February 25, 1921): 254.

31. Ibid.

32. Breitensträter appeared in *Der Held des Tages* (1921, dir. Rudi Bach). Prenzel appeared in *Und es lockte der Ruf der sündigen Welt* (1925, dir. Carl Boese). Schmeling starred in *Liebe im Ring* (1930, directed by Reinhold Schünzel) and *Knockout* (1934, directed by Karl Lamac and Hans Zerlett).

33. Ilse Friedleben, "Deutsches Damentennis: Spaziergang unter Meisterinnen," *Sport und Sonne* (1928): 83.

34. Quoted in Jacques Mortane, "Suzanne Lenglens Erinnerungen," *Sport und Sonne* (1928): 152.

35. "Was Berufssportler verdienen können," *Die Leibesübungen* (1927): 132.

36. Dr. Willy Meisl, "Das Problem des Amateurismus," *Die Leibesübungen* (1927): 129.

37. W.A. Lamprecht, "Der Tennis-Berufsspieler," *Die Leibesübungen* (1927): 146; Heinz Alexander, "Was verdienen Amateure?," *Der Querschnitt* (1932): 410.

38. Burghard von Reznicek, *Tennis: Das Spiel der Völker* (Marburg, 1932), 202.

39. Burghard von Reznicek, "Kommende Cracks?," *Sport im Bild* (1930): 725; Stratz, *Lill*, 52.

40. "Zeitlupe," *Sport und Sonne* (1928): 237.

41. Beverley Nichols, "Señorita de Alvarez oder Tennis ohne Tränen," *Der Querschnitt* (1928): 566; Nelly Neppach, "Was trägt man zum Tennis?," *Sport im Bild* (1929): 948.

42. Rudolph Stratz, *Lill: Der Roman eines Sportmädchens* (Berlin, 1929): Rudolph Stratz, *Lill: Der Roman eines Sportmädchens* (Berlin, 1929), 52.

43. Mr. Buchgeister, "Ueber Frauensport," *Der Leichtathlet* (August 24, 1926): 22.

44. Nichols, "Señorita de Alvarez," 566.

45. Stratz, *Lill*: Stratz, *Lill*, 124.

46. On the trope of sexual assertiveness in female tennis players at the time, see Erik Jensen, *Body by Weimar: Athletes, Gender, and German Modernity* (New York, 2010).

47. Paula von Reznicek, *Auferstehung der Dame* (Stuttgart, 1928), 146.

48. H. Reinking, "Der Sport und seine Eingliederung in die körperliche Erziehung des weiblichen Geschlechts" in *Die körperliche Ertüchtigung der Frau* (Berlin, 1925), 95.

X

FRIENDS OF NATURE: THE CULTURE OF WORKING-CLASS HIKING

John A. Williams

For years, historians have tended to cast Social Democratic cultural efforts during the Weimar Republic as insufficiently progressive, too "bourgeois" in outlook and everyday practice, and therefore ineffective in building a solid ground of working-class support for Germany's fledgling democracy. A general consensus has evolved, according to which the weaknesses of the moderate workers' cultural movement contributed to the Social Democrats' failure to hinder the Nazis' accession to power.[1] This chapter revisits socialist cultural mobilization in a less judgmental and less teleological way. My analysis avoids the common tendency among scholars of Weimar to begin with liberal democracy's failure and work backward in a quest to uncover the causes of that failure. I focus here on one organization within the vast network of socialist cultural organizations, the Tourist Association "Friends of Nature" (*Touristenverein "die Naturfreunde,"* TVNF).

The *Naturfreunde* movement promoted a proletarian "turn to nature" through hiking, with the goal of improving the working class's physical, mental, and political strength. This project has to be seen within the ambiguous context of postwar malaise, competition for mass support, and myriad projects of national healing that characterized everyday popular culture in Weimar. Looking at socialist cultural efforts in this way allows us both to address the old question of success vs. failure and to ask entirely new kinds of questions. How did the socialist subculture address the everyday problems and desires of Weimar's industrial workers? What relationships between moderate Marxism, the working class, and nature did the *Naturfreunde* create? To what extent was the socialist turn to nature progressive for its time?

It should be stressed from the outset that the *Naturfreunde* movement for the most part conformed to a capitalist system that forced workers to rely on their bodily health as the prerequisite for their economic survival. Nevertheless, they cannot be justifiably accused of political apathy or "embourgeoisement."[2] TVNF leaders hoped to help German workers democratize the political and economic system from below. They are a classic example of the general effort by the socialist workers' cultural movement to transform the skilled German workers into "New Human Beings," who would lead the nation toward a better future characterized by genuine popular participation and social equality.[3]

The most original contribution of the *Naturfreunde* was the notion of "social hiking." This kind of hiking took groups of workers through their regional homeland, exposing them to the environment of the countryside and the industrial town, as well as to the social conditions of rural and urban workers. Social hiking was intended to reveal how working people lived and how capitalism was preventing them from developing "an active mind in a strong, beautiful body."[4] By combining experiences of the rural landscape with a strong commitment to social justice, the Weimar *Naturfreunde* thus attempted to use leisure as a tool to raise working-class consciousness and strengthen the proletarian collective.

Organization and Ideology

The *Touristenverein "Die Naturfreunde"* was founded in 1895 by a small group of Social Democratic artisans in Vienna. From the beginning the *Naturfreunde* saw capitalism as the enemy, arguing that capitalists alienated workers from nature by claiming the natural landscape as private property. The *Naturfreunde* wanted to give workers access to the natural landscape, a goal that was reflected in their official slogan. In opposition to the powerful bourgeois Alpine Association, whose motto was "*Berg auf*" ("Up the mountain"), they adopted the populist motto "*Berg frei*" ("the mountain is free," that is, accessible to workers). By 1914 the movement had spread to Germany, where it attracted some 12,000 mostly skilled male workers and an indeterminate number of their family members.[5]

Soon after the Weimar Republic was founded, the national TVNF organizational network became fully autonomous from the movement's international leaders in Vienna. In 1923 a German leadership committee took up residence at its office in Nuremberg. It presided over a federal structure in which eighteen district branches and hundreds of local groups maintained a high degree of independence. The membership of the TVNF expanded nearly ten times in early Weimar, from 20,753 people in 1919 to 116,124 in 1923. More non-proletarian members joined, most notably employees, civil servants, educators, and artists.[6]

The TVNF invested time, energy, and money establishing collectively owned property in the form of *Naturfreunde* houses. These served members as overnight hostels and as sites of meetings and celebrations. The number of such German houses rose rapidly, from 40 in 1922 to 160 in 1926 and 230 by the end of 1931.[7] Building projects were financed through members' contributions, lotteries, and subsidies or loans from local governments; and municipal governments sometimes donated building sites or materials. The SPD and trade unions often lent their support by petitioning authorities and publicly singing the praises of local TVNF groups at their groundbreaking ceremonies. Of course, the *Naturfreunde* had to compete for state funding with myriad other organizations. One way in which they tried to solve this problem was by joining its staunchest competitor for funding, the National Federation of Youth Hostels, in 1926. In return, *Naturfreunde* houses opened their doors to all adolescents, bringing many of them into contact with socialist hikers for the first time.[8]

The *Naturfreunde* were obliged to formulate their overtures to the state in language that was as politically neutral as possible. This was not all that difficult, for they shared the Weimar state's interest in social reform in general and the welfare of young people in particular. The local group in Neustadt, for instance, used typical "youth cultivation" rhetoric, arguing that working youths needed a *Naturfreund* house "to steel the body for new work, to prevent sickness, and to encourage serious weeknight activities for body and mind without the pressure to drink and smoke." Particularly during the winter, the lack of such meeting places was "driving youths into the arms of pulp literature and all the other enervating, de-moralizing winter activities, including the immoderate enjoyment of alcohol and tobacco."[9]

Such appeals were sometimes couched in terms of the good of the nation. The same Neustadt group reminded the Palatinate state government in 1923 that the working populace was suffering from the French occupation of the Rhineland. Due to the policy of passive resistance, there were many unemployed workers who would be helped by participating in the building project. "This house will be one day be a monument that bears witness to the fact that in a time of hardship, there were men and women here who gave their all for the good of the people and the Fatherland."[10]

Figure 10.1 Young *Naturfreunde* in the Upper Bavarian district meet at the Rohrauerhaus, 1924. Courtesy of the Naturfreunde Deutschlands, Bezirk München.

In no sector of Weimar political culture (except for the far Left) was this brand of defensive nationalism unusual at the time. Its use, and the use of youth cultivation rhetoric, shows the cleverness of the *Naturfreunde* in using politically consensual language in their appeals to the authorities.

In spite of the political divide between Social Democrats and Communists that weakened the Weimar labor movement, the membership of the *Naturfreunde* was politically varied. Leaders merely expected that a member would belong to one or the other Marxist party, and a significant minority of functionaries and members belonged to the Communist or Independent Socialist parties.[11] The few available memoirs claim that the rank-and-file members, be they socialists or communists, generally got along well in the local organizations. This reflected the lack of a strict segregation between communists and socialists in everyday life; they lived often side-by-side and interacted peaceably within working-class neighborhoods.[12]

Nevertheless, finding political consensus was difficult. Ideological divisions over practical and doctrinal issues increased among the leaders and functionaries, if not in the rank and file. In 1923–1924 and again in 1930–1932, the national leaders in Nuremberg, all Social Democrats, chose to expel thousands of communist-affiliated members as punishment for their attempts to push the movement in a more radical direction. During the first open controversy in 1923–1925, the membership fell from its all-time high of over 116,000 members to 83,853 by the end of 1924. By 1926, less than one-half of the membership of 1923 remained. After 1926, the numbers stabilized, and the TVNF began a phase of slow but steady growth, reaching about 61,000 by 1929. By the late 1920s, the TVNF was a skilled workers' and lower middle-class movement that was mostly committed to moderate socialism. It might well have eventually regained its 1923 levels if the Depression, and another surge of political polarization, had not put an end to the positive trend. Membership began to fall again, albeit more gradually. There were 59,126 *Naturfreunde* in 1930, and 58,134 in 1931. Still, even as late as 1931 there remained over 800 local groups in Germany.[13]

Political disagreements were not the only source of trouble for the *Naturfreunde*. Two broad trends threatened to deprive the movement of support from industrial workers and the lower middle class. One was the rationalization of industrial labor, which was evidently both exhausting and dispiriting for many factory workers.[14] An even more significant challenge was the expansion of the mass media and mass sports in the 1920s, which offered workers more ways to spend their leisure time than they had ever had before. The *Naturfreunde* thus had to work harder to convince workers that getting up early to go hiking was both a fun and meaningful way to spend one's precious free time.

To popularize and lend meaning to their movement, *Naturfreunde* leaders and spokespersons constructed in their public discourse official narratives of progress through "turning to nature." Although they sought consensus around such narratives, this was a tall order, as we will see. Nonetheless, there was a basic pattern that any narrative of turning to nature followed. It began with a detailed diagnosis of a particular social crisis (or crises). The next step involved advocating and describing an ideal method of turning to nature. The narrative concluded with a vision of improvement for the individual, for the entire membership of the TVNF, and ultimately for the entire nation.

It was easiest for Weimar *Naturfreunde* leaders to find a consensus regarding the problems that workers were facing. The first problem that they pinpointed and continually stressed was the exclusion of the working class from access to rural nature. Indeed, since its beginning the movement had represented such access as a basic human right and had attacked the capitalist system of private property for hoarding the rural landscape. Karl

Renner, one of TVNF's founders in Vienna, voiced this critique already in 1896 as follows:

> Not a single piece of the earth belongs to us. The house in which we live, the workshop in which we toil, the fields through which we hike—everything belongs to others. The tree under which we rest, the caves in which we seek shelter from the storm, the forest whose clean air strengthens our lungs— all of nature experiences us as strangers. We are strangers on this earth, for we have no part of it! They have left only the street to us!...They have divided the earth...among themselves and have granted us only the dust of the street.[15]

This lament, and the desire to appropriate the natural world, paralleled the labor movement's more general and ongoing attempt to gain access to Germany's classical cultural traditions, as represented by the works of Goethe, Schiller, Beethoven, and others. It also paralleled the Marxist goal of appropriating the means of industrial production for the good of workers.

Another problem that the Weimar *Naturfreunde* commonly stressed in their narratives was the rationalization of industrial production. This streamlining of work processes and regimentation of the workforce commenced in some industries during the period of relative stabilization in the mid-1920s. Social Democratic and union leaders generally supported it as necessary, if not progressive.[16] Yet the TVNF took a starkly negative view of the process, not only as a cause of structural unemployment, but even more so as a threat to the worker's body and psyche. As rationalized work processes took away the individual's humanity, he sank "into night and horror." The worker was becoming a docile, easily exploitable part of the machine who just happened to be made of flesh, blood, and mind.[17] These experiences, wrote the TVNF essayist Adolf Lau, "wear down any upwards-striving powers in the human being," turning the worker into "a docile beast of burden who knows no real cultural needs and thus has no part in the lively workings of nature." The only experience of nature left to the worker, Lau concluded, was the purely biological growth and decline of the physical body.[18] Such arguments were an innovative extension of the Marxist critique of alienation: the modern worker was not only alienated from the work process, but from nature itself.

A third problem that the *Naturfreunde* diagnosed was the threat of urban life to workers' physical and mental health and, ultimately, to polit- ical health as well. The city was a "stony desert" in which "millions were striving for air and light." It distracted and weakened the working class with "its modern non-culture (*Unkultur*), its poisonous enjoyment spots, its slick streets and people, its noise and unnatural smells of factory smoke and perfume, its breeding-grounds of terrible 'culture'-sickness."[19] And like most others on the Left, the *Naturfreunde* were suspicious of the new and increasingly popular mass media, movies in particular. The cinema, they announced, was a capitalist enterprise bent on exploiting the "taste of the uneducated masses," who "willingly let themselves be betrayed and deluded."[20]

There is reason to doubt that this forceful rhetoric against mass urban culture had a great influence on the rank and file. Working people took part in many different kinds of leisure pursuits and forms of sociability including, but not limited to, organized movements like the *Naturfreunde*. Indeed, the attack on mass media simply reflected the obvious availability of the many new ways for workers to spend their leisure hours, most of which were insufficiently political from the perspective of TVNF leaders. The need to win workers' support in the face of such competition made developing the second step in their narrative of progress—the formulation of methods of turning to nature—difficult for *Naturfreunde* leaders. For there was disagreement over how to make organizational practice appealing and popular, and that, it soon became clear, was fundamentally an issue of politics.

All *Naturfreunde* leaders could agree on the need to restore and maintain physical and mental health. They agreed that hiking was a great way to improve circulation, to provide relief from the crowded atmosphere of the working-class apartment, and to refresh the mind through exposure to a diversity of sensory impressions.[21] The most controversial question was: how could hiking be used to raise the political consciousness of the rank and file and thus help them gain access to nature, resist rationalization, and avoid the ills of mass urban culture?

The Bavarian *Naturfreund* Walter Trojan described the difficulty of appropriating hiking for political purposes in a 1925 essay. The war with its 10 million dead and 10 million wounded signaled a negative turning point in world history, Trojan wrote. Would a generation come that had the energy and ability to construct a new world? Socialists had to look at present conditions clearly and pragmatically; they had to drop their utopian promise that one day "a magnificent empire of peace, freedom and fraternity and socialism" would come. Many workers were reluctant to fight capitalism directly, Trojan argued, because of their lack of freedom and their obligations to family. And workers longed for enjoyment in everyday life, because they understood that at the end of the path of life stood death. The working mass did not understand why not only work, but free time, had to involve struggle. Should their little bit of leisure also be a struggle?[22]

An overarching *Naturfreunde* narrative of turning to nature through hiking developed rhetorically within this difficult context in the course of the 1920s. According to this narrative, which had become dominant by the mid-1920s in the published discourse of the *Naturfreunde*, work itself could provide no joy to the worker. Thus emotional experience had to be sought during one's free time, and only free time could save one from slavery to the machine.[23] Sport alone was not the solution, since the entire human being, not just the body, needed relief and redemption in order to become politically strong. Hiking in a group of one's peers was the best way to restore health, to offer the worker a diversity of sensory experiences and mental stimulation, and to strengthen the solidarity and political determination of the collective.

The emphasis on emotion was strong in this narrative, but it coexisted with a stress on progress through reason. Workers needed knowledge about the natural world, since only those who were attuned to science could take up the class struggle successfully.[24] Hiking, then, was a form of self-education in the "book of nature, whose pages are turned by the feet."[25] In this way, political consciousness could be raised. "Our first duty is to give to the mass of the proletariat knowledge of nature," announced the national leaders in Nuremberg. "But we will not stop at natural knowledge and hiking; both are useless if they fail to lead to the socialist deed." This deed, according to these leaders, was exemplified by the building of *Naturfreunde* houses, which were symbolic utopian acts of collective solidarity.[26]

These national leaders in Nuremberg spoke for the moderate Social Democratic majority in the TVNF. For the radical Communist and Independent Socialist minority, however, their narrative did not go far enough. The political divisions that emerged within the *Naturfreunde* movement resulted above all from the radicals' formulation of their own alternative narrative of turning to nature, at the end of which lay not peaceful democratization through reform, but violent revolution.

This radical narrative took shape as the moderate TVNF leadership began to clamp down on the Communist minority. At the 1923 national conference in Leipzig, a majority of *Naturfreunde* delegates agreed on the programmatic separation of political work and leisure activities, thereby sidestepping the strategic question of how to combine leisure and politics. Responding to the criticisms of the left-wing minority that such a separation would lessen the movement's political strength, Carl Schreck formulated a more specific resolution that the movement would be solely concerned with "the cultural value of hiking and the processes of nature."[27] A special conference adopted Schreck's resolution in October 1924, simultaneously granting the national leadership committee the right to expel individual members as well as entire local groups. The leaders in Nuremberg first exercised that right against the entire Brandenburg district, where local groups had been joining the revolutionary communist sports movement. The also expelled local groups in Solingen, Remscheid, and Cologne for the same reason.[28]

In a special issue of their district journal entitled "Against the Current," the Brandenburg leaders presented their response to the moderates. It is here that we find the radical narrative, which was rationalistic, militant, and masculinist. The radicals rejected the notion of a "third column" according to which the workers' cultural movement should leave economic and political issues to the parties and unions. For them there was no such thing as politically neutral cultural forms. They also rejected the moderates' emphasis on emotion, which they saw as emptily sentimental "gushing about nature" (*Naturschwärmerei*). "The paths of the proletariat in the homeland of Romanticism lead not 'back to nature,' but over barricades and mountains of corpses. They are hard, stony, and shadowless." Given this emphasis on militarism, what really counted for the radicals was "the task of building, through systematic physical cultivation (*Körperpflege*), a healthy, naturally-developed troop of fighters to achieve and sustain a proletarian people's state."[29]

Radicals in the *Naturfreunde* were thus representing themselves by 1924 as forward-looking, energetic class warriors, in contrast to the allegedly weak moderate majority. However, their actual narrative of improvement through hiking was strikingly similar to that of the moderates, and it was thus somewhat at odds with the hyperrationalist and militarist verbiage. This hiking narrative began with a worker's encounter with the local natural setting of his homeland, an encounter that was simultaneously emotional and rational: "Hiking in the region of the *Heimat* reveals an unknown world to the proletarian who is eager to learn. He sees nature at work in all its restless, intermeshed, and interdependent processes; and he is seized by a great love of nature that allows him to understand it." The narrative then moved to the healing power of nature and its ability to show the hiker how unnatural capitalism was: "[Nature] heals the worker's body and mind, [and he] comes to recognize the processes at work in human society and the unnatural state of affairs in the capitalist system." This experience of a nature that was running according to natural laws of justice would then spark the worker's political anger and his will to fight: "He feels himself strong, in complete possession of his powers, and he dares to reproach society for its lack of morality, culture, and authenticity. But the worker does not restrict himself merely to criticism. He takes up the fight alongside his comrades to establish proletarian cultural values."[30]

The joining of reason, emotion, and political militancy in this rhetoric of the early 1920s reflected the aim of creating an actively fighting working class, an aim held by the radical Left throughout the Weimar years. Yet this version of the narrative was still based on a holistic notion held in common with moderate *Naturfreunde*, the belief that hiking would advance the working class not only physically and mentally, but also politically. That view remained consensual throughout the history of the Weimar *Naturfreunde*. Soon an innovative notion of "social hiking" took shape as the organization tried anew to find a way to combine politics, leisure, and nature in everyday practice.

"Social Hiking" and Representations of Nature

Even though the radicals' demand to combine leisure and politics met with failure in the short term, their critique ultimately forced the *Naturfreunde* to recognize the need to formulate a more overtly political method of turning to nature. Beginning in the mid-1920s, the *Naturfreunde* developed a consensual narrative of turning to nature politically through a new kind of "social hiking" (*soziales Wandern*). This was their most innovative and daring contribution to Weimar Social Democracy and to German culture in general.

In the process of developing the concept of social hiking, they deployed the word "social" in two senses. First, they spoke of *collective solidarity* among workers, which they believed could be created through the group nature experience. Divisions of gender and generation could be transcended, leading to mutual respect and the sense of class commitment that was necessary for the development of new leaders.[31] Social hiking was also an opportunity to learn collectively about nature. As Mathilde Hürtgen of the Rhineland *Naturfreunde* wrote, hikers should teach themselves about "historical, regional, literary history; the study of plants, animals, geography; and human cultures and traditions." The many possibilities of collective self-education, she asserted, made social hiking superior to all other kinds of proletarian sport.[32]

Second, "social" stood in this narrative for political socialism, which would grow within the individual out the experience both of nature and of one's fellow workers. Getting to know workers in other locales and professions, in other words, was a way to raise socialist consciousness. Hikers needed to study the living, working, and health conditions of other workers, their places of work and leisure, and their political attitudes and mentalities.[33] Above all, social hikers had to learn about the economic backwardness and systematic inequality that were preventing Germany's progress toward social justice. As the Rhineland *Naturfreund* essayist Theo Müller wrote, "A short trip in which we observe the activity of the farmer, the poor forestry worker, and the craftsman can teach us more than any heavy tome."[34]

Although this "social hiking" narrative of turning to nature became the dominant one in the TVNF after 1925, controversy persisted between moderates and radicals over the political efficacy of hiking in this way. In fact, whether a given local *Naturfreunde* group paid any attention to social inequalities during a hike depended on the group's political stance. Groups under a moderate leadership often found it easy to focus on everyday work processes in lieu of a critique of capitalist exploitation. For instance, in an exhibition entitled "*Heimat* and Hiking" held in Munich in 1928, the exhibit on social hiking contained an original weaver's room and pictures of other workplaces, as well as various examples of regional handicrafts. The presentation was picturesque, with no critical discussion of Bavarian workers' economic situation.[35] By contrast, more radical groups emphasized critical sociological understanding as a precondition for true social hiking. At the 1925 conference of the Württemberg district, debate raged over whether groups should read and talk about sociology alongside natural science during its meetings and hikes. Radical delegates argued that only Marxist sociology could show workers the way to liberation. Social hiking without this knowledge was not truly social. Yet this was a minority view at the conference. One of the visiting national leaders, Xavier Steinberger, spoke against the teaching of sociology, using the tried and true moderate argument that the *Naturfreunde* should avoid all overt (that is, radical) political activity. A vote followed, and the sociology resolution failed.[36]

What did social hiking look like in practice? The frequency of TVNF hikes is impressive. In the Baden district, for instance, a total of 10,554 hikes with 115,279 participants took place between 1928 and 1931. 28 percent were hikes of just a few hours; 57 percent took an entire day; and 15 percent were hikes of several days duration.[37] Anywhere from 7 to 70 men, women, adolescents, and children typically participated in a *Naturfreunde* hike. What of the solidarity-building and socialist elements of social hiking? Viola Denecke has argued that the kind of hiking in which cities were visited and political discussion took place never became popular in the TVNF.[38] But in truth, there is simply not enough surviving evidence to be sure of this. Judging by the hiking announcements listed in district journals, groups on day hikes nearly always chose to leave the town and head for the countryside, which might imply an escapist attempt to leave the city and its problems behind. Yet longer journeys of a week or more often took hikers directly through towns and cities. Sometimes they even visited factories.[39]

The extent of political discussion during *Naturfreunde* activities is also impossible to gauge. Each local group held talks and discussions, but not much of this appears to have dealt directly with socialist theory or political events. In the discussion evenings and public exhibitions of the Baden district, for instance, the focus was on the natural phenomena, geography, history, and folk traditions of southwestern Germany.[40] There is other evidence that everyday discussions dealt mainly with natural phenomena and culture. Former *Naturfreund* Georg Graser described such occasions in another memoir:

> [I remember] the weekend hiking trips and the meadows surrounding the houses where motley groups of cheerful young people would camp, interspersed with young-at-heart adult leaders, all of whom used the informal *Du* in speaking to each other. I remember the "workers' academies," where the teacher—often an older, well-known man of science—would sit naked but for a loincloth under a tree. In the grass around him would lay a crowd of tanned, naked young boys and girls. Everyone had the right to interrupt the teacher, to question and to correct him.[41]

Even if this text does not indicate overtly political consciousness-raising, it does show that social hiking was taking place in the broader sense of building an egalitarian sense of community. Moreover, less formal discussions of politics may have taken place during hikes. According to the memoirs of former member Fritz Bohne, the *Naturfreunde* in their everyday activities studied botany, cooked, sang, and "did silly things together," but there was also a great deal of political discussion.[42]

Although we cannot draw any definite conclusions about political discussion in everyday TVNF practice, it seems clear that the *Naturfreunde* concept of nature itself was both democratic and socialist. The organization was obliged to appeal to workers by developing nature concepts and narratives of progress that meshed well with industrial workers' everyday experiences. We have already seen that a vision of the rural landscape as a site of physical, mental, and emotional recovery emerged as an alternative to everyday living and working conditions in the industrial city. What else can be said about the *Naturfreunde* movement's representation of nature?

First, the movement fashioned a new socialist version of the *Heimat* concept. Often in Weimar Germany, the rhetoric of *Heimat* or "homeland" was shot through with nostalgia for pre-industrial social hierarchies.[43] But the *Naturfreunde* clearly distanced themselves from this conservative *Heimat* ideal, developing an alternative concept that represented the natural landscape of Germany as both rural and industrial and as a site of potential social equality. This was the homeland behind the social hiking idea, in which city and country, industry and agriculture are all integral parts of the modern democratic nation. No part can exist without the others, and there is a strong ideal of equality between different ways of working and living.

This representation of the *Heimat* landscape as the unifying symbol of a socially diverse nation is also found in a 1931 speech on social hiking by one Dr. Schomburg. Addressing a meeting of *Naturfreunde* youths in northern Germany, Schomburg warned his audience not to seek only the sublime and the beautiful during a hike. Instead, the social hiker had to experience all the variety of the landscape, even that which seemed ugly. Thus *Naturfreunde* needed to hike not only in the agrarian countryside, but also through industrial towns. Nor should they hike only in the friendly seasons; they had also to face the storms of winter. Schomburg, in other words, was saying that there was much more to hiking than physical and aesthetic enjoyment—it was also about embracing all aspects of nature and the nation. And his ideal of social hiking transcended even nationalism. "We must expose the people to the diversity of life, not stopping at the political borders of the nation ... Whoever wants to learn to hike in a truly social way must also hike at least once into foreign lands." This would save the hiker from arrogance, for only in this way could people recognize that every nation, including Germany, had both good and bad qualities.[44] This version of *Heimat* demonstrates that the concept could merge with both the liberal-republican ideal of the nation and with the progressive internationalist tradition of socialism.

A second typical feature in *Naturfreunde* representations of nature was a strong current of rationalism. According to the "social hiking" narrative of progress, hiking would give workers a chance to learn about the laws of nature firsthand. Such knowledge would show them that capitalist society was fundamentally at odds with natural evolution, which the *Naturfreunde* saw as an inevitable progression toward a more just human society. The authors who wrote along these lines saw humanity's evolution not primarily as a process of violent struggle, but as an orderly, egalitarian process of cooperation and symbiosis.[45] The following passage in a 1930 essay by Ludwig Ziegler constructs a parallel between nature and an ideal socialist community:

> The simple observation that there is a uniform cell structure common to all plants and animals reminds of the equality that we are striving for in society. The study of plant and animal life reveals to us the existence of mutual aid among the organisms, the kind that we desire for our highly developed human race. Concepts like the division of labor, love, freedom, and joy—they can be comprehended in the processes that take place every day along the path of the proletarian hiker.[46]

In his "hiking diary" another member drew similar political analogies to natural processes: "'Mountains are kings, and wind and weather are the forces that wear them down into the valley of democracy.' I read that somewhere once. So that would be progress? Culture? Leveling. Equalization."[47] It should be noted that such gradualism was not to the liking of the radical minority of *Naturfreunde*, who tended to see human evolution as a struggle between the classes. Bourgeois society, wrote one, was "condemned to death by nature, which only knows eternal advancement…The dispossessed are in league with nature, and the possessing class is doomed."[48]

It seems unlikely, however, that ordinary members of the TVNF perceived nature in the same rationalist and scientific way as the spokespersons quoted above. There is very little we can say about the rank-and-file members' attitudes toward the landscape; the only remaining evidence exists in the form of a tiny number of hand-written hiking journals. One report from a local group in 1927, for example, describes six men and one woman taking the train to a nearby town, then hiking further.

> After climbing a small hill we stood before the cliff wall. Beneath us was an old mill with a half-decayed water wheel covered in moss. Above us on the edge of the cliff, knotty linden trees rustled in the wind. We walked a little further and we stood before a waterfall that must present a wonderful spectacle when there is a lot of water.[49]

This matter-of-fact language is typical of such reports, in which the authors generally use prosaic words or the term "romantic" when describing the landscape. A further bit of evidence comes from the few surviving photographic collections produced by *Naturfreunde* local groups.[50] Without exception, they show people contemplating a strictly rural landscape, with no sign of towns or factories. Often people look out over a rural landscape with their backs turned to the camera, echoing the classically Romantic landscape tradition of Caspar David Friedrich and others.

What this scanty evidence does suggest is that rank-and-file *Naturfreunde* did not view nature in a very rationalistic way. Indeed, some of the leading members who published their thoughts in TVNF journals seemed to realize this. They combined their interest in natural laws with a strongly emotional emphasis on reverence and happiness. For Walter Trojan, "Reason and emotion go hand-in-hand in the hiker, and this combination alone makes the full human being."[51] And Adolf Lau of the Rhineland *Naturfreunde* offered an optimistic vision of the future in which approaching nature in both a rational and an emotional way would make nature "the wellspring (*Born*) of new life energy." "Every person will stand close to every other," Lau predicted with striking optimism, "and all these individuals' unique *internal* experiences of nature will unite, giving life to a higher community. This will be made possible by a friendship between human beings and nature that encompasses the entire world."[52] This is an extraordinary statement of solidarity among people and with nature. It demonstrates that reason and emotion, the ideal of a democratic human community across national boundaries, and protoenvironmentalist thinking could be joined together in a socialist concept of nature.

Indeed—and this is a third significant feature of TVNF concepts of nature—the Weimar *Naturfreunde* were unique in the entire Marxist labor movement in struggling against environmental destruction. At the forefront of the movement's conservationist efforts were the relatively moderate leaders. The handful of more radical figures who had anything to say about nature protection argued that only the revolutionary destruction of capitalism itself would end the overexploitation of nature. This attitude was analogous to the dominant radical view of women's rights and human rights, and it meant putting off efforts at practical change until after the revolution. Any such efforts at the present time would be a "useless waste of proletarian energies."[53]

Historian Ulrich Linse has criticized the *Naturfreunde* for allowing "bourgeois values" to enter the movement in the form of conservationism.[54] At first glance, the history of German conservationism would seem to justify such criticism. The conservation movement had originated as an elitist, conservative project of the educated bourgeoisie at the end of the nineteenth century. At its heart lay antipathy to socialism and disdain for the "masses." And yet, Linse ignores the potential of the conservationist idea itself to capture the imagination of German industrial workers, some of whom were already protesting pollution and landscape destruction in the late nineteenth century. Thus it is not surprising to find the *Naturfreunde* leadership already in 1911 adding "the cultivation of *Heimat* and nature preservation" to the organization's national statutes.[55] This version of conservationism was not "bourgeois"; rather it was an adaptation of the *Naturschutz* idea to an oppositional protest movement. Moreover, conservationist ideology had much in common with the *Naturfreunde* goal of helping the common people recover from urban and industrial life. There was nothing uniquely conservative, bourgeois, or German about this. The demand for workers' access to nature has characterized many conservationist initiatives elsewhere in the modern age.[56]

Because conservationism was not inherently conservative, then, the *Naturfreunde* were able to incorporate it into their project of creating a socialist future. They asserted that nature conservation was a practical way to counter the harmful consequences of capitalist greed. As one essayist put it, most human beings were driven by "the fanatical desire for property," so they looked at the landscape through the eyes of the "would-be owner." This attitude was devastating for nature, since plants and animals were helpless against the invasion of the "vastly more powerful human species." Conservationists in the *Naturfreunde* had to take up the struggle against this "mental condition" by popularizing a sense of community between human beings and nature.[57] This ethos of nature protection was communicated to *Naturfreunde* members in a number of ways. For instance, it was prominent in the movement's rules of correct hiking:

> Spare and safeguard nature!...Do not yell or make loud noise when moving through nature, especially in the woods. At resting spots, do not litter and do not break bottles and glasses. Anyone who likes to explore caves should avoid damaging their most beautiful ornaments, the stalactites and stalagmites. We ask all those who share our opinion in this matter to join us in the battle against false attitudes toward nature, and to help us fight hiking abuses (*Wanderunsitten*).[58]

Naturfreunde essayists also called for laws to protect relatively undisturbed natural areas, and they voiced their support for activist conservation leagues like the Nature Park Association (*Verein Naturschutzpark*). The

TVNF also undertook efforts to promote conservation in the general public through local exhibits and the distribution of flyers.[59]

More daringly, the *Naturfreunde* sometimes participated in local protests aimed at preserving recreation areas near the cities. Local groups in the Rhineland, for example, protested against the regulation of the lower Rhenish waterways, which obliterated many of the lakes close to industrial centers. Young people seem to have been particularly active in this regard, on occasion even taking on the military. The *Naturfreundejugend* in Dresden held an "anti-war hike" in 1930 that culminated in their brief occupation of an army exercise field. Their purpose was to call attention to the destruction of nature by the military.[60]

Division and Destruction, 1929–1933

The *Touristenverein "Die Naturfreunde"* offered one of those alternative pathways that make Weimar culture in hindsight so interesting, a popular project that *might* have succeeded—if only it had had more time and a more stable economic and political context. Organized socialist hiking in the Weimar Republic was grounded in firm commitments to human rights, equality, and reverence for the natural world. At their best, the Weimar *Naturfreunde* showed that reason and emotion, the ideal of a democratic human community across national boundaries, and proto-environmentalist thought could indeed join together in a liberal-republican conception of nature.

But the period of relative political stability in the *Naturfreunde* was as brief as the time of stability enjoyed by the Weimar Republic itself. The years 1925–1928 were not adequate for the TVNF to put down its roots firmly in popular culture. Unfortunately for the movement, there was a resurgence in 1928 of political struggle between the moderate majority and the radical minority within the TVNF. Following Stalin's accession to power in the USSR in 1928, the German Communist Party underwent a phase of radicalization that put an end to any chance of cooperation with the Social Democrats. The KPD more and more stridently criticized the SPD, and communist *Naturfreunde* worked to draw other members away from "social fascism," their new term for Social Democracy. In 1929 a number of local groups in Saxony, Thuringia, Württemberg, Saarland, and the Rhineland joined a newly created communist sporting federation, the Fighting League for Red Sport Unity (*Kampfgemeinschaft für rote Sporteinheit*). On the national level, an Oppositional Naturfreunde Committee was formed.[61]

The Social Democratic leaders of the TVNF realized that not only the movement's political solidarity, but also its property in the form of *Naturfreunde* houses, were under threat. The national leadership committee in Nuremberg presented an ultimatum to the radical groups: either refrain from all "party-political activity" (such as membership in the Fighting League) or face expulsion. By the national conference in Dresden of August 1930, the TVNF had expelled several local groups. At that meeting, a majority of delegates supported the leadership's policy of expulsion; and the leaders at Nuremberg passed a resolution giving themselves authority to expel local groups without the official consent of the broader organization. This put a de facto end to the federalist division of powers among the eighteen *Naturfreunde* districts; henceforth crucial powers would be in the hands of a small number of anticommunist leaders in Nuremberg. These leaders demonstrated a high degree of political hypocrisy at the conference. Xavier Steinberger announced that there was room for different political viewpoints in the organization—as long as everyone refrained from agitation in support of specific parties. Yet he went on to call on the delegates to support the SPD in the upcoming national election to be held on September 14, 1930, earning mockery from the opposition.[62]

There followed many more purges of local groups from the TVNF—no fewer than 213 by 1932. The minority communist factions schemed to draw local groups into the KPD fold, with the "hiking section" of the *Fighting League for Red Sport Unity* developing strategies to that effect. Communists, they wrote, should send representatives to meet with local groups during their discussion evenings. They should attempt to take over the discussion, making sure that current politics as well as advancements in the Soviet Union took up time. Should this tactic fail, they would smuggle in new members to undermine Social Democratic influence.[63] The national leaders in Nuremberg responded with their own "defensive measures," demanding that all new members undergo a background investigation to see whether they might be KPD spies.[64]

Yet the situation was more complex than it appears, suggesting that the political divisions of late Weimar were forced on the rank and file from above. Despite polarization at the upper echelons of leadership, the tradition of solidarity that came from communal hikes and house construction continued to stabilize the movement in the early 1930s. Communist and socialist *Naturfreunde* continued in several places to cooperate unofficially. People of differing political views could still make a local group function from day to day. Also, many groups were critical of both the moderate leaders and the radicals, committing themselves only tentatively to one side or the other. The local group in Leipzig, for instance, criticized the polarizers for losing sight of "the democratic rights of the membership," and they called for a renewed commitment to political neutrality as the basis for reunification.[65]

It seems possible that the "social hiking" consensus might have held the movement together if not for this power struggle between socialist and communist functionaries. However, in what might have been an unconscious attempt to quell emotions during this time of political strife, the spokespersons for *Naturfreunde* hiking undertook a rhetorical shift that may have further weakened the movement. This involved moving away from the aforementioned synthesis of rationalism and emotionalism that had become so integral to the "social hiking" idea. By 1929 *Naturfreunde* writers were representing social hiking as a strictly "no nonsense" practice and rejecting the reverent Romantic approach to nature as outdated, reactionary, and "bourgeois." As one wrote, "The remnants of Romantic hiking in our ranks must be overcome, because unworldly Romanticism does not suit us, and it hinders us in our battle to conquer the world . . . The socialist is not only for a planned economy, he is also for planned hiking."[66]

Of course it is impossible to prove that the draining away of emotionality from hiking discourse reduced the attraction of the *Naturfreunde* for Germany's workers. But judging by the rare bits of evidence of working-class attitudes to nature, which were often infused with emotion and (sometimes Christian or pantheistic) reverence, we can reasonably infer that jettisoning Romanticism in favor of rationalism was a mistake. Here are just some examples from surveys of working-class young people:

How beautiful, when you see God's world waking up. Then you realize how small and insignificant we are in the face of nature.[67]

My mother and grandmother still believe in God and go to church. That's not for me. If I want to pray, I can do it when I take a hike. There I see nature, and that is my God.[68]

Religion is a far-reaching idea. Many people think that it is pious to go continually to church . . . I find that repulsive; for I and my colleagues have discovered that of 50 people who go to church, only five are truly pious. The rest go only to be admired in their new clothes or to have a rendezvous. My religion is nature with its many wonders. Here I feel divinity, here God's omnipotence reveals itself, here one sees that there must be a higher power.[69]

In short, political division and, probably, the denigration of emotionality severely reduced the popularity of the *Naturfreunde*. The economic crisis that began in 1929 further contributed to the stagnation of the TVNF's membership and caused great financial difficulties for the movement. Many local groups could no longer pay their dues to the national organization, as even better off workers were falling onto hard times.[70] Things grew worse as the Depression wore on. By 1932, one local group had only two employed members left, for instance; and there was a drastic decline in the numbers of young workers in the movement.[71]

TVNF property also came under threat during these years of economic crisis. Local groups were often heavily in debt because of their building projects. Before the Depression, these debts had been met in part by fees charged to non-members to stay overnight in the houses. But such visitors declined rapidly in number after 1929, and groups began requesting help from the national leaders to save their houses from being reclaimed by creditors.[72]

Moreover, as the Nazis' political fortunes improved in the crisis situation of late Weimar, the network of *Naturfreunde* houses became one of their targets. In 1931 the leader of the Frankfurt local group received the following letter from an anonymous Nazi:

> I warn you, honorable Herr Comrade, that we are going to spoil the attempts by you pack of proletarians to contaminate the Taunus region with your so-called *Naturfreunde* houses... You dirty pack of proles belong in the factory, in prison, or at the pig-trough, but not in God's free nature. Germany awake, awake, awake![73]

Thugs undertook to vandalize some of the houses as well. For instance, in April 1932 they laid waste to one house near the northern town of Maschen and smeared it with swastikas. These attacks increased in frequency after the *Naturfreunde* entered the SPD's anti-Nazi propaganda federation, the Iron Front, in early 1932.[74]

On January 30, 1933 President Paul von Hindenburg named Adolf Hitler chancellor of Germany. The Nazis used the Reichstag fire to convince Hindenburg to pass a "Decree for the Protection of Nation and State" on February 28. Using these and other police decrees, the new regime began to clamp down on the Marxist labor movement between March and May. Underestimating the Nazis' totalitarian determination to take complete control of the state and civil society, the TVNF national leaders in Nuremberg, Xaver Steinberger and Leonhard Burger, did everything they could to save the organization. This included attempts to downplay the movement's Marxist tradition and to appease the Nazis through "self-synchronization" (*Selbstgleichschaltung*). On March 16, Burger and Steinberger sent a memorandum to all local groups advising them not to do anything that might raise the suspicion of illegal activity. The TVNF had nothing to hide, they wrote, since it had always worked legally in the service of the nation. Therefore groups must obey all state laws and decrees and must take all possible steps against attempts of the now illegal Communist Party to invade the organization.[75]

Yet the national leadership's effort to conform failed to convince the new regime. The Nazis banned the *Naturfreunde* as a threat to the nation and did their best to track down and punish the surviving remnants of local groups throughout the 1930s. Nevertheless, through the Nazi "Strength Through Joy" initiative, they offered organized hikes in an attempt to negotiate the consent of industrial workers to their rule. This was itself an ironic measure of the popularity of proletarian hiking by the 1930s.[76]

Conclusion

The decline of the *Naturfreunde* movement was due not to any inherent ideological weaknesses, but to the larger conditions of political polarization and economic collapse that weakened the Weimar Republic itself. Thus the problems of late Weimar can be seen in microcosm in the fate of the popular cultural movement that was the *Naturfreunde*. Culture and politics were intertwined then—perhaps they always are. But the history of the Friends of Nature also has something to tell us about the complex relationship between culture and nature in the modern age. This movement was a left-wing example of a broader popular tendency, in Germany and elsewhere, to seek answers to the problems of modern life in a "turn to nature." Proponents of such a turn to nature were deeply disturbed by the consequences of capitalist industrialization and urbanization. Historians have long interpreted this critical stance as simply antimodern; and in the German case, they have often accused nature movements before 1933 of setting the cultural stage for the "romantic" and antimodern nature worship that *allegedly* characterized Nazism.[77]

In fact, those cultural activists who focused on nature in the Weimar Republic were for the most part thoroughly modern and sometimes strikingly progressive for their time. The *Naturfreunde* movement's offer of improved health, intertwined as it was with their socialist critique of capitalism, held great potential to attract those workers who desired the solace that contact with rural nature and with their fellow workers undeniably offered. Moreover, the determined efforts by *Naturfreunde* leaders and publicists to instill an ethic of stewardship in the working class, as well as the organization's occasional public demonstrations in favor of nature conservation, are early examples of popular environmentalism in Germany. In this the *Naturfreunde* were swimming against the main current of Marxism, an ideology that shared with capitalism a technocratic, utilitarian notion of progress through the exploitation of nature.[78] The *Naturfreunde* saw in nature not only a realm of working-class liberation and health, but also something that had intrinsic value and beauty.

Ultimately this movement fell victim to the same crises that destroyed the Weimar Republic—the Great Depression, the polarization of political culture, and the rise to power of the National Socialists. Yet given more time and a more stable political and economic situation, the *Naturfreunde* might have succeeded in using workers' desires for a more healthy and natural life in order to strengthen the popular commitment to republican democracy.

Notes

1. See, for example, Josef Mooser, *Arbeiterleben in Deutschland, 1900–1970* (Frankfurt, 1984); David Barclay and Eric Weitz, eds., *Between Reform and Revolution: German Socialism and Communism from 1840 to 1990* (New York, 1998); Geoff Eley, *Forging Democracy: The History of the Left in Europe, 1850–2000* (Oxford, 2002). A more positive view can be found in K. H. Pohl, *Die Münchener Arbeiterbewegung* (Munich, 1992); Hans-Werner Frohn, *Arbeiterbewegungskulturen in Köln, 1890 bis 1933* (Essen, 1997). This chapter is adapted from *Turning to Nature in Germany: Hiking, Nudism, and Conservation, 1900–1940* by John Alexander Williams, © 2007 Board of Trustees of Leland Stanford Jr. University, by permission.

2. Since 1984 several German studies of the *Naturfreunde* have appeared. These are primarily organizational histories, and analyses of ideology and practice are few. Those that address ideology generally make the misleading argument that the TVNF was fundamentally "bourgeois" and thus a failure. Williams, *Turning*, 283–84.

3. On the *Arbeiterkulturbewegung*, see Rob Burns and Wilfried van der Will, *Arbeiterkulturbewegung in der Weimarer Republik* (Frankfurt, 1982); Friedhelm Boll, ed., *Arbeiterkultur im europäischen Vergleich* (Munich, 1986) and *Arbeiterkulturen zwischen Alltag und Politik* (Vienna, 1986); W. L. Guttsmann, *Workers' Culture in Weimar Germany* (New York, 1990); Peter Lösche, ed., *Solidargemeinschaft und Milieu: Sozialistische Kultur- und Freizeitorganisationen in der Weimarer Republik* (Berlin, 1990–1993, 4 vols.).

4. Theodor Waechter, "Soziales Wandern," *Aufstieg* (1929): 1.

5. Workers' wives and childern were categorized as "auxiliaries" and not counted in the TVNF's official statistics. See Williams, *Turning*, 76–77.

6. The most politically radical districts were Brandenburg and Thüringen, and there were also communist-led local groups in Berlin, Württemberg, and the Rhineland. Viola Denecke, "Der Touristenverein 'Die Naturfreunde'" in Franz Walter, et al., *Sozialistische Gesundheits- und Lebensreformverbände* (Bonn, 1991), 242–43, 273–75, 285.

7. Historische Kommission zu Berlin (hereafter HKB), NB457: TVNF Reichsleitung to Allgemeiner Deutscher Gewerkschafts-Bund (July 19, 1926); Wulf Erdmann and Klaus-Peter Lorenz, "Baumeister der neuen Zeit: Das Naturfreundehäuserwerk entsteht" in *"Mit uns zieht die neue Zeit": Die Naturfreunde*, ed. Jochen Zimmer, et al. (Cologne, 1984), 141–83.

8. HKB, NB457: "Grundsteinlegung des Naturfreunde-Ferienheimes und der Jugendherberge Am Üdersee"; Anon., *Das Naturfreundehaus auf dem Rohrberg bei Weissenburg in Bayern* (Nuremberg, 1925): 7–8.

9. Bayerisches Hauptstaatsarchiv München (hereafter BayHStAM), MK13977: TVNF Ortsgruppe Neustadt to Stadtverwaltung Neustadt (November 12, 1922). On youth cultivation, see Williams, *Turning*.

10. BayHStAM, MK13977: TVNF Ortsgruppe Neustadt to Regierung der Pfalz (July 24, 1923).

11. Ibid.

12. Denecke, "Touristenverein," 276–77; Klaus-Michael Mallmann, *Kommunisten in der Weimarer Republik* (Darmstadt, 1996).

13. Denecke, "Touristenverein," 257, 273–75. No 1932 figures are available.

14. Herbert Winkler, *Die Monotonie der Arbeit* (Leipzig, 1922); Alf Lüdtke, "'Deutsche Qualitätsarbeit,' 'Spielereien' am Arbeitsplatz und 'Fliehen' aus der Fabrik: Industrielle Arbeitsprozesse und Arbeiterverhalten in den 1920er Jahren" in Boll, *Arbeiterkultur*, 155–97.

15. Karl Renner, "Der Arbeiter als Naturfreund und Tourist," *Der Naturfreund* (1926, orig. 1896): 3–4.

16. Hans-Albert Wulf, *"Maschinenstürmer sind wir keine": Technischer Fortschritt und sozialdemokratische Arbeiterbewegung* (Frankfurt, 1987).

17. Fritz Endres, "Die ideellen und kulturellen Werte der Naturfreundebewegung," *Nordbayerischer Wanderer* (1930): 20; Karl Eckerlin, "Warum Arbeitersport- und Wanderbewegung?," *Aufstieg* (December, 1929): 1-2; Gustav Riemann, "Der Kampf um unsere Freiheit," *Nord- und Ostdeutscher Wanderer* (1930): 51.

18. Adolf Lau, "Naturfreundschaft als Faktor des kulturellen Aufstieges," *Der Naturfreund* (1926): 210.

19. Anon., "Aufwärts!," *Rheinisches Land* (1927): 149; Theo Müller, "Neue Kultur—Naturfreundschaft," *Rheinisches Land* (1926): 129.

20. Richard Kunze, "Kinokultur und richtiges Wandern," *Der Wanderfreund* (1920): 66.

21. Anon., "Des Wanderns Einfluss auf die Nerven," *TVNF, Gau Mittelrhein-Main* (December, 1921).

22. Walter Trojan, "Das Erlebnis des Zeitgeschehens," *Nordbayerischer Wanderer* (1925): 82.

23. Gustav Riemann, "Der Kampf um unsere Freiheit," *Nord- und Ostdeutscher Wanderer* (1930): 51.

24. Bruno Krause, "Wissenschaft und Klassenkampf," *Die Naturfreunde: Mitteilungsblatt für den Gau Rheinland* (November, 1924): 1.

25. Fritz Endres, "Vom Sinne des Wanderns," *"Berg frei": Mitteilungsblatt des TVNF, Gau Pfalz* (1922).

26. Bundesarchiv Berlin, Stiftung Archiv der Parteien und Massenorganisationen der DDR (hereafter SAPMO-BArch), RY22/V SUF/419: Reichsleitung to TVNF, Gau Brandenburg (July 15, 1924).

27. Quoted in ibid., 250.

28. SAPMO-BArch, RY22/V SUF/419: Reichsleitung to Gau Brandenburg; Augustin Upmann and Uwe Rennspiess, "Organisationsgeschichte der deutschen Naturfreundebewegung bis 1933" in Zimmer, et al., *Zeit*, 81–82; Denecke, "Touristenverein," 251. Solely from the standpoint of organizational unity, these expulsions were justified, as the KPD was conspiring to destabilize the TVNF by creating communist factions at the local and district levels. Bundesarchiv Berlin (hereafter BArch), R58/782: "Diskussionsgrundlage für die Regelung der Frage des Arbeiter-Wanderer-Bundes und des TVNF" in "Auszug aus Informationsblatt der KJD, Bezirk Nordbayern Nr. 5 vom 25.7.24," attached to Preussischer Minister des Innern to Polizeipräsidenten Abteilung XA (October 16, 1934).

29. SAPMO-BArch, RY22/V SUF/420: Herrmann Leupold, "Die Kultur des Proletariats und die Aufgaben der Naturfreundebewegung," *Gegen den Strom* (1924): 6–7, and Emil Jensen, "Die proletarische Kulturbewegung" in ibid., 9.

30. Jensen, "Kulturbewegung," 10.

31. Willy Buckpesch, "Der Wert des Jugendwanderns," *Luginsland* (1927): 56–57.

32. Mathilde Hürtgen, "Sollen wir Sport oder Kultur pflegen?," *Rheinisches Land* (1926): 151.

33. Werner Mohr, "Soziales Wandern," *Der Naturfreund* (1930): 218.

34. Theo Müller, "Ein 'Berg frei' dem neuen Jahr!," *Die Naturfreunde: Mitteilungsblatt für den Gau Rheinland* (January, 1925): 1–2.

35. BayHStAM, MK13977: "Heimat und Wandern," *Fränkische Tagespost* (December 21, 1928).

36. K.M., "Die Gaukonferenz in Stuttgart," *Aufstieg* (March, 1925): 1–3.

37. Heinrich Coblenz, *Geschichte der badischen Naturfreunde* (Karlsruhe, 1947), 26–27.

38. Denecke, "Touristenverein," 258.

39. Eco-Archiv im Archiv der Sozialen Demokratie der Friedrich-Ebert Stiftung (hereafter Eco-Archiv), Ortsgruppe Kuchen, *Wanderberichtsbuch*: "Tageswanderung am 4. März 1928."

40. Coblenz, *Geschichte*, 100–8.
41. Georg Glaser, *Geheimnis und Gewalt* (Stuttgart, 1953), quoted in Jochen Zimmer, "Vom Walzen zum sozialen Wandern" in *Studien zur Arbeiterkultur*, ed. Albrecht Lehmann (Münster, 1984), 161.
42. Interview with Franz Bohne, reprinted in Zimmer et al., *Zeit*, 282.
43. This rhetoric characterized the Weimar bourgeois conservationist movement, for example. Williams, *Turning*, 219–56.
44. Prof. Dr. Schomburg, "Soziales Wandern," *Der Naturfreund aus Gau Nordmark* (1932): 3–7.
45. In this they were probably influenced by Peter Kropotkin's writings on symbiosis.
46. TVNF München, *Festschrift zum 25jährigen Bestehen* (Munich, 1930), 39.
47. Lutz Lerse, "Aus meinem Wanderbuch," *Der Naturfreund* (1922): 82.
48. M. Frenzel, "Natur und Mensch," *Der Wanderfreund* (1920): 26.
49. Eco-Archiv: Eugen Bielforth, report of a hike on October 16, 1927 in Ortsgruppe Kuchen, *Wanderberichtsbuch*.
50. Magistrat der Stadt Mörfelden-Walldorf, ed., *"Der Konrad, der hat die Mandoline gespielt und ich die Gitarre": Eine kulturgeschichtliche Ausstellung zur Naturfreundebewegung der Weimarer Republik am Beispiel der Ortsgruppe Mörfelden* (Mörfelden-Walldorf, 1992), 104–5; Wulf Erdmann and Klaus-Peter Lorenz, *Die grüne Lust der roten Touristen* (Hamburg, 1985).
51. Trojan, "Erlebnis," 82.
52. Lau, "Naturfreundschaft," 212.
53. For instance, Meyer, "Für den Naturschutz!," *Der Wanderfreund* (1922): 77.
54. Ulrich Linse, "Die 'freie Natur' als Heimat: Naturaneignung und Naturschutz in der älteren Naturfreundebewegung" in *Hundert Jahre Kampf um die freie Natur: Eine illustrierte Geschichte der Naturfreunde*, ed. Jochen Zimmer and Wulf Erdmann (Cologne, 1991), 68–70.
55. Staatsarchiv Leipzig (hereafter STAL), PPL-V, Nr. 708: "Satzungen des Gesamtvereins, beschlossen auf der 7. Hauptversammlung zu München, Pfingsten 1913." On proto-environmentalist attitudes and protest in the working class, see Williams, *Turning*, 67–69.
56. Peter Coates, *Nature: Western Attitudes Since Ancient Times* (Berkeley, 1998), 161–62; Peter Gould, *Early Green Politics: Back to Nature, Back to the Land, and Socialism in Britain, 1880–1900* (Brighton, 1988).
57. Anon., "Der Sinn des Naturschutzes," *Rheinisches Land* (1926): 154.
58. SAPMO-BArch, RY 18/II 142/1: TVNF, "Schutz und Schonung der Natur" (c. 1921).
59. Markwart, "Der werdende Naturschutzpark in der Lüneburger Heide," *Der Naturfreund aus dem Gau Nordmark* (October, 1924); Anon., "Zwei deutsche Naturschutzparke," *Nordbayerischer Wanderer* (1925): 135; Die Gauleitung, "Unsere Arbeit im Jahre 1926/27," *Nordbayerischer Wanderer* (1928): 50; Hans Peter Schmitz, "Naturschutz—Landschaftsschutz—Umweltschutz:" in

Zimmer, et al., *Zeit*, 184–204; Jochen Zimmer, "Kleine Chronik 'Naturschutz und Naturfreunde'" in Zimmer and Erdmann, *Kampf*, 78–81.

60. "Um den Schutz der Natur," *Rheinisches Land* (1926): 137–39; Jochen Zimmer, "'Grüne Inseln im Klassenkampf'?" in Zimmer and Erdmann, *Kampf*, 46.

61. Upmann and Rennspiess, "Organisationsgeschichte," 85; Peter Friedemann, "Die Krise der Arbeitersportbewegung am Ende der Weimarer Republik" in Boll, *Arbeiterkultur*, 229–40.

62. While the moderate leaders in the Nuremberg central committee have been justly criticized for their behavior at the Dresden conference, the radical minority at this meeting also contributed to the polarization by, for example, demanding that leading *Naturfreunde* functionaries leave the Christian church. "Die III. Reichsversammlung der Naturfreunde Deutschlands," *Der Naturfreund* (1930): 228-29; Eco-Archiv: TVNF Ortsgruppe Weissenburg, "Rundschreiben des TVNF Reichsleitung für Deutschland" (April 5, 1933), 3-4; Denecke, "Touristenverein," 244, 254–55.

63. BArch: BArch, R58/782: "Rundschreiben Nr. 4 der Wandersparte der Roten Sporteinheit," quoted in TVNF Reichsleitung, "Anhang zum Rundschreiben an alle Ortsgruppen vom 3.2.1933: Abwehr kommunistischer Wühlarbeit," 3–4.

64. TVNF Reichsleitung, "Anhang," 7.

65. "An alle Naturfreunde Württembergs!," *Arbeiter-Wanderer: Organ der oppositionellen Naturfreunde, Gau Württemberg* (1931); Upmann and Rennspiess, "Organisationsgeschichte," 77–88; SAPMO-BArch, SgY 2/V DF VIII/70: TVNF, Ortsgruppe Leipzig, "Für die Einheit" (c. 1930).

66. Stechert, "Was ist soziales Wandern?," *Jugend und Arbeitersport* (1932): 22–23.

67. Quoted in Robert Dinse, *Das Freizeitleben der Grossstadtjugend* (Eberswalde, 1932), 96.

68. Quoted in Carl Stockhaus, *Die Arbeiterjugend zwischen 14 und 18 Jahren* (Wittenberg, 1926), 65.

69. Quoted in ibid., 66.

70. Denecke, "Touristenverein," 281.

71. STAL, Polizeipräsidium Leipzig V, Nr. 4404: testimony of former member Arno Fleischmann given to Polizeipräsidium Leipzig, Abteilung IV (May 17, 1935); E. D., "Gau-Konferenz 1932," *Der Naturfreund aus Gau Nordmark* (July, 1932): 1–2.

72. TVNF Reichsleitung, "Anhang," 8; BArch, R58/782: Polizeipräsident in Frankfurt to Gestapoamt (August 30, 1933).

73. Reprinted in Anon., "Die Nazis als Arbeiterfreunde," *Der Naturfreund* (1931): 73.

74. "Das Naturfreundehaus in Maschen durch Nazis demoliert!," *Der Naturfreund aus Gau Nordmark* (May, 1932): 7–8.

75. BArch, R58/782: TVNF, Reichsleitung für Deutschland to alle Ortsgruppenleitungen und Bezirksleitungen im TVNF Reichsgruppe Deutschland (March 16, 1933).

76. On the TVNF's destruction and the hiking component of the Nazi *Kraft durch Freude* organization, see Williams, *Turning*, 94–104. The TVNF was refounded after the Second World War, and it exists in Germany to this day.

77. Countless works of history have cast nature movements before 1933 as proto-fascist. For a critique of this historiography, see Williams, *Turning*.

78. Coates, *Nature*, 149–51.

SELECTED BIBLIOGRAPHY

Ackermann, Volker. *Nationale Totenfeiern in Deutschland: Von Wilhelm I bis Franz Josef Strauß.* Stuttgart: Klett-Cotta, 1990.

Alter, Peter, ed. *Im Banne der Metropolen: Berlin und London in den zwanziger Jahren* Göttingen: Vandenhoeck und Rupprecht, 1993.

Ankum, Katharina von, ed. *Women in the Metropolis: Gender and Modernity in Weimar Culture.* Berkeley: University of California Press, 1997.

Becker, Frank, *Amerikanismus in Weimar: Sportsymbole und politische Kultur 1918–1933.* Wiesbaden: Deutscher Universitäts-Verlag, 1993.

Bessel, Richard. *Germany After the First World War.* Oxford: Oxford University Press, 1993.

Bingham, John. *Weimar Cities: The Challenge of Urban Modernity in Germany, 1919–1933* London, 2007.

Brenner, Michael. *The Renaissance of Jewish Culture in Weimar Germany.* New Haven, CT: Yale University Press, 1996.

Buchner, Bernd. *Um nationale und republikanische Identität: Die Sozialdemokratie und der Kampf um die politischen Symbole in der Weimarer Republik.* Bonn: Dietz, 2001.

Burns, Rob and Wilfried van der Will, eds. *Arbeiterkulturbewegung in der Weimarer Republik.* Frankfurt: Ullstein, 1982, two vols.

Canning, Kathleen, Kerstin Barndt, and Kristin McGuire, eds. *Weimar Publics/ Weimar Subjects: Rethinking the Political Culture of Germany in the 1920s.* Providence: Berghahn, 2010.

Cowan, Michael and Kai Marcel Sicks, eds. *Leibhaftige Moderne: Körper in Kunst und Massenmedien 1918 bis 1933.* Bielefeld: transcript, 2005.

Eisner, Lotte. *Die dämonische Leinwand: Die Blütezeit des deutschen Films.* Wiesbaden: Der neue Film, 1955.

Eley, Geoff, ed. *Society, Culture, and the State in Germany, 1870–1930.* Ann Arbor: University of Michigan Press, 1996.

Föllmer, Moritz and Rudiger Graf, ed. *Die "Krise" der Weimarer Republik: Zur Kritik eines Deutungsmuster.* Frankfurt: Campus, 2005.

Gay, Peter. *Weimar Culture: The Outsider as Insider.* New York: Norton, 2001 (orig. 1968).

Gilliam, Bryan, ed. *Music and Performance During the Weimar Republic.* Cambridge: Cambridge University Press, 1994.

Graf, Rüdiger. *Die Zukunft der Weimarer Republik: Krisen und Zukunftsaneignungen in Deutschland, 1918–1933.* Munich: Oldenbourg, 2008.

Grossmann, Atina. *Reforming Sex: The German Movement for Birth Control and Abortion Reform, 1920–1950.* Oxford: Oxford University Press, 1995.

Guttsmann, W. L. *Workers' Culture in Weimar Germany.* New York: Berg, 1990.

Hake, Sabine. *Topographies of Class: Modern Architecture and Mass Society in Weimar Berlin.* Ann Arbor: University of Michigan, 2009.

Hardtwig, Wolfgang, ed. *Politische Kulturgeschichte der Zwischenkriegszeit, 1918–1939.* Göttingen: Vandenhoeck und Rupprecht, 2005.

Herf, Jeffrey. *Reactionary Modernism: Technology, Culture, and Politics in Weimar and the Third Reich.* Cambridge: Cambridge University Press, 1986.

Hermand, Jost and Frank Trommler. *Die Kultur der Weimarer Republik.* Munich: Nymphenburger Verlag, 1984.

Hoeres, Peter. *Die Kultur von Weimar: Durchbruch der Moderne.* Berlin: be.bra Verlag, 2008.

Isenberg, Noah, ed. *Weimar Cinema.* New York: Columbia University Press, 2009.

Isherwood, Christopher. *The Berlin Stories.* New York: New Directions, 2008 (orig. 1935).

Jarausch, Konrad and Michael Geyer. *Shattered Past: Reconstructing German Histories.* Princeton, NJ: Princeton University Press, 2003.

Jelavich, Peter. *Berlin Alexanderplatz: Radio, Film, and the Death of Weimar Culture.* Berkeley: University of California Press, 2006.

———. *Berlin Cabaret.* Cambridge, MA: Harvard University Press, 1996.

Jensen, Erik. *Body by Weimar: Athletes, Gender, and German Modernity.* Oxford: Oxford University Press, 2010.

Kaes, Anton. *Shell Shock Cinema: Weimar Cinema and the Wounds of War.* Princeton, NJ: Princeton University Press, 2009.

———, Martin Jay, and Edward Dimendberg, eds. *The Weimar Republic Sourcebook.* Berkeley: University of California Press, 1994.

Kniesche, Thomas and Stephen Brockmann, eds. *Dancing on the Volcano: Essays on the Culture of the Weimar Republic.* Rochester: Camden House, 1994.

Kolb, Eberhard. *The Weimar Republic.* London: Routledge, 2004, second ed., transl. P. S. Falla and R. J. Park.

Korte, Helmut. *Der Spielfilm und das Ende der Weimarer Republik.* Göttingen: Vandenhoeck and Rupprecht, 1998.

Kreimeier, Klaus. *The Ufa-Story: A History of Germany's Greatest Film Company, 1918–1945.* New York: Hill and Wang, 1996.

Lacey, Kate. *Feminine Frequencies: Gender, German Radio, and the Public Sphere, 1923–1945.* Ann Arbor: University of Michigan Press, 1997.

Landesmuseum für Technik und Arbeit in Mannheim. *Tanz auf dem Vulkan: Die Goldenen 20er in Bildern, Szenen und Objekten.* Mannheim: Landesmuseum für Technik und Arbeit in Mannheim, 1994.

Lenk, Carsten. *Die Erscheinung des Rundfunks: Einführung und Nutzung eines neuen Mediums 1923–1932*. Opladen: Westdeutscher Verlag, 1997.

Leonhard, Joachim-Felix. ed. *Programmgeschichte des Hörfunks in der Weimarer Republik*. Munich: dtv, 1997, two vols.

Lerg, Winfried. *Rundfunkpolitik in der Weimarer Republik*. Munich: dtv, 1980.

Lethen, Helmut. *Cool Conduct: The Culture of Distance in Weimar Germany*. Berkeley: University of California Press, 2003.

Lüdtke, Alf. ed. *Alltagsgeschichte: Zur Rekonstruktion historischer Erfahrungen und Lebensweisen*. Frankfurt: Campus, 1989.

———, Inge Marßoleck, and Adelheid von Saldern, eds. *Amerikanisierung: Traum und Alptraum im Deutschland des 20. Jahrhunderts*. Stuttgart: Steiner, 1996.

Maase, Kaspar. *Grenzenloses Vergnügen: Der Aufstieg der Massenkultur, 1850–1970*. Frankfurt: Fischer, 2007 (orig. 1997).

McCormick, Richard W. *Gender and Sexuality in Weimar Modernity: Film, Literature, and "New Objectivity."* New York: Palgrave, 2001.

McElligott, Anthony. *Contested City: Municipal Politics and the Rise of Nazism in Altona, 1917–1933*. Ann Arbor: University of Michigan Press, 1998.

———, ed. *Weimar Germany*. Oxford: Oxford University Press, 2009.

Meskimmon, Marsha and Shearer West, eds. *Visions of the "Neue Frau": Women and the Visual Arts in Weimar Germany*. Aldershot, UK: Scolar, 1995.

Metzger, Rainer and Christian Brandstetter. *Berlin: The Twenties*. New York: Harry N. Abrams, 2007.

Mommsen, Hans. *Die verspielte Freiheit: Der Weg der Republik von Weimar in den Untergang 1918 bis 1933*. Berlin: Propyläen, 1989.

Mosse, George. *Fallen Soldiers: Reshaping the Memory of the World Wars*. Oxford: Oxford University Press, 1990.

Murray, Bruce. *Film and the German Left in the Weimar Republic: From Caligari to Kuhle Wampe*. Austin: University of Texas Press, 1990.

Nolan, Mary. *Visions of Modernity: American Business and the Modernization of Germany*. Oxford: Oxford University Press, 1994.

Palmér, Torsten and Hendrik Neubauer, eds. *The Weimar Republic Through the Lens of the Press*. Cologne: Könemann, 2000.

Patrice Petro, *Joyless Streets: Women and Melodramatic Representation in the Weimar Republic*. Princeton, NJ: Princeton University Press, 1989.

Peukert, Detlev J.K. *The Weimar Republic: The Crisis of Classical Modernity*. New York: Hill and Wang, 1989, transl. Richard Deveson.

Rabinbach, Anson, *The Human Motor: Energy, Fatigue, and the Origins of Modernity*. Berkeley: University of California Press, 1992.

Rohkrämer, Thomas. *Eine andere Moderne? Zivilisationskritik, Natur, und Technik in Deutschland, 1880–1933*. Paderborn: Schöningh, 1999.

Ross, Corey. *Media and the Making of Modern Germany: Mass Communications, Society and Politics from the Empire to the Third Reich*. Oxford: Oxford University Press, 2008.

Rossol, Nadine. *Performing the Nation in Interwar Germany: Sport, Spectacle, and Political Symbols, 1926–36.* Basingstoke, UK: Palgrave Macmillan, 2010.

Rowe, Dorothy. *Representing Berlin: Sexuality and the City in Imperial and Weimar Germany.* London: Ashgate, 2003.

Saldern, Adelheid von, ed. *Stadt und Moderne: Hannover in der Weimarer Republik.* Hamburg: Ergebnisse Verlag, 1989.

Scheck, Raffael. *Mothers of the Nation: Right-Wing Women in Weimar Germany.* Oxford: Berg, 2004.

Schrader, Bärbel and Jürgen Schebera. *The "Golden" Twenties: Art and Literature in the Weimar Republic.* New Haven, CT: Yale University Press, 1978.

Schubert, Michael. *Der schwarze Fremde: Das Bild des Schwarzafrikaners in der parlamentarischen und publizistischen Kolonialdiskussion in Deutschland von den 1870er bis in die 1930er Jahre.* Stuttgart: Steiner, 2003.

Sneeringer, Julia. *Winning Women's Votes: Propaganda and Politics in Weimar Germany.* Chapel Hill: University of North Carolina Press, 2002.

Swett, Pamela E. *Neighbors and Enemies: The Culture of Radicalism in Berlin, 1929–1933.* Cambridge: Cambridge University Press, 2007.

Tatar, Maria. *Lustmord: Sexual Murder in Weimar Germany.* Princeton, NJ: Princeton University Press, 1997.

Theweleit, Klaus. *Male Fantasies.* Minneapolis: University of Minnesota Press, 1987 (orig. 1977), transl. Stephen Conway, two vols.

Usborne, Cornelie. *Cultures of Abortion in Weimar Germany.* New York: Berghahn, 2007.

———. *The Politics of the Body in Weimar Germany: Women's Reproductive Rights and Duties.* Ann Arbor: University of Michigan, 1992.

Ward, Janet. *Weimar Surfaces: Urban Visual Culture in 1920s Germany.* Berkeley: University of California Press, 2001.

Warstat, Matthias. *Theatrale Gemeinschaften: Zur Festkultur der Arbeiterbewegung 1918–33.* Tübingen: Francke, 2005.

Wedemeyer-Kolwe, Bernd. *"Der neue Mensch": Körperkultur im Kaiserreich und in der Weimarer Republik.* Würzburg: Königshausen & Neumann, 2004.

Weitz, Eric. *Weimar Germany: Promise and Tragedy.* Princeton, NJ: Princeton University Press, 2007.

Welzbacher, Christian. *Die Staatsarchitektur der Weimarer Republik.* Berlin: Lukas, 2006.

———, ed. *Der Reichskunstwart. Kulturpolitik und Staatsinszenierung in der Weimarer Republik 1918–1933.* Weimar: Weimarer Verlagsgesellschaft, 2010.

West, Shearer. *The Visual Arts in Germany, 1890–1937.* New Brunswick: Rutgers University Press, 2001.

Widdig, Bernd. *Culture and Inflation in Weimar Germany.* Berkeley: University of California Press, 2001.

Willett, John. *Art and Politics in the Weimar Period: The New Sobriety, 1917–1933.* New York: Pantheon, 1978.

Williams, John Alexander. *Turning to Nature in Germany: Hiking, Nudism, and Conservation, 1900–1940.* Stanford, CA: Stanford University Press, 2007.

Wirsching, Andreas. *Die Weimarer Republik: Politik und Gesellschaft.* Munich: Oldenbourg, 2008.

INDEX